Ludwig Nohl

Letters of Distinguished Musicians:

Gluck, Haydn, P.E. Bach, Weber, Mendelssohn

Ludwig Nohl

Letters of Distinguished Musicians:
Gluck, Haydn, P.E. Bach, Weber, Mendelssohn

ISBN/EAN: 9783744718080

Printed in Europe, USA, Canada, Australia, Japan

Cover: Foto ©Thomas Meinert / pixelio.de

More available books at **www.hansebooks.com**

LETTERS

OF

GLUCK, HAYDN, P. E. BACH, WEBER, AND MENDELSSOHN.

LONDON
PRINTED BY SPOTTISWOODE AND CO.
NEW-STREET SQUARE

LETTERS

OF

DISTINGUISHED MUSICIANS:

GLUCK, HAYDN, P. E. BACH, WEBER, MENDELSSOHN.

TRANSLATED FROM THE GERMAN BY

LADY WALLACE.

LONDON:
LONGMANS, GREEN, AND CO.
1867.

TRANSLATOR'S PREFACE.

THE PRESENT VOLUME contains some unpublished letters of MENDELSSOHN, which cannot fail to be welcomed by those who have learnt to know and to love him by reading the series of Letters long since published. Those letters possessed for all readers a singular charm, attesting a purity of thought, a vigour of fancy, and a rectitude of life rarely indeed surpassed. In them was seen the lover of beauty in all its forms, the painter and the poet whose gifts culminated in music, the great artist who, without a mission or a party, wrote down his thoughts faithfully and ingenuously as they arose within him. It was no exaggerated praise which affirmed that 'nothing more perfect than these letters has ever fallen from the pen even of those whose pen is their only instrument.'

The letters now for the first time given to the public exhibit Mendelssohn as he was when he appeared in

England,—full of life, joy, and animation, even at a time when the bodily powers were in great part exhausted. It was this singularly pure, bright, and genial character which awakened the interest felt in this country for any memorials of a man so gifted and so guileless. But although Mendelssohn was the first great German musician whom English readers learnt to value as much for their writings as for their musical works, he was not the only one whose career, so far as it was known, enlisted the sympathies or admiration of all who appreciate true greatness. Through a longer life Beethoven had struggled with greater difficulties than fell, happily, to Mendelssohn's lot; and his deafness gave him a claim on public reverence not less than that which blindness conferred on Milton. With natural powers almost more dazzling, with a play of fancy and a vigour of imagination not less wonderful, Mozart had died, like Mendelssohn, at the age of thirty-seven.

The expectation was not disappointed that the lives of these men, if they could speak in their own persons, would present materials well worthy of careful thought. The letters of Beethoven exhibited a character in which the highest artistic genius was combined with unswerving integrity and an indomitable tenacity of purpose. Those of Mozart bring before us a being full of beauty and grace alike in mind and in person, but having to fight his way among men as much beneath him intellectually as in rank they were above him, and to struggle with a poverty which his disposition left him little able to cope with. The affectionate cheerfulness which rarely flagged under constant anxieties, adds greatly to the charm of these letters, and heightens the pathos of his bright but brief career. A mournful interest gathers round the closing days of his life; but, in spite of their dreariness, the reader feels that one who had done so much to delight his fellow-men for ever was not without his reward.

The volume now placed before the English reader has been compiled and translated under the conviction that the lives of other musicians may awaken an interest as real, if not, perhaps, so deep or so acute, as those of Beethoven, Mozart, and Mendelssohn. The name of GLUCK is associated with a revolution in music. He propounded principles which were generally unacceptable, and he never faltered in what he supposed to be his duty. His letters tell the story of a man assured of the truth of his convictions, and not less sure that these convictions would in the sequel be received as undoubted principles of the art and science of music.

Of the letters of CARL P. E. BACH it may be enough to say that they are not unworthy of the son of so great a father. Those of HAYDN will probably carry with them for English readers a higher interest, will bring before them a man in whom great powers were combined with a genuine simplicity of character, and will enable them to appreciate more thoroughly the mental strength which at an age of more than sixty years could produce such works as the Creation and the Seasons.

The letters of Carl von Weber, contained in this series, are addressed with few exceptions to his most intimate friend, and may thus be regarded as introducing us to his inmost thoughts. If they do not impart much new information about his opinions, it must be remembered that he was known scarcely less as a writer than as a musician.

This volume is illustrated with portraits of Gluck, of Haydn, and of Weber, the latter having been kindly lent for the purpose by the possessor, Dr. Ayling.

October 1867.

PREFACE.

A perusal of the letters of celebrated musicians confers on us not only the enjoyment of a closer personal knowledge of the writers, but also possesses the advantage of enabling us to trace more correctly the connection between their works and their spiritual life. The recognition of the value of letters from musical men was first awakened in more extended circles by the publication of those of Mozart and Beethoven, which quickly gained the sympathies both of the public at large and of men of letters. We do not doubt, therefore, that this fresh collection will also meet with a kind reception from musicians and lovers of music; and though a very small group of the distinguished musicians of the last century is here represented, yet the number of the letters and documents given amply suffices to afford a complete insight into the peculiarities of each master.

The series appropriately opens with Christopher Willibald Ritter von Gluck, the great reformer—this master being not only the first earnestly to combine music with universal spiritual life, but, above all, the first to set forth these, his innovations, with clear conviction, striving also to expound his doctrine in plain speech. His method and his principles, being based on the true essence of art, more especially as regards the Drama, can never lose either their truth or their value. The manner, too, in which he expresses his ideas, in thoughtful words with calm deliberation, and persistent energy, cannot fail in many ways to excite fresh interest in these questions at the present day, when a new form of dramatic music is once more in the course of development. Gluck's written effusions, expressive of his ideas and tendencies, are here given for the first time in as complete a form as possible, and it is surprising to see how true and striking the expressions of the great man are, nearly without exception, and that it is his still surviving spirit that animates the finest artistic efforts of the day, and aids in the production of new works of genius. Almost every word of his seems as if only recently uttered, on subjects, too, which at this very moment possess the most vital interest for us; the imperishable charm of Truth still lives in Gluck.

Notwithstanding every effort and research, what we now offer of Gluck's contemporary, Carl Philipp Emanuel Bach, is much less valuable and important, both in number and in substance. The highly gifted son of the great Johann Sebastian may also be called a reformer in his day; carrying out in his peculiar style the work of the talented Domenico Scarlatti, with intellectual cultivation and heartfelt enthusiasm. He may with justice be designated as the founder of pianoforte music, in the same way that Gluck is that of the Musical Drama. His reforms, however, are not so clear and palpable in spiritual things as those of Gluck, who, in his analysis, invariably quotes the text of his operas, and is always prepared to portray with the most perfect lucidity the intentions of each of his works. But though C. Ph. Em. Bach's letters chiefly treat of the form of his artistic productions, still his whole mode of expressing himself has so much of universal interest, and of striking truth, that the large circle of the music-loving public cannot fail to have their sympathies enlisted. Indeed, the science and the esthetics of this art will here find many solid materials to complete the still unfinished bridge between the substance of music, and of spiritual life.

JOSEPH HAYDN! Whose heart has not been a hundred times gladdened by him, both in bright and sorrowful moods—who has not keenly felt the charm of his ingenuous natural style? From him we do not expect special reflections on his art and its effects—yet, in first learning thoroughly to know and to prize the man himself, by the series of his letters, we are tempted to many speculations as to how this simple man became so important an artist, nay, even the Father of that branch of art, in which he first thoroughly developed the full power of music, and its most profound musical signification. Haydn was the first who assumed absolute rule in that realm of love, which finds expression by the use of instruments alone, and who knew how to give life and individuality to each component part of the orchestra. Even the few esthetical expressions found in his letters are welcome, and at all events this first collection supplies a more clear and complete idea of his personality, than the brief biographical notices, and fragmentary sketches which already exist of him.

The fourth of this number, Carl Maria von Weber, has, on the other hand, written many articles and letters, being not merely a musical critic, but an author. Thus writing much, he soon learned to write well, and his nature being creative, these letters, though not intended for publication, exhibit an amiable and energetic character, and furnish a variety of intellectual and valuable opinions and judgments of his art, well worthy of preservation: indeed, it is the most confidential correspondence of our second reformer in music that I am now enabled to offer,—his letters to his friend Johann Gänsbacher. It is true that Max Maria von Weber, in his noble and most delightful biography of his father, has already made some use of the contents of these letters, but everyone must admit that their value is far from being exhausted. Many a new *trait* will gratify those friends of Weber who knew the attractiveness of his character, while the whole tendency and style of his correspondence is truly delightful and invigorating.

Felix Mendelssohn-Bartholdy, the last and youngest of our cycle, at once gained an extensive circle of readers by his former letters, from his easy and cultivated style, expressing himself with so much charm and playfulness, both with regard to his own affairs and everything connected with art. As the letters here given, though only an after-gleaning, are, however, quite new, they will, we trust, be equally welcome, and also assist in bringing vividly before us the image of the artist.

May this new collection, then, also succeed in interesting the friends of our art!

Ludwig Nohl.

Munich:

Nov. 1, 1866.

CONTENTS.

CHRISTOPH WILLIBALD GLUCK.

BORN 1714; DIED NOVEMBER 15, 1787.

CARL PHILIPP EMANUEL BACH.

BORN MARCH 1714; DIED SEPTEMBER 14, 1788.

JOSEPH HAYDN.

BORN MARCH 21, 1733; DIED MAY 31, 1809.

CARL MARIA VON WEBER.

BORN 1786; DIED 1826.

FELIX MENDELSSOHN-BARTHOLDY.

BORN 1810; DIED NOVEMBER 4, 1847.

ILLUSTRATIONS.

CHRISTOPH WILLIBALD GLUCK.

BORN 1714 ; DIED NOV. 15, 1787.

GLUCK'S LETTERS.

1.

*To the Grand Duke Leopold of Tuscany.**

(Written in Italian.)

YOUR ROYAL HIGHNESS,

When I undertook to compose music for 'Alceste,' I proposed entirely to abolish all those abuses introduced by the injudicious vanity of singers, or by the excessive complaisance of masters, which have so long disfigured the Italian opera, and instead of the most

* The Grand Duke of Tuscany, subsequently the Emperor Leopold II., was a warm friend to music, and in a certain sense an admirable *connoisseur*. Like his elder brother, the Emperor Joseph II., who so materially promoted Mozart's works, his younger brother, Maximilian Franz, Elector of Cologne, was of the greatest importance in the development of young Beethoven. Leopold appears here not only as the special patron of Gluck, but also as protecting with truly princely generosity the promising Florentine, Cherubini. He unfortunately died before that master had displayed his great gift for dramatic music, and in the very year when Beethoven, at the age of twenty-two, came to Vienna. He is the last of the House of Hapsburg who was of any material assistance in the development of music, and along with it the noble achievements of the German intellect; with him dies the appreciation of this House for the true interests of Germany, and also the art of music. The above dedication of Gluck's is therefore in some degree an honourable monument for Leopold II.

splendid and beautiful of all entertainments, thus rendering it the most ridiculous and tiresome. My purpose was to restrict music to its true office, that of ministering to the expression of the poetry, and to the situations of the plot, without interrupting the action, or chilling it by superfluous and needless ornamentation; I thought that it should accomplish what brilliancy of colour and a skilfully adapted contrast of light and shade effect for a correct and well-designed drawing, by animating the figures without distorting their contours. I wished, therefore, to avoid arresting an actor in the most excited moment of his dialogue, by causing him to wait for a tiresome *ritournelle*, or, in the midst of half uttered words, to detain him on a favourable note, either for the purpose of displaying his fine voice and flexibility in some long passage, or causing him to pause till the orchestra gave him time to take breath for a cadence. It did not appear to me that I ought to hurry rapidly over the second part of an aria, possibly the most impassioned and important of all, in order to have the opportunity of repeating regularly four times over the words of the first part, causing the aria to end where in all probability the sense did not end, merely for the convenience of the singer, and to enable him to vary a passage according to his caprice; in short, I have striven to banish the abuses against which reason and good sense have so long protested in vain.

My idea was that the overture should prepare th

spectators for the plot to be represented, and give some indication of its nature; that the concerted instruments ought to be regulated according to the interest and passion of the drama, and not leave a void in the dialogue between the air and the recitative, so that the meaning of a passage might not be perverted, nor the force and warmth of the action improperly interrupted.

Further, I thought that my most strenuous efforts must be directed in search of a noble simplicity, thus avoiding a parade of difficulty at the expense of clearness. I did not consider a mere display of novelty valuable, unless naturally suggested by the situation and the expression, and on this point no rule in composition exists that I would not have gladly sacrificed in favour of the effect produced.

Such are my principles. Fortunately, the *libretto* was wonderfully adapted to my purpose, in which the celebrated author (Calzabigi), having imagined a new dramatic plan, replaced flowery descriptions, superfluous similes, and cold sententious morality by the language of the heart, strong passions, interesting situations, and an ever varying *spectacle*.

Success has justified my maxims, and the unanimous approval of so enlightened a city (Vienna) clearly shows that simplicity, truth, and nature are the great fundamental principles of the beautiful in all artistic creations. Nevertheless, in spite of the repeated entreaties of the most highly respected persons to publish my opera, I am so fully aware of the risks I incur in combating prejudices so widely spread, and so deeply rooted, that I am under the necessity of arming myself with the mighty protection of your Royal Highness, and therefore entreat the favour of being permitted to prefix to my opera your august name, which so justly unites the suffrages of enlightened Europe.

A great protector of the fine arts, reigning over a nation which enjoys the renown of having rescued these from universal oppression, and producing the grandest models in them all, in a city always the first to cast off the yoke of vulgar prejudice in order to proceed onwards to perfection—can alone undertake the reform of the noble Drama, in which all the fine arts bear so large a share. When this is effected, the glory will at least be mine of having set in motion the first stone, and obtained the public testimony of your illustrious patronage. I have the honour to subscribe myself, with the utmost devotion, your Royal Highness's

Grateful and obedient servant,

CHRISTOPH GLUCK.

2.

*To the Duke of Braganza.**

(Written in Italian.)

Vienna, Oct. 30, 1770.

Your Highness,

In dedicating this my new work to Your Highness, I seek rather a judge than a patron. A soul superior to commonplace prejudices, with an adequate knowledge of the great principles of art, a taste formed not so much on grand models, as on the immutable foundations of the beautiful and the true—such are the qualities that I look for in my Mæcenas, and which I find combined in Your Highness. The sole reason that induced me to publish my music of 'Alceste' was the hope of finding successors, who, following the path already opened, and encouraged by the full suffrages of an enlightened public, should take courage to destroy the abuses introduced on the Italian stage, and bring it as far as possible to perfection. I bitterly feel that I have hitherto striven after this in vain. Pedants and critics, an infinite multitude, who form the greatest obstacle to the progress of the fine arts, loudly protesting against a method which, were it actually to take

* The English traveller Dr. Burney writes, in his 'Journal of a Musical Tour,' the following about the Duke of Braganza :—' This prince is an excellent judge of music ; he is a great traveller, having visited England, France, and Italy, before his arrival in Germany. He is very lively, and occasioned much mirth by his pleasantries, which were all seasoned with good humour.'

root, would at once destroy all their pretensions to supremacy of judgment, and injure their sphere of influence. They thought themselves entitled to pronounce a verdict on 'Alceste,' from some informal rehearsals, badly conducted, and even worse executed; the effect to be produced in a theatre being calculated from that in a room, with the same sagacity as in a certain city of Greece, where judgment was passed on statues at the distance of a few feet, originally intended to be erected on the most lofty columns.

A fastidious ear perhaps found a vocal passage too harsh, or another too impassioned, or not sufficiently studied, forgetting that, in their proper places, such forcible expression and striking contrasts were absolutely required. One pedant took advantage of an evident oversight, or perhaps an error of the press, to condemn it as if it had been some irremediable sin against the mysteries of harmony;* it was likewise decided in full conclave, that this style of music was barbarous and extravagant. It is true that other scores are judged by a similar criterion, and judged too with almost the certainty of infallibility; but Your Highness will at once perceive the cause of this. The more truth and perfection are sought after, the more necessary are precision and exactness.

The differences are almost imperceptible that dis-

* 'Theory of music,' as it is now called, or, according to the current expression of the country, 'thorough bass.'

tinguish Raphael from the common herd of painters, and the slightest alteration in an outline, that would not destroy the likeness in a caricature, entirely disfigures the portrait of a lovely woman. Very little would suffice, by merely changing something in the expression of my aria 'Che farò senza Euridice?' to turn it into a *saltarello* for *fantoccini*. A note more or less sustained, a neglected *rinforzo* in the time or voice carelessly omitted, an *appoggiatura* out of place, a shake, a passage, a run, may ruin a whole scene in such an opera; whereas such things do no harm, or, indeed, rather embellish the common run of operas. The presence, therefore, of the composer at the performance of this class of music is as indispensable, so to speak, as the presence of the sun to the works of nature. He is its absolute soul and life, and without him all must be confusion and darkness. But we must be prepared for such obstacles so long as there are in the world people who consider themselves authorised to decide on the fine arts, because they enjoy the privilege of possessing eyes and ears, no matter what the quality of these may be. The mania of discussing those very subjects which they least understand, is unhappily a failing only too prevalent among men, and, very recently, one of the greatest philosophers of the age presumed to write about music, and to bring forward as oracles 'blind dreams and romantic follies'*

* A quotation from Arteaga's 'History of the Italian Opera,' 1780,

Your Highness has no doubt read the drama of 'Paride,' and must have observed that it does not offer to the composer those violent passions, those grand images, or tragic situations, which agitate the spectators in 'Alceste,' furnishing such opportunities for great effects in harmony; thus the same power and energy cannot assuredly be expected in the music,—just as in a picture in a full blaze of light, the same force of *chiaroscuro* and the same sharp contrasts are not to be exacted, that the painter can employ on a subject which permits him to choose a subdued light. This opera does not treat of a wife about to lose her husband, and who, in order to save him, has the courage to invoke the infernal gods in a wild forest, amid the black shades of night, trembling even in her last death-struggle for the fate of her children, and forced to tear herself away from the husband whom she adores. In the present work we see a loving youth combating for a time the conscientious scruples of a haughty and noble woman, and at last triumphing over them by all the arts of a vehement passion. I have striven to find some variety of colouring, seeking it in the diverse characters of the two nations, Phrygia and Sparta, contrasting the wild and rude nature of the one with the delicate and indolent nature of the other. I thought that singing in an opera being only a substitute for

a learned Jesuit, born at Madrid in 1750, and well versed in the ancients; he lived for some time in Bologna, and died at Paris in 1799.

declamation, ought to imitate in Elena the native ruggedness of her country; and that, in order to preserve this character in the music, it would not be thought a defect on my part to descend even to trivialities. When truth is sought, it must be varied in accordance with the subject we have to work out, and the greatest beauties of melody and harmony become defects and imperfections when out of place. I do not expect greater success from my 'Paride' than from 'Alceste,' at least in my purpose to effect the desired change in musical composers; on the contrary, I anticipate greater opposition than ever; but, for my part, this shall never deter me from making fresh attempts to accomplish my good design; and, if I gain the approval of Your Highness, I shall gladly say, *Tolle siparium; sufficit mihi unus Plato pro cuncto populo.*

I have the honour to be, with the most profound respect, Your Highness's humble, devoted, and obliged servant, LE CHEVALIER CHRISTOPH GLUCK.

3.

To the Editor of the 'Mercure de France.' *

(Written in French.)

Sir,

I might justly be reproached by others, and should also severely reproach myself, after reading the letter

* The letter in question was addressed to one of the directors of the opera at Paris, and dated August 1, 1772, and written by M. Bailly du

written to one of the directors of the Royal Academy of Music, inserted in your 'Mercury' of last October, the subject of which is 'Iphigenia'—and, after expressing my gratitude to the author of that letter for the praise which he has been pleased to lavish on me—were I not eager to declare that his friendship, and far too favourable impressions of me, have no doubt carried him away, and I am very far from flattering myself that I merit the eulogies he bestows on me. I should reproach myself even more keenly, were I to allow the invention of this new style of Italian opera, the success of which has justified the attempt, to be attributed to myself. The principal merit is due to M. Calzabigi; and if my music has produced any sensation, I ought to acknowledge that it is he who has enabled me to develop the resources of my art. This author, full of genius and talent, has followed a path little known by Italians in his *libretti* of 'Orpheus,' 'Alceste,' and 'Paride.' These works are overflowing with those happy situations, and terrible and pathetic events, which

Rollet, secretary to the French Embassy in Vienna, to M. le Chevalier Antoine d'Auvergne, in order to pave the way for the reception at the Grand Opera of 'Iphigénie in Aulis,' the text of which Du Rollet himself had written to suit the French taste, thus encouraging Gluck to compose music in the French dramatic style. Gluck's answer to this letter, which could scarcely have been written without his knowledge, and the appearance of which in the 'Mercure' no doubt caused him much satisfaction, bears evident traces of Du Rollet's helping hand. The flattering expressions, too, applied to the French, are only designed to awaken the attention of the public, and to render the performance of the opera possible.

supply the composer with the means of expressing ardent passion, and creating energetic and touching music. Whatever talent a composer may possess, he can only write indifferent music, if the poet does not excite in him that enthusiasm, without which the productions of every art must be feeble and languid. The imitation of nature is the acknowledged aim which all ought to seek. This it is that I strive to attain; always simple and natural, so far as I can possibly make it so, my music only tends to enhance the expression, and to add force to the declamation of the poetry. For this reason I do not employ those *shakes*, *passages*, and *cadences*, of which Italians are so lavish. Their language, therefore, which quite suits this style, is, in this respect, by no means advantageous for me: no doubt it has many other merits, but, born in Germany, I do not consider that any study on my part, of either Italian or French, entitles me to appreciate the delicate shades which cause a preference for one beyond the other, and I think that a foreigner ought to abstain from judging between them; but I may be allowed to say, that the language which suits me best, is that which enables the poet to furnish me with the most varied means of expressing the passions; and such is the advantage I found in the words of 'Iphigenia,' the poetry of which appeared to me to have all the energy calculated to inspire good music. Though I never had occasion to offer my works to any theatre, I cannot be displeased with the writer of the letter in question to one of the directors, for having proposed my 'Iphigenia' to your academy of music. I must confess that I would gladly have brought it out in Paris, because, by its effect and with the aid of the celebrated M. Rousseau of Geneva, whom I purposed to consult, we might perhaps, acting in concert, and seeking a noble, touching, and natural melody—the declamation too being in exact accordance with the prosody of each language, and the character of each people—have succeeded in establishing the system I have in view, that of producing music appropriate to all nations, and thus abolishing the ridiculous distinctions of national music. My studies of the works of this great man on music, and among others the letter in which he analyses the monologue in Lully's 'Armida,' prove to me the sublimity of his knowledge and the accuracy of his taste, and fill me with admiration. The result is the most entire conviction on my part, that if he had chosen to apply himself to the exercise of this art, he might have realised the prodigious effects that antiquity attributes to music. I am charmed to take advantage of the present occasion to render to him publicly that tribute of praise which I think he deserves.

I request, Sir, that you will be so obliging as to insert this letter in your next 'Mercury.'

I have the honour to be, Sir, &c.,

CHEVALIER GLUCK.

4.

*To Padre Martini.**

(Written in Italian.)

Vienna, Oct. 20, 1773.

Reverend Father and Friend,

It has been intimated to me by Herr Taiber † that your Reverence is desirous to have my portrait. Sensible as I am of the honour you thus confer on me, I deeply regret not being able to go myself to Bologna, in the hope of finding there some clever artist, feeling persuaded that the pleasure of seeing you would tend to embellish me.

His Excellency Count Durazzo, Imperial Ambassador at Venice, my kind patron for many years, intends to have a copy taken from a portrait done of me in Rome, on the occasion of my last visit there, and he has caused a young *protégé* of his to alter it in accordance with my present appearance and physiognomy.

Of the compositions named to you, I believe 'Orfeo' alone is known there. The others have met with considerable approval at our Court, and I am now on the eve of going to Paris to produce the last of my

* The signature only is in Gluck's hand. Padre Martini was the well-known and most renowned of all teachers of composition of the previous century, who also plays a part in Mozart's letters.

† Mozart also, in a letter of April 16, 1789, speaks of an Antoine Teyber, at that time organist in Dresden, perhaps a pupil of the world-famed Padre. But as there were several musical Teybers, it is difficult to decide which is here meant.

works, 'Iphigenia in Aulis,' on the great opera stage there. The enterprise is certainly a bold one, and the obstacles will be great, because I must infallibly come into collision with national prejudices; and against such, reason avails little.

If I can be of any service to you here, pray command me. I have also to thank His Excellency the Ambassador for offering to forward the portrait to you on his return to Venice. He loves and patronises the fine arts, and has a particular esteem for yourself, even without knowing you personally.

I have the honour to be, with high consideration and friendship,

Your Reverence's obedient servant,

Cavaliere Christof Gluck.

Padre Martini was by no means insensible to Gluck's politeness. When, some time afterwards, the well-known musical feud broke out in Paris, Martini replied to a letter of the Abbé Arnaud, Feb. 28, 1777, by a communication preserved at Vienna in the Imperial Library, from which we give the following extract:—'In your letter you bestow just and well-deserved eulogiums on the energy and merits of Herr Ritter *Cluck*. (!) In the three dramas of his with which I am acquainted, he has strived to bestow on the words the most lively and powerful expression, combined with the most exciting emotions, and his efforts have been rather directed to the music being adapted to the words than these to the music; and, on the occasion of his presence at the opening of the new theatre in Bologna, when he honoured me by a visit, I congratulated him on having succeeded in combining the most beautiful aspect of Italian music with that of the French, as well as with the finest instrumental music of Germany.'

Gluck's friends were careful that this letter from so world-renowned an authority should be widely circulated, and there can be no doubt that the writer intended it for publication.

5.

To Louis XVI. of France.

Sire,

When, following the example of the Greeks, Augustus, the Medici, and Louis Quatorze fostered and remunerated the arts, they had a more important object in view than that of multiplying amusements and pleasures; they considered this phase of human knowledge as one of the most precious links of the political chain; they knew that the arts alone possess the advantage of civilising man without corrupting him, and of disposing him to submission without degrading him.

From the hour of your accession to the throne, Sire, you have shown yourself to be animated by the same principles and by the same views. While Your Majesty incessantly labours for the welfare and happiness of your subjects, you do not disdain the homage I presume to offer you; and in bestowing on me the first proofs of your patronage of art, you confer happiness and renown on a foreigner, but one whom no Frenchman can surpass in zeal, in gratitude, and in devotion towards your august person.

With these sentiments, combined with the most profound respect, I am, Sire, Your Majesty's devoted humble servant, LE CHEVALIER GLUCK.

The following dedication to Marie Antoinette, who had caused Gluck to be summoned to Paris, and always continued his especial benefactress, is from the original score of 'Orphée et Euridice: Tragic Opera in Three Acts, dedicated to the Queen by M. le Chevalier Gluck, given for the first time by the Royal Academy of Music on Tuesday, August 2, 1774, at Paris, chez Des Lauriers.'

6.

To Marie Antoinette.

Madam,

Loaded by your benefits, the most precious in my eyes is that which has fixed my abode in the midst of a nation worthy to possess you, from knowing the full value of your virtues. Honoured by your protection, I no doubt owe to this advantage the applause I have received. It has been no pretension of mine, though some have thought fit to reproach me with it, to come here to give lessons to the French in their own language, nor to prove to them that until now they have had no author worthy of their admiration or their gratitude.

Some pieces exist among them to which I award the praise they merit; several of their living authors are worthy of their reputation. I thought that I might attempt with French words the new style of music that I have adopted in my three last Italian operas. I see with satisfaction that the language of nature is the universal language; M. Rousseau has employed it with the greatest success in his simple style. His 'Devin du Village' is a model which no author has yet imitated. I cannot tell how far I have succeeded in mine; but I have the approval of Your Majesty, who has permitted me to dedicate to you this work, and for me this is the most flattering success. The style that I attempt to introduce seems to me to restore to art its primitive dignity, and music will no longer be restricted to those cold conventional beauties to which authors were formerly forced to confine themselves.

It is with sentiments of the most profound respect that I am, Madam, Your Majesty's humble and obedient servant, LE CHEVALIER GLUCK.

With regard to the relations that existed between Gluck and his former pupil in singing, Marie Antoinette, we have further information in the recently published correspondence with her mother and sister. On August 26, 1774, she writes from Versailles to Marie Christine thus:—

'A glorious triumph, at last, my dear Christine. On the 19th we had the first performance of Gluck's "Iphigénie." I was quite enchanted with it, and nothing else is talked of. On this subject an amount of excitement everywhere prevails in society, which is the most extraordinary thing that you can conceive. It is quite incredible; people quarrel and fight as if some religious question were at stake; at Court too, though I have openly pronounced in favour of this work of genius, most vehement partisanship and animated discussions are carried on, and in the city I am told that things are even worse. I conversed with Herr Gluck before the last rehearsal, when he himself developed to me the plan of his thoughts, in order to establish the true character of what he calls operatic music, and to restore it to nature. If I may judge by the effect produced on myself, his design has succeeded even beyond his expectations. The Dauphin was startled out of his usual repose, and continually applauded, but in the course of the performance some parts (just as I expected) quite transported him. The audience seemed puzzled, and indeed time is required to become accustomed to the new system, after being so long familiar with one so totally opposite. Now all the world wish to see the piece, which is a good sign, and Gluck seems well satisfied. I am sure you will rejoice as much as I do at this occurrence.'

The diary too of the unfortunate Princesse de Lamballe offers on this subject a few notices very little known, and useful in explaining the foregoing dedication, as well as some of the letters hereafter to be given of the master himself.

'During the period of her happiness and power, Marie Antoinette sent for the celebrated Gluck to Paris. His presence cost the state nothing, for the Queen paid all his expenses from her own privy purse, besides presenting him with the receipts of his operas, which brought in enormous sums to the theatre.

'Gluck composed his "Armida" in order to make a flattering allusion to Marie Antoinette's beauty. I never saw Her Majesty display so much interest in any event as in the success of this piece. She really became quite a slave to "Armida," and she had the unusual complaisance to hear every piece of Gluck's before it was rehearsed in the theatre. Gluck often told her that he always improved his music according to the impression that it made on the Queen.

'One day, after the rehearsal of a piece that he had just laid before Her Majesty for her approbation, on his leaving Marie Antoinette I followed him, wishing him joy of the increasing success that attended each representation of his opera. "Ah! my dear Princess," cried he, "all I now want to be raised to the seventh heaven is two such beautiful heads as that of Her Majesty and your own." "If that is all you want," answered I, "we can be painted for you, Herr Gluck." "No, no; you do not understand me, I mean living heads; my actresses are very ugly, and Armida, as well as her confidante, ought to be very lovely."

'Great as the public success was of "Armida," being one of the finest operas ever given on the French stage, no one prized this work more highly than the composer himself. Gluck was passionately enamoured of it; he said to the Queen that the air of France had redoubled the powers of his musical genius, and the sight of Her Majesty had given such a wonderful impetus to his ideas, that his compositions had become, like herself, angelic and sublime.

'The first representation of the part of Armida was Madame Sanct-Huberti. The Queen much admired her talent; she was *prima donna* of the French Opera, though a German by birth. Gluck highly commended the natural qualities of her voice, and, at the request of the Queen, he took the trouble to instruct her himself in the part of "Armida." Sacchini was trained in the noble style of the Italian school, and Mdlle. Bertin, the Queen's dressmaker and milliner, was commanded by Her Majesty to prepare a complete costume for the part.

'Gluck had the most thorough conviction of the value and dignity of his works,*—a feeling which threw obstacles in the way of putting "Armida" on the stage, having excited the jealousy of the great Vestris, the composer affording him very little opportunity for displaying the fascinations of his art. Several serious disputes arose between the two rivals, both of whom equally shared the enthusiastic admiration of the Parisians. It was at one time feared that the success of "Armida" might suffer, if the dancers were not allotted an equal share in the representation. But Gluck, whose German obstinacy would not permit him to leave out one single note, said to Vestris that if he composed a ballet, the stage would in that case be left entirely at his disposition; but that an artist, whose sole talent lay in his heels, had no right to kick down such an opera as "Armida." "My subject," added Gluck, "is taken from the immortal author of the 'Gerusalemme Liberata.' I have composed the music in accordance with the rules of art and the prompting of my own genius, so there cannot be much space for *entrechats*; and if Tasso had wished to make Rinaldo a dancer, he would not have displayed him in the guise of a warrior."

* Madame Campan too, in her 'Memoirs,' relates that when the Queen at her *toilette* asked him about 'Armida,' he drew himself up to his full height, and said, in his German accent: 'Madame, il est bientôt fini, et vraiment ce sera superbe.'

'Rinaldo was the part that Vestris wanted for his son, whom the Parisians called "Le Dieu de la Danse." At length, owing to the intervention of the Queen, Vestris wisely consented to play the part just as Gluck had written it.'

7.

To Klopstock.

I hope you duly received through Graf v. Cobenzl the arias you wished to have; I sent them by him to save you the expense of carriage. I was obliged to omit any remarks, not knowing how to express myself as I desired. I believe you would find it equally difficult were you to attempt to instruct any one by letter what expression to give to a declamatory passage from the 'Messiah;' all that kind of thing depends on feeling, and cannot well be explained; and this you know even better than I do. I strive to lay a foundation here, but have hitherto been unable to do much, for scarcely had I arrived in Vienna when the Emperor left it, and is not yet returned. We must therefore await a favourable moment in order to effect anything: at these great Courts there is seldom an opportunity for doing any good, though I hear that an academy of arts and sciences is about to be established here, and that the receipts from their newspapers and almanacks are to furnish a portion of the funds, and help to pay the expenses. When I have further information on the subject, I shall not fail to let you know all about it. In the meantime continue to love me a little till I am so happy as to see you again. My wife and daughter send you their compliments, and were delighted to hear something of you. I remain your devoted

GLUCK.

The original of the above letter is in the Berlin State Library; it was first published in Riedl's 'Literarische Monaten' in 1776, then in Forkel's 'Musical and Critical Library,' vol. ii. p. 368; and by Schmidt, who thus relates the circumstance that gave rise to the foregoing letter:—

'Gluck, on his way back from Paris, with his wife and niece in the spring of 1775, met Klopstock in Strasburg, and made his niece sing to him various pieces from the "Herrmanns-Schlacht." The poet, quite enchanted, gave the musician a rendez-vous eight days later at Rastatt, and there, in a brilliant society, wrote out the following agreement, signed by Gluck's niece, and by all present, among whom were some very distinguished persons:—

'"I, the undersigned, enchantress of the Holy Roman Empire, and also of the unholy Gallic Empire, hereby confirm what I have already promised, and do again promise Klopstock, which is, that as soon as I, arch-enchantress, return to the arch-city of the Arch-Imperial family, called Vienna, and have rested after my journey for the space of three days and nights, undertake at once, and without further pause or delay, to send him, 1st, the aria, in which Orpheus invokes Eurydice; 2ndly, the aria in which Alceste invokes her children, adding a few words to express, in so far as words can express them, the style and manner, the construction and peculiarity, and also the light and shade of my musical mode of delivery, in order that the aforesaid Klopstock may, on his part, send these my words, as well as the airs, to his niece in Hamburg, who, according to his account, is also addicted to sorcery.

' " Signed, sealed, and delivered at Rastatt, March 17, 1775." ' *

The English Dr. Burney, in his 'Journal of a Musical Tour' in 1773 (vol. ii. p. 257), gives the following ac-

* D. F. Strauss gives an interesting account, furnished by a merchant of Karlsruhe, of the meeting of these two great men:—'During Klopstock's stay here, the Chevalier Gluck appeared one fine morning with his wife and niece; they brought letters of introduction to me from Rath Riedel in Vienna, and were announced by me at Court, where, on two successive evenings, they charmed the Court with their divine music, to which, however, with the exception of two cavaliers, Klopstock and myself, no one was admitted. Old Gluck sang and played *con amore* many passages from the "Messiah," set to music by himself; his wife accompanied him in a few other pieces; and his amiable niece sang several times Klopstock's song, "Ich bin ein deutsches Mädchen" in the most enchanting manner. Klopstock remained all the time standing in a corner, or imbibing incense, which he was very chary of bestowing on these people in return. They left us for Paris, provided with rich princely gifts. When, in the course of a certain time, they returned from thence, the minister Von Edelsheim invited them to dinner on their arrival, and sent to say that I might also come. I could not, however, make my

count of a visit he made to Gluck, with Countess Thun, at his house in the Faubourg St. Marc :—

'He is very well housed there; has a pretty garden and a great number of neat and elegantly furnished rooms. He has no children. Madame Gluck, and his niece who lives with him, came to receive us at the door, as well as the veteran composer himself. He is much pitted with the small-pox, and very coarse in figure and look, but was soon got into good humour; and he talked, sang, and played, Madame Thun observed, more than ever she knew him at any one time.

'He began upon a very bad harpsichord by accompanying his niece, who is but thirteen years old, in two of the capital scenes of his own famous opera of

appearance till dinner was nearly over. When I arrived, the minister desired me to seat myself between Mdlle. Gluck and Herr v. M., the present *Hof-Marschall*. "You have come just at the right moment," said the lively girl, "and you shall decide between Herr Klopstock and myself." "Et de quoi s'agit-il?" asked I. "Whether the French nation is amiable or not? Klopstock persists in asserting the latter, and will not give way on the point, notwithstanding Herr v. P. (he sat at her right) and Herr v. M. are both opposed to him." "Et vous, mademoiselle?" "Oh! I cannot tell you to what an extent I was *fêtée* by all Paris, from the highest to the lowest, and loaded with favours, polite attentions, and presents." "Then the question is decided," was my answer; "all who are really acquainted with the nation find them most amiable, which the French certainly are, *malgré la haine du Nord*; those may despise them who do not know them, but this is in itself a sufficient punishment." The girl jumped up and kissed both my cheeks. "Dear X.," said she, "you are the man for me!" casting a glance of compassion on Klopstock. All applauded, and I made a little hit at Klopstock, saying to him: "*Apprenez, cher poète, à mieux juger les nations, et à faire le complaisant vis-à-vis le sexe.*" "Just what I thought," was his sole answer, and he continued as obstinate as before.

"Alceste." She has a powerful and well-toned voice, and sang with infinite taste, feeling, expression, and even execution. After these two scenes from "Alceste," she sang several others by different composers, and in different styles, particularly Traetta.

'I was assured that Mdlle. Gluck had learned to sing but two years, which, considering the perfection of her performance, really astonished me. She began singing under her uncle, but he, in a precipitate fit of despair, had given her up; when Signor Milico arriving at Vienna about the same time, and discovering that she had an improvable voice and a docile disposition, begged he might be allowed to teach her. Her performance now is an equal proof of the sagacity and penetration of Signor Milico. Mdlle. Gluck is thin, seems of a delicate constitution, and as she sings so much in earnest, I should fear for her health if she were to make singing a profession, but she is not intended for a public performer.

'When she had done, her uncle was prevailed upon to sing himself, and, with as little voice as possible, he contrived to entertain and even delight the company in a very high degree; for with the richness of accompaniment, the energy and vehemence of his manner in "Alceste," and his judicious expression in the slow movements, he so well compensated for the want of voice, that it was a defect which was soon entirely forgotten. He was so good humoured as to perform almost his whole opera of "Alceste," many admirable things in a still later opera of his, "Paride ed Elena," and in a French opera from Racine's "Iphigénie," which he has just composed. This last, though he had not yet committed a note of it to paper, he sang with as much readiness as if he had had a full score before him.'

It is notorious that at that period in Paris there was a very powerful Italian party, to which Louis XV. and his celebrated favourite, Madame Dubarry, belonged. When Marie Antoinette took her countryman Gluck under her special protection, Madame Dubarry was doubly incited to set up a rival in opposition to him, and for this purpose she selected her old *protégé* Nicolo Piccini, a Neapolitan; and she succeeded, through the administration of the Grand Opera, in having the composition of 'Roland' entrusted to him, although an agreement had already been concluded with Gluck on the subject. His friend Du Rollet mentioned it to Gluck, who sends him the following sarcastic and energetic reply:—

8.

To M. Bailly du Rollet.

(Written in French.)

I have just received, my dear friend, your letter of January 15, in which you exhort me to continue to work at the opera of 'Roland;' this is no longer possible, for when I learned that the administration of the Opera, who were perfectly well aware that I was occupied with 'Roland,' had handed over the work to M. Piccini, I burned all that I had already written of it, which perhaps was of no great value, in which case the public ought to be obliged to M. Marmontel for having prevented their hearing bad music. Moreover, I am not the man to enter into rivalry with any one. M. Piccini would have too great an advantage over me; for, in addition to his personal merits, which are assuredly very great, he would also have that of novelty, I having given four works at Paris, whether good or bad, no matter. This must exhaust the imagination; besides, I have shown him the way, and he has only to follow me. Of his patrons I say nothing. Sure am I that a certain politician of my acquaintance [the Marchese Carraciolo, Neapolitan Ambassador in Paris] will give dinners and suppers to three-fourths of Paris, for the purpose of gaining proselytes for him; and that Marmontel, who knows so well how to write tales, will relate to the whole kingdom the exclusive merits of M. Piccini.

I do really pity M. Hebert [Director of the Grand Opéra] for having fallen into the hands of such persons; the one an exclusive amateur of Italian music, and the other the dramatic author of operas supposed to be comic. They will make him see the moon at midday. I am sincerely grieved, for this M. Hebert is an excellent man, for which reason I feel inclined to give him my 'Armide;' on the conditions, however, that I named in my previous letter. I must repeat that the most essential are, that, when I come to Paris, I am to have at least two months to train my actors and actresses; that I am to be empowered to have as many rehearsals as I shall consider necessary; that no part is to be doubled; and that another opera is to be held in readiness, in case any actor or actress should be indisposed. These are my conditions, and without their fulfilment I will keep my 'Armide' for my own pleasure. I have written the music in a manner which will prevent its soon growing old.

You tell me, my dear friend, in your letter, that nothing will ever equal 'Alceste,' but, for my part, I do not join in your prophecy. 'Alceste' is a complete tragedy, and I own I think it very near perfection; but you have no conception of how many shades and different paths music is susceptible. The whole combinations of 'Armide' are so different from those of 'Alceste,' that you will scarcely believe they are by the same composer, and I have also put forth the little strength still left me in order to finish 'Armide.' I have striven in it to be rather a poet and a painter than a musician; in short, you will be able to judge for yourself, if they choose to let it be heard. I must confess that I should like to finish my career with this opera. True it is that the public will require at least as much time to comprehend it as was necessary for them to understand 'Alceste.' There is a certain delicacy in 'Armide' which is not to be found in 'Alceste;' for I have discovered the means of making the personages speak, so that you know at once, from their mode of expression, when Armida is speaking, when the confidante, &c. &c. I must conclude, or you will think that I have become either a *charlatan* or a lunatic. Nothing has so bad an effect as to praise one's self: it was only admissible in the great Corneille; but when Marmontel or I do so, people ridicule us, or laugh in our faces. You are quite right, however, in saying that French composers have been too much neglected; for, unless I am much mistaken, Gossec and Philidor, who know the requirements of the French opera, would, in my opinion, suit the public infinitely better than the best Italian authors, were it not for the amount of enthusiasm for everything that has the *prestige* of novelty. You also say, my dear friend, that 'Orphée' loses when compared with 'Alceste.' Good heavens! how can there be any comparison between two works which have nothing in common? The one may please more than the other, but were you to see 'Alceste' performed by your inferior actors, and any other actress than Mdlle. Le Vasseur, and on the other hand 'Orphée' by the very best you have, you would then admit the balance to be in favour of 'Orphée:' the best composed works, when badly executed, become of all others the most insupportable. No comparison can exist between these two works of an opposite nature. If, for example, Piccini and I each composed the opera of 'Roland,' then people could judge which of us had succeeded the best, but different poems must necessarily produce different music, which with respect to the expression of the words may be all that is most sublime, each in its own sphere, but then any comparison must be a *lame* one. I almost tremble at the idea of people comparing 'Armide' and 'Alceste;' poems forming such a contrast, the one making you weep, and the other causing solely thrilling sensations. If this should occur, my only resource will be to pray to the Almighty that the worthy city of Paris may recover its good sense. Adieu, my dear friend, &c. GLUCK.

In a pamphlet of the Abbé Arnaud, 'La soirée perdue à l'Opéra,' the composer Sacchini was reproached with having in his 'Olympia' made use of passages taken from Gluck's 'Alceste.' A friend of Sacchini, and a partisan of the Italian party, the dramatic poet Framery, extracted the passage, and published it in an article accusing Gluck, on the other hand, of being a plagiarist from Sacchini. Gluck's answer is the more bitter inasmuch as Sacchini was the queen's singing-master, and also in certain respects a rival of Gluck. His letter was immediately published in the 'Journal de Paris.'

9.

Reply of M. le Chevalier Gluck to an Article published by le Sieur Framery in the 'Mercure de France,' September 1776.

In the 'Mercure de France,' of September 1776, appears a letter from a certain Sieur Framery on the subject of M. Sacchini, who is much to be pitied, if he requires such a defender to sustain his reputation. Almost everything that M. Framery thinks fit to say about M. Gluck, M. Sacchini, and M. Milico, is false. The Italian 'Alceste' of M. Gluck never was performed, either at Bologna or in any other Italian city, owing to the difficulty of executing the work when M. Gluck is not present to direct it.

He only gave it at Vienna in Austria in 1768. At the revival of this opera, M. Milico sung the part of Admete. It is true that M. Sacchini inserted the contested passage in his air, 'Se cerca, se dice,' a musical phrase to be found in the Italian 'Alceste' of M. Gluck, 'Ah! per questo già stanco mio cuore,' published at Vienna in 1769. We may also state that another passage towards the end of the same air is taken from 'Paride ed Helena;' it occurs in the aria 'Di scordami,' also published at Vienna. M. Framery is not aware that an Italian composer is very often forced to accommodate himself to the caprice, and the voice, of a singer, and it was M. Milico who prevailed on M. Sacchini to insert the said phrases into his aria. M. Gluck himself reproached his friend Milico with this, for at that time M. Gluck had not yet given his 'Alceste' at Paris, although he had every intention to do so. M. Sacchini's genius, so replete with fine conceptions, has no occasion to despoil others, but from courtesy towards Milico, he borrowed those passages in which the singer thought he would shine the most. The reputation of M. Sacchini has been so long established that it has no need whatever of vindication, but it may possibly be tarnished owing to his airs written for Italian words being parodied by arranging them with French words, taking into account the difference between the two melodies and the two prosodies. M. Framery is a man of letters, and might be better employed than in thus confounding the national character of the French and Italians, and writing mongrel music, by arranging airs, which, though endured in the Opéra Comique, are not suitable to the Grand Opéra.

La Harpe, celebrated for his eloquence, and who had also written some poetry, but was far from being well versed in music, gives a minute description of the first performance of Gluck's 'Armide,' on September 23, in the 'Parisian Journal of Politics and Literature,' Oct. 5, 1777. He represents the effect as very indifferent, and states that the first act alone and part of the fifth were applauded, while the rest was very coldly received. The opera was too noisy, and every minute the same clamour recurred, just as in 'Iphigénie' and 'Alceste; there could be no doubt that both these operas were too loud; in 'Armide,' also, from first to last, the same monotonous tiresome *criaillerie* was renewed; the composer had made her a Médée, forgetting that Armide ought to be a syren, &c. &c.—*Tout comme chez nous!*—*Tempora mutantur*; whereas we always remain the same towards the creations of genius. We seem to be reading a *Tristan* criticism of 1865. La Harpe, however, acknowledged that Gluck was *un homme de génie*; he therefore thought it worth while again to unsheath his bright blade. In the course of eight days the following severe retort appeared:—

10.*

To M. de la Harpe.

Oct. 12, 1777.

It is impossible for me, sir, not to agree to the very judicious observations you have recently made on my operas, in your 'Journal de Littérature,' October 5; and I find nothing, absolutely nothing, to say in reply.

Hitherto I had the simplicity to believe that in music, as in other arts, all the passions were within its sphere, and that it ought not to please less in expressing

* This letter appeared in the 'Journal de Paris,' of Oct. 12, 1777.

rage and fury, and the cry of grief, than in depicting the sighs of love—

> Neither serpent nor monster is so odious
> As not to please when counterfeited by art.

I thought this axiom true in music as well as in poetry. I was convinced that singing imbued with the colouring of the sentiments to be expressed ought to be modified in accordance with them, and assume as many different accents as the poetry had different tints, in short, that the voice, the instruments, every sound, and even silence itself, ought all to tend to one single aim, that of *expression*, and the union between the singing and the words be so close that the poem should not appear to be less composed for the music, than the music for the poem.

These were not my only errors: it seemed to me that the French language was not much accentuated, and had no determined quantity like the Italian tongue. I was also struck with another discrepancy between the singers of the two nations: if I found in the one voices more soft and flexible, the others seemed to me to put more force and energy into their action; thence I concluded that Italian singing would not suit the French.

In subsequently looking over the scores of some of your old operas, in spite of the shakes, cadences, and other defects, with which these airs are overloaded, I found enough of real beauties in them to make me believe that the French have their own resources within themselves.

These, sir, were my ideas before reading your observations. Instantly light dissipated darkness; I was confounded to find that you had learned more of my art in some hours of reflection, than I had done after having exercised it for forty years. You prove to me, sir, that it suffices to be a man of letters to entitle you to pronounce on all subjects. I am now fully convinced that the music of the Italian masters is music par excellence, is, in fact, *music*; that singing, in order to please, ought to be regular and methodical, and that even in those moments of excitement, when the personage singing, animated by different passions, passes successively from one to another, the composer ought always to preserve the same *motif de chant.*

I agree with you that, of all my compositions, 'Orphée' is the only one that is tolerable. I humbly ask pardon from heaven for having *deafened* my auditors by my other operas; the number of times they have been performed, and the applause the public has thought fit to bestow on them, does not prevent my seeing that they are pitiable; I am so convinced of this that I intend to write them afresh, and as I perceive that you are all for tender music, I propose to put into the mouth of the furious Achilles a song so touching and sweet, that the spectators shall be moved by it even to tears.

With respect to 'Armide,' I must beware of leaving the poem as it now is, for, as you judiciously observe, 'the operas of Quinault, though full of beauties, are composed in a manner unfavourable to music; they are very fine as poems, but very bad as operas.' If, therefore, they must become very bad poems (evidently, in your opinion, the only mode to make good operas), I must entreat you to procure me the acquaintance of some *rhymer* who will set to work at 'Armide,' and insert a couple of arias in every scene. We can together settle the quantity and the measure of the verse, and, provided the number of syllables be complete, I shall not trouble myself further. I, on my side, will work at the music, from which, of course, I must scrupulously banish all noisy instruments, such as kettledrums and trumpets; it is now my desire that only hautboys, flutes, French horns, and violins (with *sourdines*, of course) should be heard in my orchestra; while my sole object shall be to arrange the words to suit these airs, which will not be difficult, having previously taken their exact dimensions. Then the part of Armide will no longer be a monotonous and tiresome *criaillerie.* She will no longer be a Médée, a sorceress, but an *enchantress.* I intend that in her despair she shall sing an air so *regular* and *methodical,* and at the same time so tender, that the most delicate *petite maîtresse* may listen to it without the smallest shock to her nerves.

If some blockhead should say to me, 'Sir, pray

remember that Armide in a state of fury should not express herself like Armide enamoured,' I should reply to him, 'Sir, I do not wish to *offend the ear* of M. de la Harpe; I do not wish to *adhere* to nature, but rather to *embellish* it; instead of making Armide utter cries of anguish, I wish her to *enchant* you.' If he were to persist, and to declare that Sophocles, in the finest of all his tragedies, did not scruple to present to the Athenians Œdipus with blood-shot eyes, and that the recitative or species of declamation introduced, by which the eloquent complaints of that unhappy king were expressed, were no doubt uttered in the liveliest accents of grief, I would again reply that M. de la Harpe objects to hear the cry of a man who *suffers.*

Do I not, sir, thus define the spirit of the doctrine that pervades your remarks? I have procured for several of my friends the pleasure of reading them. One of them said to me on returning your pamphlet, 'You ought to be grateful, M. de la Harpe gives you some valuable hints, he makes the confession of his musical faith, do the same in return; send for his poetical and literary works, and through friendship for him note down in them all that does not please you. Many people are of opinion that criticism produces no other effect on art, than that of wounding the artist whom it attacks, and to prove this, they say that never have poets had more censors, or been more indifferent, than in the present day; but consult the journalists on the point, and ask them if there is anything more useful to the state than journals. People may object that it does not become you, a musician, to decide about poetry; but is that more startling than a poet, a man of letters, who judges despotically of music?'

Thus spoke my friend; but notwithstanding my gratitude to you, sir, I feel on due consideration that I cannot follow his suggestions without incurring the fate of him who, in the presence of Hannibal, made a long harangue on the art of war.

11.

To M. J. B. Suard.

Sir,

Having always considered music not only as the art of pleasing the ear, but as one of the best means of touching the heart, and exciting the affections, and having consequently adopted a new method, I also occupied myself with the dramatic action. I sought grand and forcible expression, and, above all, I wished that each part of my work should be duly connected. I soon found that all the singers, male and female, and a great number of professors, were against me; but men of letters and talent, without exception, both in Germany and Italy, more than consoled me by the praise and marks of esteem they conferred on me. This is by no means the case in France, for though there are men of letters there whose suffrages might indeed well compensate me for losing others, still there are many who have declared themselves hostile to me.

It seems that those gentlemen are more successful when they write on other topics, for, if I may judge by the reception the public have kindly given to my works, no great stress is laid on their remarks or their opinions. But what do you think, sir, of the fresh attack M. de la Harpe has made on me? This M. de la Harpe is a very pleasant doctor, truly. He speaks of music in a manner that would excite the contempt of the most juvenile chorister in Europe, and yet he says, *I will it so*, and talks of *my doctrine*, '*Et pueri nasum rhinocerontis habent.*' Cannot you, sir, say a few words to him, you who defended me so advantageously against him? Ah! if my music has given you any degree of pleasure, I entreat that you will place me in a position to prove to my friends, the connoisseurs in Germany and Italy, that among the men of letters in France, there are some who, in speaking of the arts, know at least what they are saying.

I have the honour to be, sir, with the highest esteem and gratitude, your obedient,

LE CHEVALIER GLUCK.

A society of musical friends in Paris had mentioned to Gluck that there was a scene from 'Armide' in their repertoire which Cambini (who is also named in

Mozart's letters) had composed two years previous to the appearance of Gluck's 'Armide.' From a feeling of modesty and appreciation of the admirable treatment of this very scene by Gluck in his opera, Cambini had never again given his own aria. His friends, however, were of opinion that both scenes were equally in their place, the one in the theatre, and the other at a concert; so they applied to Gluck, hoping that he would send them an answer such as might induce Cambini once more to enjoy the applause his aria excited in their concerts. Gluck's reply is as follows:—

12.

To the Friends of Music in Paris.

Jan. 12, 1778.

M. Gluck is very sensible of the politeness of *messieurs les amateurs* and M. Cambini; he has the honour to assure these gentlemen that it will give him much pleasure to hear the performance of M. Cambini's scene from 'Armide.' It would indeed be tyranny in music to seek to prevent authors bringing forward their productions. M. Gluck enters into no rivalry with anyone, and it will always be a pleasure to listen to music better than his own. The progress of art ought to be the sole object sought after.

LE CHEVALIER GLUCK.

13.*

To Marie Antoinette.

Madame,

In deigning to accept the homage that I venture to offer you, Your Majesty fulfils my every wish. It was of great moment to my happiness to make it known that the operas I have composed for the express purpose of contributing to the pleasures of a nation, of which Your Majesty forms the delight and the ornament, have merited the attention, and obtained the approval, of a refined and enlightened Princess, who loves and protects all the arts; who, in applauding every style, can discriminate between them, and who knows how to bestow on each the degree of esteem it deserves.

I am, with the most profound respect, Your Majesty's humble and devoted servant,

LE CHEVALIER GLUCK.

14.

To Herbert von Dalberg.†

Paris, June 8, 1779.

Sir,

I duly received your esteemed letter of the 14th of last month; I had previously read with much pleasure

* 'Iphigénie en Tauride,' tragédie en 4 actes, given for the first time by the Académie Royale de Musique, on May 18, 1779.

† The signature alone is autograph.

the poem of Cora sent to me by Graf Seau, and the information that you are its author gives it fresh value in my eyes. I wish very much that I could accept your obliging invitation to Mannheim, but as my business here has already detained me beyond the appointed time, on its conclusion I must take the shortest route to return to Vienna. With regard to the musical composition of the above poem, we must first of all ascertain the views of Graf Seau as to the performance of the piece, the talents of the proposed singers, and be made fully acquainted with the qualities of their voices. On my way through Munich, I will discuss these points with Graf Seau, and after this preliminary information, it will be an easy matter to decide by letter, the various alterations and additions you may consider requisite during the progress of the work. I only regret that my present position deprives me of the advantage of making your personal acquaintance. It would, however, be most agreeable to me if the fulfilment of your intentions were to bring me into more intimate connection with you, and thus enable me more frequently to express my due sense of your merits, and the entire esteem with which I have the honour, sir, to subscribe myself, your obedient humble servant,

RITTER GLUCK.

15.*

To M. Gersin.

Vienna, Nov. 30, 1779.

Sir,

I am very sensible of the honour you do me in sending me the sketch of a tragedy for which I am to compose the music. I consider it well calculated to produce great effects, but you are evidently not aware that henceforth I mean to write no more operas, and that I have finished my career; my age and the annoyances I lately met with in Paris about my opera 'Narcisse' have for ever disgusted me from again writing operas. It would be a pity, however, were you not to finish your work, for you will certainly find musicians in Paris of great merit, and capable of satisfying all your requirements.

I have the honour to be, sir, with much esteem, your humble and obedient servant,

RITTER GLUCK.

16.

To Herbert von Dalberg.

Vienna, Jan. 19, 1780.

M. le Comte,

I received the letter you did me the honour to address to me, and have read with pleasure the opera

* A faithful facsimile of this letter, autograph throughout, now lies before me, and I find inscribed on it—*communiqué par la famille de M. Gersin.*

that you were so good as to forward to me, but, as I am not acquainted with the singers who are to execute it, I cannot undertake to write the music. As soon as the opera that I am arranging here, and which I had already the honour to mention to you, is completed, I shall have the pleasure of sending it to you, and we can then enter more fully into the subject.

I have the honour to be, M. le Comte, your very humble and obedient servant,

CHRISTOPH GLUCK.

17.*

Gluck's Will.

April 2, 1786.

As nothing is more certain than death, nor more uncertain than the time of it, I, the undersigned, being in the full possession of all my faculties, give my last instructions as follows:—

1. I commend my soul to the infinite mercy of God; my body to be interred according to the rites of the Holy Catholic Church.

2. I bequeath the sum of twenty-five florins for fifty masses for my soul.

3. I bequeath to the poor-house one florin, to the general hospital one florin, to the burgher hospital one

* Taken from the original by Schmid; the master died on Nov. 15, 1787.

florin, to the normal school one florin — four florins in all.

4. Further I bequeath to each of my domestics still in my service at the time of my death, one year's wages.

5. I leave it entirely to the will and pleasure of my heir general to give anything to my brothers and sisters.

6. As the fundamental principle of every testament is the appointment of an heir, I hereby appoint my dear wife, M. Anna von Gluck, née Bergin, as my sole and exclusive heir; and that no doubts may arise as to whether the silver and other personal property be mine or my wife's, I hereby also declare all the silver and other valuables to be the sole property of my wife, and consequently not included in my previous bequests. Should, however, this my last will and testament not prove valid, I hope that it may be considered legal as a codicil. Lastly, I appoint my highly esteemed cousin, Joseph von Holbein, Royal Hofrath, executor to this my will, and I bequeath to him a snuff-box as a remembrance.

Signed and witnessed, &c.

CHRISTOPH GLUCK.

CARL PHILIPP EMANUEL BACH.

Born March 1714; died September 14, 1788.

BACH'S LETTERS.

1.

AUTOBIOGRAPHY.

I, Carl Philipp Emanuel Bach, was born in Vienna, in March 1714. My late father, Johann Sebastian Bach, was Capellmeister at different courts, and finally music director at Leipzig. My mother, Maria Barbara Bach, was the youngest daughter of Johann Michael Bach, a solid and profound composer. After finishing my studies at the Thomas School in Leipzig, I applied myself to the law in that town, and afterwards at Frankfort-on-the-Oder. At the latter place, I directed a musical academy, also conducting and composing for public concerts and all the different festivities. I never had any other master for composition or pianoforte playing than my father. When my academical course ended in 1738, I went to Berlin, where a very advantageous offer was made to me to visit foreign countries, as companion to a young gentleman; but an unexpected and gracious summons to Ruppin from the then Crown Prince (now King of Prussia) caused my proposed journey to be given up. Owing to certain circumstances, however, it was the year 1740 (on the accession of his Prussian Majesty to the throne) when I was first formally installed in his service, and I had the honour to accompany him on the piano, the first solo on the flute played by his Majesty. From that time till November 1767, I continued steadily in the Prussian service, although I had more than one opportunity of accepting excellent offers elsewhere. His Majesty was so gracious as to render this unnecessary by adding a considerable sum to my salary. In 1767 I was offered the situation of the deceased Capellmeister Telemann, as director of music in Hamburg. After many respectful applications,* I at last received my discharge from the King, and the sister of his Majesty, Princess Amelia of Prussia, did me the honour before my departure to appoint me her Capellmeister.

Since my residence here, I have had some flattering overtures made to me, which, however, I have invariably declined. My duties in the Prussian service never allowed me any spare time to travel in foreign countries, so I have always remained in Germany, and have only made a few expeditions in my fatherland. The absence of foreign travel would have been more prejudicial to me in my profession, if I had not from my youth upwards enjoyed the rare good fortune to have at home, and likewise to hear there, the most admirable of all species of music, to make acquaintance with many masters of the very highest class, and to gain their

* An application to the Royal Prussian House Archive Direction in Berlin to communicate these representations remained unanswered.

friendship. I had the same privilege in my youth at Leipzig, for hardly any professor of music passed through that city without making the acquaintance of my father, and playing before him. The grandeur of my father in composition, and in organ and pianoforte playing, so peculiarly his own, was too widely known for any musician of note to miss the opportunity of associating, if possible, on an intimate footing with that great man. I need not say much of all that wa to be heard at that period, especially in Berlin and Dresden; who does not know that epoch, when in music, as well as in its more accurate and delicate mode of execution, a new period commenced, by which the art of harmony attained such a height, that my feelings lead me to fear that it has even already very much deteriorated. I believe, and so do many far-seeing men, that the gay comic style, now so popular, has the greatest share in this, without quoting men who might perhaps be reproached with having written little or nothing really humorous. I will name one of the greatest living masters in that style, Signor Galuppi, who in my house at Berlin entirely agreed with me, relating to me on that occasion many ludicrous incidents that he had witnessed in some Italian churches. In short, I was obliged to rest satisfied, and was quite willing to be satisfied, by hearing, in addition to all the great masters of our fatherland, the best class of every kind sent to Germany by foreign countries, and I think there is scarcely one species of music in which I have not heard the greatest proficients.

It would not be difficult for me to fill up a large space with the names of those composers, singers, and instrumentalists of all sorts whom I have known, if I chose to be diffuse, and to exert my memory to recall them. But this I do know to a certainty, that among them were men of genius, whose equals in their own style and grandeur have never again appeared. In spite of all this, I do not deny that it would have been a very great pleasure, as well as an advantage to me, if I could have met with an opportunity to visit foreign lands.

In the year 1744, I married, in Berlin, Johanna Maria Dannemann, daughter of a wine merchant there, the fruits of this marriage being two sons and a daughter, all now living. My eldest son practises here (in Hamburg) as a lawyer; my daughter is still at home with us, and my youngest son is now in Saxony, studying his profession as a painter, in the Leipzig and Dresden academies. The following works of mine have been published with my consent and knowledge :—

In the year 1731, a minuet with the hands crossing over, arranged for the piano, a simple and at that time popular effect [introduced chiefly by Domenico Scarlatti]. This minuet I engraved myself on copper. [A list follows of his other compositions till the year 1773; he then continues:] Having been obliged to compose most of my works for particular individuals, and for the public, I have been thus placed under more restraint than in the few pieces I wrote for my own pleasure. Sometimes, indeed, I have been compelled to follow very ludicrous instructions; still it is possible that these far from agreeable suggestions may have inspired my genius with a variety of ideas, which probably would never otherwise have occurred to me.

I never approved of any great monotony, either in style or in composition, having heard so much that was excellent of every kind, and as it has always been my opinion that we ought to appreciate what is good wherever it is to be found, or in however small a proportion it may exist in a piece; it is probably owing to this, and also by the aid of the natural talents with which God has endowed me, that the great variety remarked in my works may be attributed. I must take advantage of this occasion to observe that critics, even when they write without prejudice, which is, however, seldom the case, very often treat the compositions they criticise too unmercifully, not being aware of the circumstances, requirements, and various causes from which the pieces originate. How seldom we meet with a proper amount of sympathy and knowledge, honesty and courage, in a critic; four qualities which they ought, at all events, to a certain extent, to possess. It is, therefore, very sad for the realm of music that criticism, in many respects so useful, should often be the occupation of heads by no means gifted with these qualities.

Among all my works, especially for the piano, there are only some trios, solos, and concertos, that I wrote in all freedom, and for my own use.

My chief study, particularly in later years, has been directed to arrange for the piano (in spite of its deficiency in sustaining power), so that playing should resemble singing as much as possible. This is no very easy task, if the ear is not to be left void, nor the noble simplicity of the song injured by too much noise.

My idea is that music ought to move the heart with sweet emotion, which a pianist will never effect by mere scrambling, thundering, and arpeggios, at least not with me.

The above sketch, so interesting in many respects, written by the founder of our pianoforte music, whom Haydn and likewise Mozart regarded as their direct predecessor and teacher, was published by the Hamburg bookseller Bode in 1773, in the third volume of a translation of the 'Journal of a Tour,' by Dr. C. Burney. That celebrated Englishman had been for some years travelling through France, Germany, and Italy, for the purpose of collecting materials for a general history of music; and in the year 1772 he went to Hamburg also, solely, as he informs us, for the purpose of visiting Carl Phillip Emanuel Bach, adding, 'Hamburg is not at present possessed of any musical professor of great eminence except C. P. E. Bach, but he is legion!—and I wanted no other musical temptation to visit that city.'

Amongst other things, he mentions the following, which brings the man personally nearer to us than even his autobiography; so it may find a place here, inasmuch as the book in question is now rather rare.

'When I went to his house, I found with him three or four rational and well-bred persons, his friends, besides his own family, consisting of Madame Bach, his eldest son, who practises the law, and his daughter. The instant I entered, he conducted me upstairs into a large and elegant music room furnished with pictures, drawings, and prints, of more than a hundred and fifty eminent musicians, among whom there are many Englishmen, and original portraits in oil of his father and grandfather. After I had looked at these, M. Bach was so obliging as to sit down to his *Silbermann clavichord*, and favourite instrument, upon which he played three or four of his choicest and most difficult compositions, with the delicacy, precision, and spirit, for which he is so justly celebrated among his countrymen. In the pathetic and slow movements, whenever he had a long note to express, he absolutely contrived to produce from his instrument a cry of sorrow and complaint such as can only be effected upon the clavichord, and perhaps by himself.

'After dinner, which was elegantly served, and cheerfully eaten, I prevailed upon him again to sit down to a clavichord, and he played with little intermission till near eleven o'clock at night. During this time, he grew so animated and *possessed* that he not only played but looked like one inspired. His eyes were fixed, his underlip fell, and drops of effervescence distilled from his countenance. He said if he were to be set to work frequently in this manner, he should grow young again. He is now fifty-nine, rather short in stature, with black hair and eyes, and brown complexion, has a very animated countenance, and is of a cheerful and lively disposition.

'His performance to day convinced me of what I had suggested before from his works, that he is not only one of the greatest composers that ever existed for keyed instruments, but the best player in point of *expression*; for others, perhaps, have had as rapid execution; however, he possesses every style, though he chiefly confines himself to the expressive. M. Bach showed me two manuscript books of his father's composition written on purpose for him when he was a boy, containing pieces with a fugue in all the twenty-four keys, extremely difficult, and generally in five parts, at which he laboured for the first years of his life without intermission.'

I have unhappily not succeeded in discovering any important letters in the correspondence of this gifted man—among all the celebrated German musicians probably the first!—who had also entire command of his own language in writing. I am obliged, therefore, to rest satisfied with giving only a portion of his business letters, and even those are of no great value. There is no doubt, however (which is proved by the last of his letters given here), that a private correspondence was carried on by him connected with the most pure affections, and intellectual relations, and we would here earnestly implore the possessors of such letters to communicate them as soon as possible to the public, in order that the personal type and disposition of this highly distinguished master of characteristic music, may be made as complete as possible.

2.

To Herr Eschenburg.

Hamburg, June 26, 1771.

Sir,

I gladly repeat my cordial thanks for your kind assurance that you will take charge of the payment of my subscriptions. Our small choir is now quite complete; I therefore regret that it is not in my power to profit by your obliging proposal, which would at any other time have been so agreeable to me. You will always find me at your command, and I have the honour to be, sir, your obedient servant,

BACH.

3.*

To Herr Forkel.

Hamburg, April 27, 1776.

Dearest Herr Forkel,

If you are still in the land of the living, be so good as to let me know as soon as possible the names of those amateurs whom you so kindly procured for me as subscribers, and as they are not merely on the list of subscribers, but pay at once, pray send the money due for my sonatas.

I have all the other lists except yours, and I wish to fix the size of the edition, and also the directions for the sonatas.

Pray continue your regard for your faithful friend,

BACH.

The remaining letters are addressed to the music publisher Artaria, in Vienna, whose grandson, Herr D. Artaria, with his usual urbanity, permitted me to copy the autograph letters. The Baron von Swieten, named in the first letter, had a great and peculiar veneration for the works of Bach, and in 1774 ordered from him six grand orchestral symphonies, in which the composer strictly complied with the wishes of the Baron, regardless of the difficulty of their performance.

* To the well-known musical historian Forkel.

4.

To Herr Artaria.

Hamburg, July 14, 1779.

Sir,

I rejoice, through the medium of Baron von Swieten, to have the opportunity of making your acquaintance; and the more so as I may at once inform you that, in the course of a few days, Herr Breitkopf will forward to you direct to Vienna, the twelve sonatas and the twelve sacred pieces you wished to have. The unusual shape of the sacred pieces delayed their publication. The Baron v. Swieten has mentioned to you, sir, the usual discount I allow on the sale of my works, and I understand you expressed yourself satisfied with it, namely, one copy in eleven. The subscription price of the sonatas is two imperial gulden for each copy, and the set of sacred music two imperial gulden and a half, also for each copy. You, sir, may sell these for any price that suits you.

If I can be of any further service to you in any way, or in your business, I am quite at your disposal.

I have the honour to be, sir, &c.

BACH.

5.

To Herr Artaria.

Hamburg, Nov. 10, 1779.

Sir,

I regret much that our correspondence goes on so slowly. The great distance at which we live from each other, and pressure of business, is no doubt the cause of this. All those compositions that you desired me to forward to you through Herr Breitkopf were at once packed up, and, to save the expense of carriage, will be sent by the first opportunity from here. The settlement of the accompanying bill had better be remitted, according to Baron von Swieten's plan, through Herr Friesen to Messrs. Perserot and Dörner here. I have marked the price in louisd'ors, because, according to our present rate of exchange, you will rather gain than lose by it; my subscribers have now all paid up, and there remains only the trifling sum due, sir, by you; as I always pay the whole expense of publishing at once, but not till all subscriptions come in, it would be doing me a favour to remit the small sum still due from your subscription; and as I know your mode of thinking too well to believe that you have any distrust of me, in order to spare time and correspondence, the whole amount of the enclosed note can be settled at once, without your having the slightest cause for uneasiness, even though my packet should be a few days later in reaching you.

In the hope of soon receiving a satisfactory reply, I am, sir, with sincere esteem, your obedient servant,

C. P. E. Bach.

All my works were paid according to the different currencies, so you can fix what prices you please, as no particular price is marked.

6.

À M. Schwickert, Libraire très-renommé à Leipzig.

Hamburg, April 10, 1780.

Sir,

You have probably mislaid one of my letters, in which I gave every detail of the matter, and of the value of my 'Essay on Pianoforte Playing;' at that time I named 800 single volumes. At present I can state with certainty that I have 260 copies of the first part, and 564 of the second. In the letter to which I have alluded, I also stated that I sell them separately, that each separate part can only be bought for three dollars, and that the first part *in any event* can alone be useful to a person not wishing to study harmony; the second part, however, which I wrote with great care, cannot be properly understood without the first, as in the second part I almost every moment refer to the first without further repetition or explanation. You wish that I should make a demand; our desperately heavy currency renders our transaction more difficult, because we cannot get nearly as much for it here as we do in Berlin, Leipzig, &c. for your currency; hence it is that if you have a louisd'or in your pocket, or a well-filled purse, in the foreign fashion, you get rid of its contents in a moment, scarcely knowing why or wherefore! My transactions, especially with my works, are chiefly carried on in the North—that is, in Russia, Livonia, Courland, Sweden, Denmark, Holstein, Hanover, Mecklenburg, Lauenburg, and Lübeck, and these are always paid in our heavy currency. Still it is your wish that I should name a price. Well, then! you must give me for the above 824 separate volumes, the 27 copperplates, and the stock of engravings, 186 louisd'or. In *our* currency, this makes not quite a dollar for each part or book, and in your light currency rather more than a dollar, which I sell for three dollars in our heavy currency. A sale is by no means a necessity for me, as little as the purchase is to you; we shall remain good friends at all events. I remain your devoted. BACH.

P.S.—If we come to an agreement, I promise to give you considerable additions to both parts, *over and above,* which I have in manuscript, and am now willing to publish. The plates for the second part are more than complete for 500 copies, and those for the first part are at present complete for 50; but that is of little consequence. Payment expected *at once* on delivery of the copies. I thank you much beforehand for the seventeen symphonies.

7.

To Artaria.

Hamburg, Oct. 15, 1782.

Dear Sir,

I take the liberty to request your kind support for my new collection, which is entirely different from the others; being easier, sweeter, and more ample, and containing seven pieces.* May I beg you to give the enclosed to the Baron as soon as possible. I am, dear sir, with high consideration, your obedient servant,

BACH.

8.

To Artaria.

Hamburg, Nov. 27, 1783.

Dear Sir,

As Klopstock† is so much beloved in Vienna, I send you the announcement of a new work, which is both for

* This was 'Fourth Collection of Sonatas for Connoisseurs and Dilettanti.'

† Bach was intimately acquainted with Klopstock, and had much personal intercourse with him.

singing and for the piano. I await your commands, and am, with sincere esteem, yours,

BACH.

9

To Artaria.

Hamburg, July 19, 1784.

Dear Sir,

You have no doubt received from Herr Breitkopf the thirteen copies of Klopstock's 'Morning Song.'* You were so good as to order twelve. I beg you will send the thirteenth to Baron v. Braun, but on no account accept payment for it. Be so kind as to forward the enclosed letter, free of charge, to the son of that gentleman. If you are disposed to order any copies of the work in the annexed advertisement, you will much oblige me.

I remain, with sincere esteem, your obedient,

BACH.

The following last letter of Bach's, the original of which is in the State Library in Munich, is written in trembling and almost illegible characters, Bach being at that time seventy-two years of age. Two years afterwards, on September 14, 1788, he died. Nothing has as

* Nottebohm in Vienna possesses a copy of this composition, with these words written in pencil by the hand of Beethoven, 'written by my dear father.' The words seem to me to be written by Beethoven himself, at the time when he was still in Bonn.

yet been discovered about the friend to whom this letter is addressed, but it is evident that they were on the most familiar terms, and the third collection of 'Sonatas for Connoisseurs and Amateurs' is dedicated to a person of the same name.

10.

À M. M. de Grotthuss, Seigneur de Gieddutz, par Memel, à Mietau.

Hamburg, Sept. 4, 1786.

Best of all the good,

And dearest of all benefactors—Oh! how long have you left us burning at a slow fire! I relied on M. F. v. Lieben and Herr v. Müller to give me news of you, but in vain! The joy we felt on receiving tidings of you to-day from yourself was indescribable. Believe me, we all pray for you, and God, I doubt not, will restore you to health. As for us, we are pretty much as we were, sometimes rather indisposed, and then well again. We every day hope for good accounts of the Baroness and yourself, and the young Baron. Pray express to them all our devotion [?], and believe me in life or in death, wholly yours,

BACH.

Do you still remember our Esculapius, Herr Liebe?

JOSEPH HAYDN.

Born March 21, 1733; died May 31, 1809.

HAYDN'S LETTERS.

1.*

Mademoiselle,

You must not take it amiss that I send you a kind of medley in complying with your wish. To describe such things requires time, and this I do not possess. I thought it best, therefore, not to write myself to M. Zoller, which I hope you will excuse.

I only offer you a rough sketch, for neither pride nor the love of fame, but solely the great kindness, and marked satisfaction, that so learned a national society has displayed towards my works, have induced me to comply with their request.

I was born on the last day of March in 1733, in the market town of Rohrau, near Prugg, on the river Leitha, in Lower Austria. The calling of my late father was that of a wheelwright (in the service of Count Harrach). He was a great lover of music by nature, and played the harp without knowing a note of music, while as a boy of five, I sang all his short simple pieces very

* The name of the lady to whom this letter is addressed is not given by the possessor of the original, J. F. Weigl, in Vienna. The date, from its contents, appears to be previous to 1779, when Swieten had returned from Berlin.

fairly; this induced my father to send me to the rector of the school at Haimburg, a relative of ours, in order to learn the first elements of music and other juvenile acquirements. Our Almighty Father (to whom above all I owe the most profound gratitude) had endowed me with so much facility in music that even in my sixth year I was bold enough to sing some masses in the choir, and also played a little on the piano and the violin. In my seventh year the late Capellmeister von Reutter, when passing through Haimburg, heard by chance my weak but pleasing voice. He forthwith took charge of me, and placed me in the Capell-Haus [in Vienna], where, in addition to my other studies, I learned singing, the piano, and the violin, from very good masters. I sang soprano both at St. Stephen's and at Court with great applause, till my sixteenth year, when I finally lost my voice, and was forced for eight whole years to gain a scanty livelihood by giving lessons; many a genius is ruined by this miserable mode of earning daily bread, as it leaves no time for study. This I, alas! know too well myself from experience, and I could never have accomplished even what I did, if in my zeal for composition I had not pursued my studies through the night. I wrote diligently, though not quite correctly, till at length I had the good fortune to learn the genuine rudiments of composition from the celebrated Master Porpora (who was at that time in Vienna).

At length, by the recommendation of the late Herr von Fürnberg* (from whom I received unusual kindness), I was appointed director at Count v. Morzin's, and subsequently Capellmeister to his Highness Prince Esterhazy, in whose service I hope to live and die.

Among my works, the following have been most approved of—the operas of 'Le Pescatrici,' 'L'Incontro improviso,' performed in the presence of his Imperial Majesty, and 'L'Infedeltà delusa'; the oratorio of 'Il Ritorno di Tobia,' given in Vienna; also a 'Stabat Mater,' for which I received, through a kind friend, a testimonial from our great musician Hasse, containing many undeserved eulogiums. This letter I will treasure up like gold as long as I live, not owing to its contents, but for the sake of so admirable a man.

I have had the good fortune to please almost all nations (except, indeed, the Berliners) in chamber-music, as testified by the public papers, and by letters addressed to myself; I only marvel that those judicious Berlin gentlemen preserve no *medium* in their criticism of my works, as in one weekly paper they laud me to the skies, and in another bury me sixty fathoms deep in the earth, and without any valid reason; but I know why it is: because they are unable to perform these pieces of mine, and are too conceited to give themselves the trouble to understand them properly, and from other

* Haydn wrote his first quartett at the instigation of Fürnberg.

causes which, God willing, I will bring forward at the right time. Capellmeister von Dittersdorf, in Silesia, recently wrote, entreating me to defend myself against their cruel attacks, but I replied that one swallow does not make a summer; that perhaps one of these days some impartial authority would stop their tongues, which happened to them once before when they had accused me of *monotony*. In spite of this, they eagerly strive to get all my works, which I was told only last winter by the imperial ambassador at Berlin, Baron von Swieten; but enough of this.

Dear Mademoiselle Leonore, you will be so good as to give this sketch, with my kind regards, to M. Zoller, for his consideration; my highest ambition consists in being regarded by the world as the honest man I really am.

I offer up to Almighty God all eulogiums, for to Him alone do I owe them. My sole wish is neither to offend against my neighbour nor my gracious Prince, but above all our merciful God.

I remain, Mademoiselle, with high esteem, your sincere friend and obedient servant,

JOSEPHUS HAYDN.

We think it will certainly contribute much to the interest in our 'maestro,' if we introduce here a little biographical sketch of his youth, which, though not written actually by himself, is founded on his own nar rative, and thus proceeds, at least at second hand, from himself. It was published in Vienna, May 1805, in the 'Journal of Fashion,' and is written by a correspondent in Vienna, who states that it was noted down 'from the lips of the simple-minded patriarch himself.' It is supposed to be written by the Saxon Legationsrath G. A. Griesinger, who had long resided in Vienna, and written a great deal in journals on the subject of music. He is also the author of a 'Biographical Notice of Joseph Haydn' that appeared in 1810. The charming simplicity and modesty of the master are also displayed in this sketch, and many interesting details given, indicative of his own quaint humour, the peculiar heritage of our nation, and which lends so great a charm to the creations of Haydn, and, indeed, in spite of Philipp E. Bach, was first employed by him in our art. The notice is as follows:—

'Haydn's father, a poor common wheelwright, had learned to play the harp during his travelling years, at Frankfort-on-the-Maine. On Sundays, it was his custom to play over his songs, while Haydn's mother sang them. Even now (1805), seventy-two years afterwards, Haydn still knows almost all these songs by heart. As a child of five years, our Sepperl (little Joseph) used to sit beside his parents, and, taking a piece of wood in his right hand, scrape away at his left shoulder, pretending to play the violin. A schoolmaster from the neighbouring little town of Haimburg, a distant relation of Haydn, was once present by chance at a concert of this kind, and observed that little Joseph marked the time with great exactness. This seemed a good omen, and he advised the father to devote his boy to music. The father, who greatly venerated the church, earnestly wished to consecrate his son to that calling, and to learn music was one of the first steps towards it. In his needy condition, he could not, however, afford to spend much on the education of his children. The more then was he rejoiced when the school rector of Haimburg took the little six year old Joseph with him, to instruct him in his school. Here Haydn was taught to read and write; he also received religious instruction, and applied himself to learn singing, the violin, the kettle-drum, and other instruments. He used to say that he had cause to thank this schoolmaster, now in his grave, for having made him begin so many different things, though he got more blows than victuals from him.

'Haydn had been about two years in Haimburg when the Court-Capellmeister Reutter, who also directed the music of St. Stephen's Church in Vienna, came to visit his friend the dean, in Haimburg. Reutter* told the dean

* Georg von Reutter, born 1705, died 1772, was an almost inexhaustible church composer, whose works ruled supreme in all the church choirs of the Imperial States almost to the present century. Even in 1823, Beethoven, who was to write a mass for the Emperor Francis, was recommended to adopt the style of that antique 'powder and pigtail' composer, for Reutter had always been an especial favourite with this Chinese emperor.

that he must try to replace some of his former choir-boys, who were beginning to lose their voices, and that he was in search of new ones. The dean proposed little Haydn, at that time eight years old, and Reutter immediately sent for him and his schoolmaster. Haydn, according to the custom of the day, and for the sake of cleanliness, wore a bob wig, and his dress was as poor as possible. 'I was a queer little urchin,' says Haydn himself. There happened to be some cherries on the dean's table; the scantily fed Haydn could not take his eyes off them. Reutter, who observed this, gave him several handfuls in his hat, and made him sing some Latin and Italian strophes, the meaning of which Haydn did not in the least understand. Reutter seemed satisfied, but asked him if he could execute a shake? "No!" answered Haydn; "nor can my cousin here either." The schoolmaster looked annoyed, and Reutter burst out laughing. Reutter then showed him how to press his tongue against his teeth, and gave him many other hints. Haydn imitated him, and succeeded at the third attempt. "You shall remain with me," said Reutter; and thus Joseph Haydn, at the age of eight, became a chorister-boy in St. Stephen's Church in Vienna.

'Here he was instructed by first-rate teachers in singing and in different instruments, as well as in the theoretical part of music. He also heard a great many fine musicians, and his own fancy was already so fertile that he even attempted eight and sixteen-part composition. "At that time," says he, "I thought it was all right if the paper was pretty well filled. Reutter gave me many a hearty scolding for my unripe productions, and lectured me for attempting sixteen-parts when I did not even understand two-part composition." When Haydn was sixteen, he received his discharge from the choir of St. Stephen's Church, his voice having given way. He contrived to maintain himself, though poorly enough, during a succession of years in Vienna. He lived in a sixth story, and his room in the garret had neither stove nor window; in winter his breath froze on his coverlet, and the water that he fetched himself from the spring in the morning for washing was frequently changed into lumps of ice before his arrival in these elevated regions. Haydn gave lessons, and played in orchestras, by which he earned something, but his poverty estranged him from other people, and his sole happiness consisted in an old worm-eaten piano. He continued to compose bravely on it nevertheless, for his genius would not let him rest. He gave lessons in singing and playing to a certain Fräulein Martinez, a connection of Metastasio (the celebrated poet), and in return he boarded with her gratis for three years. Subsequently he removed to the Vorstadt. At this period he received 60 gulden a year for conducting the music at the "Brothers of Mercy," in the Leopoldstadt, which obliged him to be in church at 8 o'clock in the morning on Sundays and fête-days; at 10 o'clock, he played the organ in Count Haugwitz's chapel, and at 11 o'clock, he sang in St. Stephen's Church, this religious service being paid by 17 kreuzers (about two shillings). Haydn speaks Italian with tolerable fluency, and is always ready to admit that he owes a great deal to an Italian artist named Porpora.* If I am not mistaken, he made his acquaintance at the house of a lady in Memersdorf. Haydn served this Porpora during three months almost in the capacity of a menial, solely with a view to learning something from him. Porpora taught the lady singing, while Haydn accompanied on the piano, and got his compositions revised from time to time.'

After Haydn became Prince Esterhazy's Capellmeister in 1760, he seldom quitted the prince's property at Estoras, and Eisenstadt, to come to Vienna; for his master, unlike most Hungarian magnates, did not care to display the wealth of his house during the winter in the imperial city; and when he did go there, he could not bear to stay long, and was always too glad to cut short his visit unexpectedly, even before the period originally fixed. At the same time, though Haydn, as we shall often enough see, was strictly

* Nicolo Porpora, born at Naples, 1685, where, in 1731, he established that celebrated school for singing in which Farinelli, Caffarelli, &c., the famed soprani, were trained. Porpora died in Naples, in 1767, at the age of eighty-two, in great necessity.

chained to his official duties yet he contrived to form business connections, in addition to the artistic ones of which he had so many in the German central point of music, inasmuch as his very wealthy master, for whose gratification he year by year, nay almost day by day, had to compose something new, by no means placed him in such a pecuniary position as to enable him to decline all other receipts. And even though the prince was sometimes exceptionally liberal with his assistance, as for instance rebuilding entirely the small dwelling of the Capellmeister, which was twice burnt down, and Haydn's wants remained through life simple to a degree, still he had a misfortune at home which the richest resources could never fully supply, an extravagant wife. This is why in the following letters we shall see him rather eager after gain, and even particular to a *groschen*, which is not in accordance with his character; and the constant necessity for the utmost economy caused him in after days to be reproached with avarice, when he no longer required to be so careful, but continued so from long habit. We shall, however, learn that few indeed attached less value to money than Haydn; on the contrary, his secret and almost lavish benevolence proves a degree of generous feeling that, in spite of the homely frugality of his life and position, was always peculiar to him.

His constant absence from Vienna gave rise to a correspondence on business with the music publisher Artaria, some of the most interesting portions of which we are about to givė; and although they treat principally of business matters, still we may, on the one hand, find that these pages are not unimportant to the enquirer, as fixing the chronological dates of Haydn's works, a problem yet to be solved; while, on the other hand, we see here, in matters however minute, the simple, honest, and modest nature, as well as the just and artistic self-consciousness, of a master so renowned in his day—one, too, whom Mozart, as we well know, so highly revered.'

2.

To Artaria.

Sir, Estoras, Feb. 8, 1780.

I send herewith the fifth and last sonata, requesting you to return the whole to me for revision; at all events, I hope to gain some credit by this work with the intellectual world. It is only those who are envious (and there are many such) who will find fault with it; should they have a good sale, I hope to prove by my future compositions that it will always be my endeavour to serve you. I am, sir, your humble servant,

JOSEPHUS HAYDN, Capellmeister.

3.

To Artaria.

Sir, Estoras, Feb. 25, 1780.

I now return you the six sonatas carefully corrected, and request that strict attention may be paid to them. The approval of Fräulein Auenbrugger* is most important in my eyes, as her style of playing and her genuine insight into music equal that of the greatest masters. Both deserve to be mentioned in the public papers, and thus be made known in all Europe. By-the-bye, I consider it advisable, in order to anticipate the criticisms of any witlings, to print in large letters on the other side of the titlepage what follows :—

'NOTICE.

'There are only two movements in these six sonatas in which the same subject occurs through several bars. The author has done so intentionally, to exemplify various modes of treatment.'

For, of course, I could have taken a hundred other ideas besides the one in question, but in order that the whole work may not be exposed to blame on account of this well-weighed passage (which the critics, and, above all, my enemies, might pervert), I think it right to annex this 'Notice,' or something of the kind, to prevent any injury to the sale of the work. I, however, submit the question entirely to the judicious decision of the Demoiselles v. Auenbrugger, to whom I beg my respectful regards.

I hope soon to have an answer on the above point, and have the honour to be, yours, &c.

J. HAYDN.

* Probably the daughter of the celebrated physician of that day, and author of some medical works, Dr. Leopold v. Auenbrugger, in Vienna.

4.

To Artaria.

Estoras, May 27, 1781.

Sir,

I am exceedingly obliged to you for the four neatly engraved copies. With regard to the songs, I have composed these fourteen with particular care, and the number would long ago have been completed if I had the words for them; and I cannot understand why Herr v. Greiner * does not send them again to me; at the time they were in my hands, I only wished to have his opinion with regard to the expression, and for which purpose I sent them to him by Herr Walther, the organ-builder, and I can get no answer either from one or the other. Will you oblige me by trying to urge on the matter through Herr Walther, for I can assure you that these songs in point of variety, simplicity, and ease, probably surpass all I have hitherto written. I have some doubt, however, whether you will yourself undertake them, for, in the first place, I ask 30 ducats for them; secondly, I require six copies; and, thirdly, the following dedication:—

* The Greiner family were at that time one of the most devoted to art in Vienna, whose house was frequented by all celebrities in art and science, both native and foreign. Caroline Pichler, one of the daughters, in her 'Denkwürdigkeiten,' especially names Mozart, Haydn, Salieri, Paesiello, and Cimarosa.

COLLECTION OF GERMAN SONGS

FOR THE PIANO,

DEDICATED

AS A MARK OF PECULIAR HOMAGE

TO

MADEMOISELLE CLAIR

BY

HERR JOSEPH HAYDN,

CAPELLMEISTER TO PRINCE ESTERHAZY.

Between ourselves, this young lady is the idol of our Prince, so you will at once see what impression such things will make! If you agree to these conditions, you may rely on my completing the remaining ones by degrees. The songs, however, must appear on Elizabeth's Day, being the name-day of the above fair lady.

Now about Paris: M. le Gros, Director of the 'Concerts Spirituels,' wrote me a great many fine things about my 'Stabat Mater,' which had been given there four times with great applause; so this gentleman asked permission to have it engraved. They made me an offer to engrave all my future works, on very advantageous terms, and are much surprised that my compositions for the voice are so singularly pleasing; I, however, am not in the least surprised, for as yet they have heard nothing. If they could only hear my operetta 'L'Isola disabitata,' and my last Shrovetide opera, 'La Fedeltà premiata,' I do assure you that no such work has hitherto been heard in Paris, nor perhaps in Vienna either. My great misfortune is living in the country.

Pray send me Herr Boccherini's letter without delay, and present my compliments to him. No one here can tell me where this place Arenas is. It cannot, however, be far from Madrid; so I beg you will try to find it out for me, as I wish to write to Herr Boccherini myself.

I am, with esteem, &c. J. HAYDN.

My portrait is highly approved of by many. Send me the picture back in the same case.

The Luigi Boccherini here alluded to was born at Lucca about 1730, and, after making some short journeys in his own country, came to Paris, where in 1768 he published 'Six Symphonies,' that is, violin quartetts, with violoncello obbligato. His fame in this new style of music soon extended beyond the boundaries of France, and Frederick William II. of Prussia was such a lover of Boccherini's quartetts and quintetts, that he settled on him a salary for life, on condition of his sending some new compositions of the kind every year to Berlin. His mode of writing is the easy, melodious, and flowing style of the Italians of that day, although he knew how to season and to enrich his works by German harmony also. He had a particular esteem for Haydn, as the founder of the quartett form, and carried on a friendly correspondence with him from Madrid, where he had met with a distinguished reception, and was appointed chamber virtuoso and composer to the Infant of Spain; this well known fact is further confirmed by these letters.*

He died in 1805. His quartetts are now-a-days only played by those who attach more value to historical traditions than to the vitality and progress of art.

5.

To Artaria.

Estoras, June 23, 1781.

I was exceedingly pleased to receive the picture, and likewise the twelve copies of the beautifully engraved portrait. But my Prince felt even more strongly on the subject, for, as soon as he saw them, he asked me to give him one. As these twelve copies are not sufficient, I beg you will send me six more, and charge them to me; you can deduct the price from the payment of the songs, six of which I am to deliver to you next week.

Fifteen only are finished, but one of these may possibly be objected to by strict censorship. It is one

* I wrote to Madrid on the subject of this correspondence, but received an answer from the director of the State Library there, to say, that no letters of Haydn are extant there, and that the grand-children of Boccherini, who are living there, possess none either.

that you gave me yourself, the words of which you shall have in a few days. I should deeply regret this, as I have written a remarkably appropriate air for it. I have not yet received the other songs from Herr von Greiner, and, no doubt, they are lost. You would therefore very much oblige me by procuring a dozen others from Hofrath Greiner, but good, and diversified, so that I may have sufficient to choose from ; for it does so happen that many a poem has a veritable antipathy to the composer, or the composer to the poem.

I agree, moreover, to the proposal of a ducat for each. But no one is to know this. I would rather receive no money till the corrections are all made. I am still in doubt about the dedication—whether to dedicate it to one or to another; at all events, it is a point that I reserve, and shall expect twelve copies.

When I come to Vienna, I hope you will be so kind as to present me to the excellent Herr v. Mansfeld. I thank you once more sincerely for the copies and portraits, and remain, &c.

J. Haydn.

6.

To Artaria.

Estoras, July 20, 1781.

I send herewith the first twelve songs, and will endeavour to transmit the two dozen to you as soon as possible; some of them are written twice over, in case my writing should not be quite legible. With regard to the third song, observe that at the close of the text below, N. B. must be engraved, and in the same way as marked by me under the text.

You will find the words of the fourth, eighth, and ninth in Friebert's songs, published by Herr v. Kurzböck; if, however, you cannot get them, I will send them to you. The same three songs have (between ourselves) been set to music wretchedly by Capellmeister Hofmann, and just because this braggart thinks that he alone has climbed to the summit of Mount Parnassus, and tries in every case to run me down with certain circles of the great world, I have composed these same three songs, to show this *pretended* great world the difference—*Sed hoc inter nos.**

You will find the words of the tenth and twelfth songs among those you sent me, and which I now enclose. The words of the twelfth are those about which I am dubious as to the censorship.

I particularly request that you will not allow anyone to copy or to sing these songs at present, or alter them in any way whatever, for, when finished, I intend myself to superintend their being sung to critical audiences; a master must maintain his rights by his presence, to ensure the proper execution of his works. They are in-

* This Capellmeister is no doubt the one in St. Stephen's, in Vienna, whose adjunct Mozart was in 1790.

deed merely songs, but not *street songs* like those of Hofmann, devoid of ideas, of expression, and, above all, of melody.

You again make me your debtor for the portraits, but do they sell? I am curious to know. At all events, the frame-makers and gilders have profited by those you have sent me.

I beg, when you have an opportunity, that you will return me the pasteboard portfolio in which the songs were packed, for that kind of thing is not to be got here.

I am, &c. J. HAYDN.

7.

To Artaria.

Estoras, June 4, 1782.

Sir,

I read with surprise in the Vienna *Diario* that it was your intention to publish my quartetts four weeks hence; I wish you had shown sufficient consideration for me to delay this announcement till I had left Vienna. Such a proceeding redounds very little to my credit, and is most injurious to me, and it is certainly a very Jewish step on your part. You ought at least to have withheld the advertisement till the entire work was completed, as I have not yet satisfied all my subscribers. M. Hummel [a music publisher] wished to become one of my subscribers, but I would not behave so shabbily, and I did not send them to Berlin entirely out of respect towards yourself and our further transactions. By Heavens! you have wronged me to the extent of more than fifty ducats, not having yet fulfilled my engagements with many of my subscribers. This step must cause the cessation of all further transactions between us.

I am, &c. J. HAYDN.

8.

To Artaria.

Estoras, Jan. 20, 1782.

I regret having written my last letter to you in a moment of hasty passion, and I do hope that, in spite of it, we shall remain good friends. There is no doubt that I gave you my quartetts with a view to their being published, but it never for a moment occurred to me that you would at once put this into the papers. The thing is now done; another time we must both be more cautious. I intend shortly to forward you some songs. I thank you for those you send, and remain, &c.

J. HAYDN.

9.

To Artaria.

Estoras, Feb. 15, 1782.

I am engaged in a most disagreeable correspondence with Herr Breunig, to whom I sent a copy of your own words as to my quartetts offered to you by him, and who has sent me the offensive paper I enclose, with the impertinent threat that, if I do not at once forward the paper to you for his satisfaction, Herr Breunig must believe me to be a liar! You will, therefore, I trust, defend both yourself and me from such an imputation; but the less I have to do with Herr Breunig the better pleased shall I be.

Yours, &c. J. HAYDN.

P.S.—I beg you will have a little patience for a short time about the songs. I should like to see a single copy of my quartetts.

10.

To Artaria.

August, 1782.

On the very day that I received yours of the 2nd ult. I had the misfortune to injure my left foot so seriously by a fall, that I have never since been able to leave the house, and my close confinement has delayed my answer to you.

The unpleasant consequences of M. Hummel's becoming a subscriber to the quartetts, I as thoroughly foresaw, as you will now see, the evil consequences entailed on me, for Baron van Swieten, in his last letter, gives me distinctly to understand that I henceforth ought to dedicate my compositions to the public. I hope you will perceive that such conduct is entirely owing to your over-hasty advertisement, and it was this very circumstance that obliged me to offer my quartetts to other people. I send you both letters. I regret that I cannot at present write to Boccherini, but when occasion offers, pray present my devoted respects to him.

As to the pianoforte sonatas with violin, you must still have a good deal of patience, because I have to compose a new Italian opera, as the Grand Duke and Duchess and perhaps his Majesty the Emperor [Joseph II.] are coming here.

Your defence against Breunig is admirably done. It was delivered to him, and he gave a receipt for it.

I am, yours, &c. J. HAYDN.*

11.

To Artaria.

Estoras, Sept. 29, 1782.

I at last send you the five symphonies you wished for, neatly and correctly written, and also well constructed; I tried them over myself with my orchestra; and

* On August 16, he writes: 'many thanks for the cantata, which is neatly engraved.' As to the symphony (or overture) of his new opera, he could not let him have it till after the opera had been performed; 'but if you would like two other works of mine that no living soul has as yet seen, you can have them for six ducats each.'

I do assure you that, the shortness of the pieces making the engraving very cheap, you will have a considerable profit by their publication. Now I beg you will put the 25 ducats, full weight, into a little box, seal it up, and wrap or sew it into an oil cloth cover, and write nothing on it except *à Mons. Haydn,* for I do not desire that any of the family here should know of my transactions. You can deliver the box to the Prince's porter, and only tell him that it contains money, and then I shall receive it quite safely from him. You must of course ask for a receipt from the porter, to say that he has been entrusted with the box by you.

I am, &c. J. HAYDN.

12.

To Artaria.

Estoras, Oct. 20, 1782.

I cannot understand why you have not received my last letter, written a fortnight ago, in which I mentioned that, when I was last in Vienna, I had myself made an agreement with your partner [Coppi] for five ducats each piece, and which Herr Artaria willingly agreed to give. I also wrote that instead of *symphonies* you were to put *overtures*; so this solves your doubts. I have been much provoked by the delay, inasmuch as I could have got forty ducats from another publisher for these five pieces, and you make too many difficulties about a matter by which, in such short compositions, you have at least a thirtyfold profit. The sixth piece has long had its companion; so pray make an end of the affair, and send me either my music or my money.

J. Haydn.

13.

To Artaria.

Estoras, April 8, 1783.

I now send you the symphony, which was so full of mistakes, that the fellow who wrote it in such a slovenly manner, ought to have his hand chopped off. The last, or fourth, movement is not practicable for the piano, and I think it advisable to have this remark printed with it. The name of Laudon [the celebrated field marshal] will contribute more to the sale than ten finales. My continued unhappy condition, having had an operation for a polypus on my nose, makes me as yet incapable of all work; you must, therefore, have patience about the songs for another week or fortnight, until my enfeebled head, by God's help, regains its former vigour. Please say to Count Durazzo that I cannot remember the subjects of his trios, or having received any of them. I searched minutely through all my music and papers, but could find no trace whatever of them; I will, however (if the Count pleases), send him the catalogue of all my trios. Hoping for a favourable answer, I am, &c.

J. HAYDN.

14.

To Artaria.

Estoras, June 18, 1783.

I send the Laudon symphony, for which the violin part is not at all required. I thank you much for Clementi's sonatas; they are very beautiful. If the author is in Vienna, pray take the opportunity to present my compliments to him.

Yours,

J. HAYDN.

P.S.—You must again have patience as to the pianoforte sonatas, with violin and bass, as I am at this moment writing a new *opera seria.*

From this period the correspondence between the composer and the publisher assumes a more friendly aspect. It is evident that the sale of Haydn's works became every year better, and the master's fame had even at that time attained very great eminence. His dramatic works, indeed, especially the *fantoccini* operas, written for his Prince's theatre, were not even known beyond the boundaries of Hungary. He was obliged to rest satisfied with the applause of his immediate circle. That this, however, was by no means wanting, we learn from the following note to Artaria :—

15.

To Artaria.

Estoras, March 1, 1784.

My very dear Friend,

Yesterday my 'Armida' was given for the second time with universal applause. It is thought the best work I have yet written. I ask pardon from Fräulein Nanet Peyer, whom I embrace a thousand times for my remissness; she may rest assured that my mass of business is to blame for this, and not myself.

I am, &c.

J. HAYDN.

16.

To Artaria.

Estoras, April 5, 1784.

I have always received more than 100 ducats for my quartetts by subscription, a sum that Herr Willmann also promised to give me, but I agree to accept the 300 florins with the following stipulations: first, that you will wait patiently till July, &c. &c. The next post day, I will send you some published things, and also an analysis of my cantata, which has been engraved, and appears to have been received with unusual applause, according to the article sent to me by Professor Cramer, from Kiel.*

Yours, in haste, &c.

HAYDN.

The following letter to the music publisher Nadermann, in Paris, discovered by C. A. Mangold, and published in the 'Neue Zuschrift für Musik,' proves how much Haydn's instrumental music was appreciated in France also. We shall hear more on this point.

17.

To Herr Nadermann.

Estoras, Oct. 25, 1784.

Sir,

As you accepted three symphonies of my composition last year, I now offer you three new and very carefully composed symphonies, neatly and correctly written out, for the sum of 150 ducats, payable at the end of November. If you, sir, agree to this proposal, I shall not fail to take advantage of the earliest opportunity to send you the piece you desire for the piano, in your last letter.

I am, &c.

HAYDN.

* It appeared in Cramer's 'Magazine of Music,' in 1783, under the title of 'The Beauties and Expression of Passion in a Cantata of Haydn,' written by C. F. Cramer himself, forty-two pages long.

18.

To Artaria.

Estoras, Dec. 10, 1785.

Mon très-cher Ami,

I received the pianoforte sonatas yesterday, and was not a little surprised at the bad engraving and the numerous glaring errors I discovered, especially in the pianoforte part. I was at first so enraged that I intended to have returned you the money, and sent off the score of the sonatas instantly to Herr Hummel, in Berlin, for being here and there illegible, and certain passages improperly inserted and omitted, I felt that I should gain very little credit, and you very little profit. Everyone who buys these sonatas must, in playing them over, curse the engraver, and give them up (particularly page 8). I would far rather pay for two new plates out of my own pocket than see such confusion. Even a master would be obliged to study before disentangling a passage; so what is to become of a *dilettante*? I spent the whole of yesterday and half of to-day in corrections, and yet I have only looked them over superficially.

My dear friend, pray take care that all this be amended, or little honour will accrue to either of us. I hope we shall soon meet.

Yours, &c.

HAYDN.

19.

To Artaria.

Estoras, Feb. 27, 1787.

Mon très-cher Ami,

As to the Paris letter you sent me, I must candidly confess that, after due consideration, I do not feel disposed to agree to it, for the following reasons. In the first place, by so doing, I should highly offend the Cadiz gentlemen, who were the original cause of these sonatas being written, and who paid me for them; in the second place, the French gentlemen would be still more offended were I to accept payment for a work to be published in three weeks, from which work, you, my good friend, will assuredly derive great profit, and the more so as it can be sold as a whole as well as quartetts.

Further, I yesterday received a letter from Herr v. Jacoby, Royal Prussian Resident, in which he says as follows:—'What is this affair about some pieces of yours, that Herr Artaria proposes to send to the King at Berlin. I shall be glad to receive an explanation on this point from yourself, and therefore beg you to write to me.' I cannot believe that you have any intention of dedicating the sonatas in question to His Majesty, either as quartetts or with all the parts, for such a thing would be contrary to common sense. I believe that he must allude to the new quartetts, which I highly approve of, if you are of the same opinion.

I beg you will let me hear from you on the subject, to allay my suspicions; I would fain hope that you will not altogether disgust me by such a step, as I have always been your attached friend, and hope ever to continue so.

I am, &c. HAYDN.

20.

To Artaria.

Estoras, March 7, 1787.

Dearest Friend,

I have nothing to say against any of the proceedings you propose about the sonatas, although motives of policy must prevent my signing the letter to the Concert Spirituel. But if you choose to make the offer in your own name, I have no objection. I approve of your reserving to yourself the right of publishing, and quite see what a great advantage it will be to you. I do not grudge it you, for I know you will not be stingy with me on other occasions. Herr v. Jacoby only wished to know what kind of work you intended to dedicate to the King of Prussia. I wrote to him I believed it was the new quartetts.* I send you the first of the three quartetts.

Yours,

HAYDN.

* Haydn received a ring for the dedication of the 'six new quartetts.'

21.

To Artaria.

Estoras, April 26, 1787.

My dearest Friend,

Thank you a thousand times for the twelve ducats, which were quite unexpected—a proof of your friendship, and your labours, as well as my own. I hope often to earn the same by my industry, especially if, as a true friend and honest man, you will candidly tell me who it was that offered you my new symphonies. I swear to you on my honour not to say one word to the person on the subject; but as such a theft cannot fail to distress me very much, and might also cause you hereafter considerable loss of your fair profits, it is your own interest to tell me the truth on the subject, and to give me timely information of such a dangerous fraud, and I do assure you I shall be most grateful to you, if you will do so. I await your speedy reply, feeling much annoyed, and on hearing from you, I will explain further about the symphonies.

The following explains the contents of the above letter, related in the biography of the well known Capellmeister Adalbert Gyrowetz (Vienna, 1848) who was in Paris in 1789. 'When Gyrowetz brought the music to the aforesaid gentlemen (the music publishers), a day was fixed to rehearse the pieces. The first artists in the orchestra of the Grand Opéra were invited to be present, when Gyrowetz saw with what love of music, nay, with what passion, the French artists strove to comprehend and to execute it properly. Thus two symphonies were performed with the utmost success, and with hearty applause. Gyrowetz then proceeded to produce a third symphony in G for rehearsal, on which they all stared at him in a searching and somewhat suspicious manner, asking him significantly whether this symphony was really and truly his own composition, and on his assurance that it certainly was so, they asked to examine the score, and after looking at it minutely, bar by bar, and finding everything tally correctly, they all began to congratulate Gyrowetz, telling him at the same time that the symphony was already published; that this very symphony had been played, as a favourite piece, in all the theatres and concerts, but had been engraved under the name of Joseph Haydn. Gyrowetz naturally showed considerable surprise, and asked how such a thing could possibly have occurred; and who could have dared to engrave his work in Paris, under a strange name; on which they all told Gyrowetz that a great honour had been conferred on him, by his symphonies having been mistaken for the work of Haydn, and that the publisher was Herr Schlesinger.

Gyrowetz went off instantly to Herr Schlesinger to learn the true story of the affair, and heard from him, that a German virtuoso on the violin, of the name of Tost, had come from Vienna to Paris, bringing with him three symphonies, which he sold to Schlesinger as compositions of Haydn, and thus it was that they were published under Haydn's name. Tost was music director in Prince Esterhazy's band, and after the Prince had got Gyrowetz's symphonies, Tost had copied them, and brought them to Paris, where they were received with great applause, and performed at all the theatres and concerts.

Gyrowetz then requested that his name, being that of the real author, should be placed on those symphonies, which was at once promised, but as a vast number of printed copies were in circulation, even to this day, many of these symphonies appear under Haydn's name.

Some years later, the affair was cleared up for Haydn too, as we shall see further on.

22.

To Artaria.

Estoras, May 2, 1787.

I heartily rejoice to hear that it is an untruth about my symphonies. I daily expect a letter from Paris, and as soon as I obtain permission, no one shall have them but you. Pray send the enclosed letter to Wallerstein.* I should like to know by and by who this Ludwig is; but there is no hurry about it. You will shortly hear of a present that I received quite unexpectedly from a great man.

I am, &c.

HAYDN.

P.S.—A young composer in Vienna, Joseph Eybler, has shown me three pianoforte sonatas of his composition, by no means badly written, and he requested me at the same time to recommend them to you for publication. The young man is very promising, plays the piano well, and has much knowledge of composition. If you have any wish to see these works, to secure yourself against loss, you can converse with him on the subject. [Eybler was, in Beethoven's day, Hofcapellmeister in Vienna.]

23.

To Artaria.

Estoras, June 21, 1787.

I have revised and corrected the 'Seven Words' throughout, and also the quartett and pianoforte ar-

* Prince v. Oettingen-Wallerstein, in Swabian Ries, was a very great musical amateur: Mozart also visited him at the time of his great journey in 1778. His chief favourite, however, whom he highly valued both as a pianist and a composer, was Major von Beecke, Kammerherr, and musical intendant, who lived at Wallerstein with the Prince. We shall repeatedly hear of this Prince.

rangement. I regret that the Berliners have anticipated you, but it is your own fault, for they never received it through me. As for the dedication of the quartetts to His Majesty the King of Prussia, I should prefer your having it written by some intelligent person in Vienna, but brief and to the point. The Minister, Herr v. Jacoby, could assist you in this best of all. You can also apply to him in my name, and I will write to him myself next Monday.

I am, &c.

HAYDN.

24.

To Artaria.

Estoras, Oct. 7, 1787.

Mon très-cher Ami,

I will send you by the first opportunity the quartetts which I caused to be played over to-day. I was quite astounded by your letter mentioning the theft of the quartetts. I do assure you, upon my honour, that they never were copied by my copyist, who is the most honest fellow imaginable; whereas *your* copyist is a rascal, for he offered mine eight species ducats this winter to let him have the 'Seven Words.' I am sorry that I cannot go to Vienna myself on purpose to have him arrested. My plan would be to cause Herr Laugh to summon him to appear before Herr v. Augusti, the burgomaster, and to make him confess from whom he received those quartetts. Herr v. Augusti is a kind old friend of mine, and would, no doubt, give me his aid in the matter, as he did once before in a similar affair. Notwithstanding your having everything written out on your own premises, you may be deceived, because these rascals have music paper *à parte*, and in this way they contrive by degrees to steal the parts placed before them. In future I will take the precaution to send you my own copyist.

I am, &c.

HAYDN.

25.

To Artaria.

Estoras, Nov. 27, 1787.

Pray excuse my not having answered you sooner, for want of a good opportunity. You wish me to give you a certificate for the six quartetts. I now enclose it. That I gave a separate certificate to Herr Forster, making over the sole right to him, is false; but that I sent the quartetts to him, after being engraved, is true enough. The blame rests with yourself, for you might have sent Herr Langmann the quartetts, and the sole right to them, three months ago. Your having withheld them proceeds entirely from the greatest selfishness; no one can blame me for striving to derive some profit from my pieces when published, being very inadequately paid for my works, and my rights also greater than those of any other negotiator. Owing to this, you must now set to work more cautiously with our contract, and put it in writing, while I shall take care that I am sufficiently remunerated. If, on the whole, you are a loser by this, which, however, I can scarcely credit, I will strive to compensate you in some other way.

I am, &c.

HAYDN.

The following very beautiful letter, addressed to the Provincial Oberverwalter Roth, in Prague, is inserted by Professor Niemtscheck, of Prague, in the sketch he wrote of his friend Mozart's life. It requires no comment, only we ought to say that it was written in December 1787, the year in which Mozart first put his 'Don Juan' on the stage in Prague. I have not hitherto discovered any trace of the original.

26.

To Herr Roth.

December, 1787.

You wish me to write an *opera buffa* for you. Most willingly, if you are inclined to have a vocal composition of mine for yourself alone, but if with a view to produce it on the stage at Prague, I cannot in that case comply with your wish, all my operas being too closely connected with our personal circle (Prince Esterhazy's, in Hungary), so they could never produce the proper effect, which I calculated in accordance with the locality. It would be very different if I had the invaluable privilege of composing a new opera for your theatre. But even then I should risk a great deal, for scarcely any man could stand beside the great Mozart.

I only wish I could impress on every friend of music, and on great men in particular, the same depth of musical sympathy, and profound appreciation of Mozart's inimitable music, that I myself feel and enjoy; then nations would vie with each other to possess such a jewel within their frontiers. Prague ought to strive to retain this precious man, but also to remunerate him; for without this the history of a great genius is sad indeed, and gives very little encouragement to posterity to further exertions, and it is on this account so many promising geniuses are ruined. It enrages me to think that the unparalleled Mozart is not yet engaged by some imperial or royal court! Forgive my excitement; but I love the man so dearly! *

I am, &c.

HAYDN.

* At that very time Mozart had succeeded to the situation of Gluck (who had recently died), at the imperial court of Vienna, with a salary of 800 florins.

27.

To Artaria.

Estoras, Feb. 16, 1788.

You will not, I hope, be offended that want of time has latterly prevented my writing to you about the oratorio; if it is already transcribed, which I hope may be the case, pray give it to our porter. By-the-bye, I am very much obliged to you for the capital cheese you sent me, and also the sausages, for which I am your debtor, but shall not fail, when an opportunity offers, to return the obligation. I beg you will send me C. P. E. Bach's two last pianoforte works.

Yours, &c.

HAYDN.

28.

To Artaria.

Estoras, May 22, 1788.

My dear Friend,

I should be both unjust and ungrateful were I so coolly to set aside your friendship. I can never forget that you gave me the preference over so many, although I well know that I deserved it more than some others; as soon as my present engagements are at an end, you shall have the first offer of my works as formerly. If you can write to me again before your departure, in time to receive an answer from me, I shall be glad for various reasons. My time is too short to-day.

Yours,

HAYDN.

29.

To Artaria.

Estoras, Aug. 10, 1788.

My manifold affairs have hitherto prevented my answering your last letter to me. I repeat that it will always be a pleasure to me to supply you with my works. As I am now in a position when I require a little money, I propose writing for you, by the end of December, either three new quartetts or three pianoforte sonatas, with violin and violoncello, and I beg you will send me by our messenger an *à conto* of twenty-five gold ducats; for which this letter must be your security. You shall have the receipt for the sum next Monday. Of course, it is an understood thing that I am then to complete the other three quartetts, or pianoforte sonatas; that, as usual, the half-dozen may be included in one edition.

N.B.—For six quartetts, the same price as formerly, one hundred ducats. For six pianoforte sonatas, three hundred florins. In the hope of a favourable answer, I am, yours, HAYDN.

30.

To Artaria.

Estoras, Aug. 17, 1788.

Many thanks for the twenty-five ducats. The care I have bestowed on the three pianoforte sonatas bespoken by you, with violin and violoncello, is an earnest of my wish to retain your friendship.

Yours,

HAYDN.

31.

To Artaria.

Estoras, Oct. 26, 1788.

In order to compose your three pianoforte sonatas particularly well, I have been obliged to buy a pianoforte. Now as you, no doubt, have long known that even philosophers occasionally stand in need of money, which is precisely my case at present, I would politely request you to pay into the hands of the organ and pianoforte-maker, Wenzl Schanz, at the Laimgruben, Blaue Schiff, No. 22, thirty-one gold ducats, which shall be repaid by me with thanks, by the end of January, 1789.

To convince you that I mean to keep my word, I enclose a little bill, of which I have to-day given notice. Should you, however, have any doubts of my integrity, I will send you, by the next post, a bond for

1,000 gulden signed by my Prince himself. I am unwilling to be in debt to tradesmen, and, thank God! I am free from this burden, but as great people keep me so long waiting for payments, I have got rather into difficulty. This letter, however, will be your security, and is valid in any court. I will pay off the interest with my *notes.* Confident that you will not refuse my request, I wrote to the organ-builder, who will certainly call on you to receive his money.

Pray excuse this liberty; your kindness is bestowed on a grateful man, who will always be your obliged,

HAYDN.

P.S.—I shall have the pleasure of seeing you in Vienna towards the end of December.

32.

To Artaria.

Estoras, March 8, 1789.

The sudden resolution of my Prince to leave hated Vienna caused my hasty journey to Estoras, and prevented my being able to take leave of the greater number of my friends; I hope, therefore, you will forgive me.

On the day of my journey, I was seized with such a violent cold that I was laid up for three weeks, but now, thank Heaven! I feel better. I will send you the third sonata a week hence.

Yours,

HAYDN.

33.

To Artaria.

Estoras, March 29, 1789.

Mon très cher Ami,

I send the third sonata, which I have rewritten, with variations to suit your taste. I beg you will press forward the publication as much as possible, for many are eagerly awaiting its appearance.

In my leisure hours I have composed a new capriccio for the pianoforte, which, from its taste, singularity, and elaborate finish, cannot fail to be received with approbation by the learned and the unlearned. It is only one piece, rather long, but by no means very difficult: as I always give you the preference in my works, I offer this one to you for twenty-four ducats; the price is rather high, but you are sure to derive good profit from it; besides, as I am your debtor, you can deduct your claim from the sum.

I am yours, &c.

HAYDN.

The following letters to Frau v. Genzinger were discovered by Th. G. von Karajan, in Vienna, and published in 1861 in the 'Jahrbuch für vaterländische Geschichte,' and afterwards republished as a separate pamphlet, with the necessary notes and explanations. The originals are in the imperial library in Vienna. The following will serve to explain these letters.

The 'Ladies' Doctor,' Peter Leopold v. Genzinger, in Vienna, during the long winter evenings, was in the habit of assembling professional musicians and amateurs, in his house at Schattenhof, where on Sundays such men as Mozart, Haydn, Dittersdorf, Albrechtsberger, &c. were welcome at his table, and produced their newest works. As physician in ordinary to Prince Nicolaus Esterhazy of Galantha, he was often obliged to pay long visits to Eisenstadt, where he became intimate with Haydn, so that, when the latter came to Vienna, he was his guest every Sunday at dinner. His wife, Marianne, née v. Kayser, an intellectual lady and most accomplished singer, appreciated and sought after at that time by all the musical circles in Vienna, was naturally attracted more closely to the amiable *maestro* from her love of music, and although she was nearly forty years of age, a personal connection was gradually developed in the course of their musical intercourse that eventually touched their hearts, and gave rise to a bright bond of friendship between the lady, happily married, and blessed with five promising children, and the old though still youthful *maestro,* whose marriage was childless and far from happy. The correspondence originated in the following note from the music-loving lady, dated January, 1789 :—

Dear M. v. Haydn,

With your kind permission, I take the liberty to send a pianoforte arrangement of the beautiful andante in your admirable composition. I arranged it from the score quite alone, and without the least help from my master. I beg that, if you should discover any errors, you will be so good as to correct them. I do hope that you are in perfect health, and nothing do I wish more than to see you soon again in Vienna, in order to prove further my high esteem.

Your obedient servant,

MARIA ANNA v. GENZINGER,

née v. Kayser.

Haydn answers from Estoras as follows :—

34.

To Madam v. Genzinger.

Estoras, June 14, 1789.

Dear Madam,

In all my previous correspondence, nothing was ever so agreeable to me as the surprise of seeing your charming writing, and reading so many kind expressions; but still more did I admire what you sent me—

the admirable arrangement of the adagio, which, from its correctness, might be engraved at once by any publisher. I should like to know whether you arranged the adagio from the score, or whether you gave yourself the amazing trouble of first putting it into score from the separate parts, and then arranging it for the piano, for, if the latter, such an attention would be too flattering to me, and I feel that I really do not deserve it.

Best and kindest Frau v. Genzinger! I only await a hint from you as to how, and in what way, I can serve you; in the meantime, I return the adagio, and hope that my talents, poor though they be, may ensure me some commands from you.

I am yours, &c.

HAYDN.

35.

To Artaria.

July 5, 1789.

Dear Sir,

I thank you much for the three sonatas and the fantasia you sent me; I only regret that here and there some mistakes have crept in which can no longer be corrected, as they are already in circulation and for sale. It is really very annoying for me that no single work of mine, published under your auspices, is ever free from errors. On former occasions, you invariably sent me the first copy before general publication, and in this you acted wisely; I could not make a proper example of the only copy you sent me of the sonatas, as I did not wish to soil it, and was also afraid of not getting another for a long time, or perhaps losing mine altogether, which must always be very irritating to an author. I must still beg a little indulgence as to my debt of thirty-nine florins; I am in hopes of being paid a debt of seven years' standing by the Archduke of Milan, when I will repay you at once. Be so good meanwhile as to forward three copies of the sonatas to me.

I now wish to learn the truth from you, as to the person from whom you received the two new symphonies which you recently advertised, whether you bought them direct from Herr Tost, or got them already published through Herr Siebert from Paris. If you purchased them from Herr Tost, I earnestly entreat you to furnish me with an *à parte* written assurance of the fact, as I hear that Herr Tost declares I sold these two symphonie to you, which caused him great loss.

I am, &c.

HAYDN.

Here follows a letter from Hadyn's fair musical friend.

Vienna, Oct. 29, 1789.

Dear Herr v. Haydn,

I hope you duly received my letter of September 15, and also the first movement of the symphony (the andante of which I sent you some months ago), and now follows the last movement, which I have arranged for the piano as well as it was in my power to do; I only wish that it may please you, and earnestly beg that, if there are any mistakes in it, you will correct them at your leisure, a service which I shall always accept from you, my valued Herr Haydn, with the utmost gratitude. Be so good as to let me know whether you received my letter of September 15, and the piece of music, and if it is in accordance with your taste, which would delight me very much, for I am very uneasy and concerned lest you should not have got it safely, or not approve of it. I hope that you are well, which will always be a source of pleasure to me to hear, and commending myself to your further friendship and remembrance, I remain, your devoted friend and servant,

Maria Anna v. Genzinger,
née v. Kayser.

My husband sends you his regards.

To this Haydn replies as follows:—

36.

To Frau v. Genzinger.

Nov. 7, 1789.

Dear Madam,

I beg your forgiveness a million times for having so long delayed returning your laborious and admirable work: the last time my apartments were cleared out, which occurred just after receiving your first movement, it was mislaid by my copyist among the mass of my other music, and only a few days ago I had the good fortune to find it in an old opera score.

Dearest and kindest Frau v. Genzinger! Do not be displeased with a man who values you so highly; I should be inconsolable if by the delay I were to lose any of your favour, of which I am so proud.

These two pieces are arranged quite as correctly as the first. I cannot but admire the trouble and patience you lavish on my poor talents, and allow me to assure you in return that, in my frequent evil moods, nothing cheers me so much as the flattering conviction that I am kindly remembered by you; for which favour I kiss your hands a thousand times, and am, with sincere esteem, your obedient servant,

JOSEPH HAYDN.

P.S.—I shall soon claim permission to wait on you.

Another letter from his fair friend has been preserved, which, we think, ought not to be omitted. It is so rarely that we can procure the full and faithful correspondence of distinguished individuals.

Vienna, Nov. 12, 1789.

My valued Herr v. Haydn,

I really cannot tell you all the pleasure I felt in reading your highly prized letter of the 9th. How well am I rewarded for my trouble by seeing your satisfaction! Nothing do I wish more ardently than to have more time (now so absorbed by household affairs), for in that case I would certainly devote many hours to music, my most agreeable and favourite of all occupations. You must not, my dear Herr v. Haydn, take it amiss that I plague you with another letter, but I could not but take advantage of so good an opportunity to inform you of the safe arrival of your letter. I look forward with the utmost pleasure to the happy day when I am to see you in Vienna. Pray continue to give me a place in your friendship and remembrance.

Your sincere and devoted friend and servant.

37.

To Frau v. Genzinger.

Estoras, Nov. 18, 1789.

Dear Lady,

The letter which I received through Herr Siebert gave me another proof of your excellent heart, as instead of a rebuke for my late remissness, you express yourself in so friendly a manner towards me, that so much indulgence, kindness, and great courtesy cause me the utmost surprise, and I kiss your hands in return a thousand times. If my poor talents enable me to respond in any degree to so much that is flattering, I venture, dear madam, to offer you a little musical *potpourri.* I do not, indeed, find in it much that is fragrant, perhaps the publisher may rectify the fault in future editions. If the arrangement of the symphony in it be yours, oh! then I shall be twice as much pleased with the publisher; if not, I venture to ask you to arrange a symphony, and to transcribe it with your own hand, and to send it to me here, when I will at once forward it to my publisher at Leipzig to be engraved.

I am happy to have found an opportunity that leads me to hope for a few more charming lines from you.

I am, &c.

JOSEPH HAYDN.

Shortly afterwards, the master seems to have been again in Vienna, when those agreeable musical meetings were renewed, and Haydn's newest quartetts in particular rehearsed. No doubt Herr v. Häring is the banker so well known as a clever violin-player to all musical *virtuosi.* In 1807 he became the leader of a numerous orchestra consisting almost entirely of amateurs, and gave crowded public concerts. Haydn writes again to his friend as follows :—

38.

To Frau v. Genzinger.

Jan. 23, 1790.

Dear kind Frau v. Genzinger,

I beg to inform you that all arrangements are now completed, for the little quartett party that we agreed to have next Friday. Herr v. Häring esteemed himself very fortunate in being able to be of use to me on this occasion, and the more so when I told him of all the attention I had received from you, and your other merits.

What I care about is a little approval. Pray don't forget to invite the Pater Professor. Meanwhile I kiss your hands, and am, with profound respect, yours, &c.

HAYDN.

This happiness did not, however, last long, for, on February 3, the master was obliged sorrowfully to announce his departure.

39.

To Frau v. Genzinger.

Feb. 3, 1790.

Noblest and kindest Lady,

However flattering the last invitation you gave me yesterday to spend this evening with you, I feel with deep regret that I am even unable to express to you personally my sincere thanks for all your past kindness. Bitterly as I deplore this, with equal truth do I fervently wish you, not only on this evening, but ever and always, the most agreeable social 'réunions'—mine are all over—and to-morrow I return to dreary solitude! May God only grant me health; but I fear the contrary, being far from well to-day. May the Almighty preserve you, dear lady, and your worthy husband, and all your beautiful children. Once more I kiss your hands, and am unchangeably while life lasts,

Yours, &c.

HAYDN.

On February 9, a most dismal epistle follows from dreary Estoras, in which all his dejection, and vexation, and longing for his distant but sympathising friend, are poured out in the warmest though playful strain.

40.

To Frau v. Genzinger.

Estoras, Feb. 9, 1790.

Much esteemed and kindest Frau v Genzinger,

Well! here I sit in my wilderness; forsaken, like some poor orphan, almost without human society; melancholy, dwelling on the memory of past glorious days. Yes; past, alas! And who can tell when these happy hours may return? those charming meetings? where the whole circle have but one heart and one soul —all those delightful musical evenings, which can only be remembered, and not described. Where are all those inspired moments? All gone—and gone for long. You must not be surprised, dear lady, that I have delayed writing to express my gratitude. I found everything at home in confusion; for three days I did not know whether I was *capell* master, or *capell* servant; nothing could console me; my apartments were all in confusion; my pianoforte, that I formerly loved so dearly, was perverse and disobedient, and rather irritated than soothed me. I slept very little, and even my dreams persecuted me, for, while asleep, I was under the pleasant delusion that I was listening to the opera of 'Le Nozze di Figaro,' when the blustering north wind woke me, and almost blew my nightcap off my head. I lost 20 lbs. in weight in three days, for the effects of my good fare at Vienna disappeared on the journey. Alas! alas! thought I to myself, when forced to eat at the restaurateur's, instead of capital beef, a slice of a cow 50 years old; instead of a ragout with little balls of

* Mozart's 'Figaro' had been again placed on the stage in Vienna in 1789, and received with great enthusiasm. The first performance also of 'Cosi fan tutte' took place on Jan. 21, 1790, and was repeated on Jan. 28 and 30. It is remarkable that Haydn makes no allusion to this latest work of his revered friend. It does not appear, however, to have had any great run.

forced meat, an old sheep with yellow carrots; instead of a Bohemian pheasant, a tough grill; and instead of good and juicy oranges, Hungarian salad; instead of pastry, dry apple-fritters, and hazelnuts, &c. Alas! alas! thought I again to myself, would that I now had many a morsel that I despised in Vienna! Here in Estoras, no one asks me, Would you like some chocolate, with milk or without? Will you take some coffee, with or without cream? What can I offer you, my good Haydn? will you have vanille ice or pine-apple? If I had only a piece of good Parmesan cheese, particularly in Lent, to enable me to swallow more easily the black dumplings and puffs! I gave our porter this very day a commission to send me a couple of pounds.

Forgive me, dear lady, for taking up your time in this very first letter by so wretched a scrawl, and such stupid nonsense; you must forgive a man spoilt by the Viennese. Now, however, I begin to accustom myself by degrees to country life, and yesterday I studied for the first time, and somewhat in the Haydn style too.

No doubt, you have been more industrious than myself. The pleasing adagio from the quartett has probably now received its true expression from your fair fingers. I trust that my good Fräulein Peperl may be frequently reminded of her master, by often singing over the cantata, and that she will pay particular attention to distinct articulation, and correct vocalisation, for it would be a sin if so fine a voice were to remain imprisoned in the breast. I beg, therefore, for a frequent smile, or else I shall be much vexed. I advise M. François* too to cultivate his musical talents. Even if he sings in his dressing-gown, it will do well enough, and I will often write something new to encourage him. I again kiss your hands in gratitude for all the kindness you have shown me. I am, &c.

HAYDN.

41.

To Frau v. Genzinger.

Estoras, March 14, 1790.

Most valued, esteemed, and kindest Frau v. Genzinger,

I ask your forgiveness a million times for having so long delayed answering your two charming letters, which has not been caused by negligence (a sin from which may Heaven preserve me so long as I live), but from the press of business which has devolved on me for my gracious Prince, in his present melancholy condition. The death of his wife overwhelmed the Prince with such grief that we were obliged to use every means in our power to rouse him from his profound sorrow. I therefore arranged for the three first days a selection of chamber-music, but no singing. The poor Prince, how-

* Josepha and Franz, the eldest children of Frau v. Genzinger.

ever, the first evening, on hearing my favourite adagio in D, was affected by such deep melancholy that it was difficult to disperse it by other pieces.

On the fourth day we had an opera, the fifth a comedy, and then our theatre daily as usual. We were also commanded to study Gassmann's old opera, 'L'Amor Artigiano,' as our master had recently expressed a wish to hear it.* I composed three new 'arias' for it, which I will shortly send you, not on account of their beauty, but to show you my industry. You shall receive the new symphony I promised in April, so that it may be performed at the Kees music.†

You must now permit me to kiss your hands gratefully for the rusks you sent me, which, however, I did not receive till last Tuesday; but they came exactly at the right moment, having just finished the last of the others. That my favourite 'Arianna' [Ariadne] has been successful at Schottenhof is delightful news to me, but I recommend Fräulein Peperl to articulate the words clearly, especially in the words 'che tanto amai.'

* Written by Salieri and Joseph II., a very favourite operetta of its day, in which Beethoven's grandfather made great effect in the electoral theatre at Bonn.

† G. B. Ritter von Kees was one of the most distinguished friends of music at that time in Vienna. Gyrowetz, in his 'Autobiography,' relates that he gave society concerts twice a week in his house, 'where the first *virtuosi* then in Vienna, and the best composers, such as Joseph Haydn, Mozart, Dittersdorf, Hoffmeister, Albrechtsberger, Chiarnowichi, &c. assembled. There Haydn's symphonies were performed. Mozart usually played chiefly on the piano.'

I also take the liberty of wishing you all possible good on your approaching nameday, begging you to continue your favour towards me, and to consider me on every occasion as your wn, though unworthy, master. I must also mention that the teacher of languages can come here any day, and his journey will be paid. He can travel either by the diligence or by some other conveyance, which can always be heard of in the Madschaker Hof. As I feel sure, dear lady, that you take an interest in all that concerns me (far greater than I deserve), I must inform you that last week I received a present of a handsome gold snuff-box, the weight of thirty-four ducats, from Prince Oetting v. Wallerstein, accompanied by an invitation to pay him a visit this year, the Prince defraying my expenses, His Highness being desirous to make my personal acquaintance (a pleasing fillip to my depressed spirits). Whether I shall make up my mind to the journey is another question.

I beg you will excuse this hasty scrawl.

I am always, &c.

HAYDN.

P.S.—I have just lost my faithful coachman; he died on the 25th of last month.

42.

To Frau v. Genzinger.

Estoras, May 13, 1790.

Best and kindest Frau v. Genzinger,

I was quite surprised, on receiving your esteemed letter, to find that you had not yet got my last letter, in which I mentioned that our landlord had accepted the services of a French teacher, who came by chance to Estoras, and I also made my excuses both to you and your tutor on that account. My highly esteemed benefactress, this is not the first time that some of my letters and of others also have been lost, inasmuch as our letter-bag, on its way to Oedenburg (in order to have letters put into it), is always opened by the steward there, which has frequently been the cause of mistakes, and other disagreeable occurrences. For greater security, however, and to defeat such disgraceful curiosity, I will henceforth enclose all my letters in a separate envelope to the porter, Herr Pointner. This trick annoys me the more because you might justly reproach me with procrastination, from which may Heaven defend me! At all events, the prying person, whether male or female, cannot, either in this last letter or in any of the others, have discovered anything in the least inconsistent with propriety. And now, my esteemed patroness, when am I to have the inexpressible happiness of seeing you in Estoras? As business does not admit of my going to Vienna, I console myself by the hope of kissing your hands here this summer. In which pleasing hope, I am, with high consideration, &c. yours,

HAYDN.

43.

To Frau v. Genzinger.

Estoras, May 30, 1790.

Kindest and best Frau v. Genzinger,

I was at Oedenburg when I received your last welcome letter, having gone there on purpose to enquire about the lost letter. The steward there vowed by all that was holy that he had seen no letter at that time in my writing, so that it must have been lost in Estoras! Be this as it may, such curiosity can do me no harm, far less yourself, as the whole contents of the letter were an account of my opera 'La Vera Costanza,' performed in the new theatre in the Landstrasse [a suburb of Vienna], and about the French teacher who was to have come at that time to Estoras. You need, therefore, be under no uneasiness, dear lady, either as regards the past or the future, for my friendship and esteem for you (tender as they are) can never become reprehensible, having always before my eyes respect for your elevated virtues, which not only I, but all who know you, must reverence. Do not let this deter you from consoling me sometimes by your agreeable letters, as they are so highly necessary to cheer me in this wilderness, and to soothe my deeply wounded heart. Oh! that I could be with you, dear lady, even for one quarter of an hour, to pour forth all my sorrows, and to receive comfort from you. I am obliged to submit to many vexations from our official managers here, which, however, I shall at present pass over in silence. The sole consolation left me is that I am, thank God, well, and eagerly disposed to work. I only regret that, with this inclination, you have waited so long for the promised symphony. On this occasion it really proceeds from absolute necessity, arising from my circumstances, and the raised prices of everything. I trust, therefore, that you will not be displeased with your Haydn, who, often as his Prince absents himself from Estoras, never can obtain leave, even for four-and-twenty hours, to go to Vienna. It is scarcely credible, and yet the refusal is always couched in such polite terms, and in such a manner, as to render it utterly impossible for me to urge my request for leave of absence. Well, as God pleases! This time also will pass away, and the day return when I shall again have the inexpressible pleasure of being seated beside you at the pianoforte, hearing Mozart's masterpieces, and kissing your hands from gratitude for so much pleasure.

With this hope, I am, &c.

J. Haydn.

44.

To Frau v. Genzinger.

Estoras, June 6, 1790.

Dear and esteemed Lady,

I heartily regret that you were so long in receiving my last letter. But the previous week no messenger was despatched from Estoras, so it was not my fault that the letter reached you so late.

Between ourselves! I must inform you that Mademoiselle Nanette has commissioned me to compose a new sonata for you, to be given into your hands alone. I esteem myself fortunate in having received such a command. You will receive the sonata in a fortnight at latest. Mademoiselle Nanette promised me payment for the work, but you can easily imagine that on no account would I accept it. For me the best reward will always be to hear that I have in some degree met with your approval. I am, &c.

HAYDN.

The following testimonial is in the Imperial Library at Vienna. It is rather interesting to compare it with what Mozart wrote in behalf of the same young artist, the same year:—'I, the undersigned, hereby certify that I consider the bearer, Herr Joseph Eybler, a pupil worthy of his renowned master, Albrechtsberger, a solid composer, equally versed in chamber-music and in sacred music, experienced in the art of singing; also a finished organ and pianoforte player; in short, I have found him a young musician such as we can only lament so seldom to meet with.—(Signed) MOZART.' Haydn, who, on May 2, 1787, had previously tried to procure a publisher for him, is also very kind and persuasive in his testimonial, and shows such zealous good-nature that we cannot but smile; he says:—

45.

Testimonial.

Estoras, June 9, 1790.

I, the undersigned, cannot refuse, at the request of Herr Joseph Eybler, to furnish him with a testimonial of his remarkable talents, and the assiduous study he has hitherto bestowed on music. He is not only well versed in all those musical and theoretical acquirements indispensable to sustain creditably a strict examination before any musical tribunal, but also in the more practical branches, being an excellent pianist and violin player, competent to gain the approval of every *connoisseur*. In the former capacity, he can honourably fill the situation of a Capellmeister, and in the latter become a very useful member of chamber-music.

Finally, as regards composition, I think I can award him no higher praise than to say, that he is a scholar of the far-famed Albrechtsberger. Endowed with all these qualities, what he now stands in need of is a generous Prince, to place him in a position where he can further develop and utilise his talents: a result on which the undersigned would be happy soon to congratulate him.

JOSEPH HAYDN,
Capellmeister to Prince Esterhazy.

46.

To Frau v. Genzinger.

Estoras, June 20, 1790.

Dear kind Friend,

I take the liberty of sending you a new pianoforte sonata with violin or flute, not as anything at all remarkable, but as a trifling resource in case of any great *ennui.* I only beg that you will have it copied out as soon as possible, and then return it to me. The day before yesterday I presented to Mademoiselle Nanette the sonata commanded by her. I had hoped she would express a wish to hear me play it, but I have not yet received any order to that effect; I, therefore, do not know whether you will receive it by this post or not. The sonata is in E flat, newly written, and always intended for you. It is strange enough that the final movement of this sonata contains the very same minuet and trio that you asked me for in your last letter. This identical work was destined for you last year, and I have only written a new adagio since then, which I strongly recommend to your attention; it has a deep signification which I will analyse for you when opportunity offers. It is rather difficult, but full of feeling; what a pity that you have not one of Schanz's pianos, for then you could produce twice the effect.

N.B.—Mademoiselle Nanette must know nothing of the sonata being already half written before I received her commands, for this might suggest notions with regard to me that I might find most prejudicial, and I must be very careful not to lose her favour. In the meanwhile I consider myself fortunate to be the means of giving her pleasure, particularly as the sacrifice is made for your sake, my charming Frau v. Genzinger. Oh! how I do wish that I could only play over these sonatas once or twice to you; how gladly would I then reconcile myself to remain for a time in my wilderness! I have much to say and to confess to you, from which no one but yourself can absolve me; but what cannot be effected now will, I devoutly hope, come to pass next winter, and half of the time is already gone. Meanwhile I take refuge in patience, and am content with the inestimable privilege of subscribing myself your sincere and obedient friend and servant,

J. HAYDN.

47.

To Frau v. Genzinger.

Estoras, June 27, 1790.

Highly esteemed Lady,

You have no doubt by this time received the new pianoforte sonata, and, if not, you will probably do so along with this letter. Three days ago I played the sonata to Mademoiselle Nanette in the presence of my gracious Prince. At first I doubted very much, owing to its difficulty, whether I should receive any applause, but was soon convinced of the reverse by a gold snuff-box being presented to me by Mademoiselle Nanette's own hand. My sole wish now is, that you may be satisfied with it, so that I may find greater credit with my patroness. For the same reason, I beg that either you or your husband will let her know 'that my delight was such that I could not conceal her generosity,' especially being convinced that you take an interest in all benefits conferred on me. It is a pity that you have not a Schanz pianoforte, which is much more favourable to expression; my idea is that you should make over your own still very tolerable piano to Fräulein Peperl, and get a new one for yourself. Your beautiful hands, and their brilliant execution, deserve this, and more. I know that I ought to have composed the sonata in accordance with the capabilities of your piano, but, being so unaccustomed to this, I found it impossible,* and now I am doomed to stay at home. What I lose by so doing you can well imagine: it is indeed sad always to be a slave—but Providence wills it so. I am a poor creature, plagued perpetually by hard work, and with few hours for recreation. Friends? what do I say? *one* true friend; there are no longer any true friends, but one female friend. Oh yes! no doubt I still have one, but she is far away. Ah well! I take refuge in my thoughts. May God bless her, and may she never forget me. Meanwhile I kiss your hands a thousand times, and ever am, &c.

HAYDN.

Pray forgive my bad writing. I am suffering from inflamed eyes to-day.

* In the 'Jahrbuch der Tonkunst,' of Vienna and Prague, we find the following remarks on Schanz 'pianos:'—'Their tone is not so loud as those of Walter, but quite as distinct, and generally more pleasing, and they are likewise easier to handle, as the keys are not so deep or so broad as the others. They are, in fact, a close imitation, almost a complete copy, of Stein's pianos in Augsburg.' Mozart gives a very minute description of the latter in one of his letters from Augsburg, Oct. 17, 1777. In the 'Jahrbuch,' there is also an account of the Walter pianos described by Haydn in a subsequent letter. 'His pianofortes have a rich bell tone, a distinct touch, and a strong full bass. The tone at first is rather dull, but after being played on for some time, the treble in particular becomes very clear. But if very much played on, the tone soon becomes sharp and metallic. There is frequently a fault in the instruments of this maker, which ought to be guarded against in selecting one, viz. that the treble and bass do not in all of them preserve their relative proportion in tone. In some of them the bass is too loud for the treble, and in others too metallic. The price this maker asks for his instruments varies from twelve to fifty ducats.'

48.

To Frau v. Genzinger.

Estoras, July 4, 1790.

Most esteemed and valued Lady,

I this moment receive your letter, and at the same time the post departs. I sincerely rejoice to hear that my Prince intends to present you with a new piano, more especially as I am in some measure the cause of this, having been constantly imploring Mademoiselle Nanette to persuade your husband to purchase one for you. The choice now depends entirely on yourself, and the chief point is that you should select one in accordance with your touch and your taste. Certainly my friend, Herr Walter, is very celebrated, and every year I receive the greatest civility from him ; but, *entre nous*, and to speak candidly, sometimes there is not more than one out of ten of his instruments which may be called really good, and they are exceedingly high priced besides. I know Herr Nickl's piano; it is first-rate, but too heavy for your touch ; nor can every passage be rendered with proper delicacy on it. I should, therefore, like you to try one of Herr Schanz's pianos, for they have a remarkably light and agreeable touch. A good pianoforte is absolutely necessary for you, and my sonata will also gain vastly by it.

Meanwhile I thank you much, dear lady, for your caution with regard to Mademoiselle Nanette. It is a pity that the little gold box she gave me, and had used herself, is tarnished, but perhaps I may get it polished up in Vienna. I have as yet received no orders to purchase a pianoforte. I fear that one may be sent to your house, which may be handsome outside, but the touch within heavy. If your husband will rely on my opinion, that Herr Schanz is the best maker for this class of instruments, I would then settle everything at once. In great haste, yours, &c.

HAYDN.

We have another letter to give from his fair friend, as follows:—

49.

Vienna, July, 1790.

Dear Herr v. Haydn,

I duly received your letter of July 4, and trust wholly to you to choose me a first-rate pianoforte, for Mademoiselle, as soon as she arrives, will give you a commission in the name of the Prince to select one. I am also quite willing (as you think it best) that you should order one from Herr Schanz, but it would be more satisfactory to me were you to try it yourself before I take it, fearing that, having so little knowledge myself, I might not choose a really good one.

The sonata pleases me exceedingly: there is only one passage that I should like to be altered (if, indeed, it does not detract from the beauty of the piece); I mean the passage in the second part of the adagio, where the hands must be crossed over: not being accustomed to anything of the kind, I find it rather puzzling, so pray suggest to me in what way this could be obviated.

I will return the other sonata in a few days, it is likewise very beautiful. I must, however, earnestly entreat one thing, which is, that I am not to be deprived by this sonata of the symphony you promised to compose solely and expressly for me, and which I look forward to with such delight. As you have so recently taken so much trouble, I ought not, indeed, to plague you, but I cannot resist doing so, from the exceeding pleasure I feel in your charming works.

I trust you are in the enjoyment of good health. As for myself, I have not yet quite recovered from my cold, and I have been taking Seltzer water and milk for the last few days; and I hope, God willing, soon to feel the good effects of this remedy. I now conclude, and remain with much veneration your sincere friend,

A. M. GENZINGER.

A considerable time now elapses before Haydn's answer to his 'highly esteemed, best, and kindest Frau v. Genzinger,' whose nameday (Marianne), Ascension Day, gives rise to the following letter:—

50.

August 15.

I ought to have written to you last week in answer to your letter, but as this day has been long enshrined in my heart, I have been striving earnestly all the time to think how and what I was to wish for you; so thus eight days passed, and now, when my wishes ought to be expressed, my small amount of intellect comes to a standstill, and (quite abashed) I find nothing to say; why? wherefore? because I have not been able to fulfil those musical hopes for this particular day that you have justly the right to expect Oh, my most charming and kind benefactress! if you could only know, or see into my troubled heart on this subject, you would certainly feel pity and indulgence for me. The unlucky promised symphony has haunted my imagination ever since it was bespoken, and it is only, alas! the pressure of urgent occurrences that has prevented its being hitherto ushered into the world! The hope, however, of your lenity towards me for the delay, and the approaching time of the fulfilment of my promise, embolden me to express my wish, which, among the hundreds offered to you to-day and yesterday, may perhaps appear to you only an insignificant interloper; I say *perhaps*, for it would be too bold in me to think that you could form no better wish for yourself than mine. You see, therefore, most kind and charming lady, that I can wish nothing for you on your nameday, because my wishes are too feeble, and therefore unproductive. As for me, I venture to wish for myself your kind indulgence, and the continuance of your friendship, and the goodness that I so highly prize. This is my warmest wish! But if any wish of mine may be permitted, then mine shall become identical with your own, for thus I shall feel assured that none other remains, except the wish once more to be allowed to subscribe myself your very sincere friend and servant, HAYDN.

P.S.—I expect an answer to-morrow about the piano; and you shall at the same time receive the alteration in the adagio.

Between this and the ensuing letters to his 'beloved and valued friend' an event occurred, of great importance to Haydn's future life, as well as in some degree to the general development of music—the master's engagement in London.

Prince Nicolaus died rather suddenly. Haydn received a pension for life of 1,000 florins, to which the new Prince Anton added 400 florins, without demanding any service in return; thus after a long and laborious life, Haydn was now placed in a condition of the most pleasing repose, and just as he was considering how he could best employ his future time, a stranger one day came into his room at Vienna, whither he had at once betaken himself, and said abruptly, 'I am Salomon, from London, and am come to carry you off with me; we will strike a bargain to-morrow.'

This celebrated violinist was travelling in the interests of the theatrical manager Gallini, to engage singers for the Haymarket Theatre, and on hearing at Cologne of the death of Prince Esterhazy, he hurried off to Vienna, having long had Haydn in his eye for the London concerts, but hitherto failed in engaging him, owing to Haydn's fidelity to his Prince; and even now his answer was, 'If my Prince chooses, I will go with you.'

Prince Anton at once agreed; so the master, at the age of sixty, instantly prepared to set out in the hope of gaining fame and fortune on the other side of the Channel. His friends at home, however, felt considerable misgivings on the subject, and even Mozart said, 'Papa, you have had no training for the great world, and can speak too few languages.' 'Oh!' replied Haydn, 'my language is understood all over the world!'

They set off on their journey, December 15, 1790. Mozart would not leave his revered friend the whole day. He dined with him, and, at the moment of their separation, said with tears in his eyes, 'We shall, no doubt, now take our last farewell in this life!' Haydn, too, was deeply affected, interpreting these words as referring to himself, the old man; but scarcely had a year elapsed when he had to make the following entry in his diary, 'Mozart died, December 5, 1791.'

His diary, now in the possession of the Imperial Rath Schmidtler, in Vienna, who kindly allowed me to see it, contains much that is interesting. On the first page is a list of commissions, which display Haydn's complaisance in a very amusing manner. It is well known how highly prized English goods were at that time; so we see 'needles, knives, and scissors for Frau v. Kees; spectacles for Riswagner, suitable for a man between fifty and sixty; nail scissors for Hamberger, a larger pair ditto; a French chain, various articles for Frau v. Genzinger.'

Of course, the earliest and most numerous descriptions of the journey were addressed to that dear friend whose society he had recently enjoyed more than ever. The first letter, however, is dated from Calais, Dec. 31, 1790, whereas we know that Haydn went to Munich with Salomon, and there became acquainted with Mozart's friend, Capellmeister Cannabich: they proceeded thence to Bonn, Salomon's native city, where the musical brother of Joseph II., the Elector Maximilian Franz, presented his whole band to the celebrated *maestro*, and among the number was Beethoven, then twenty years old; and even at that time conferences were held, to arrange that this latest genius of that great epoch of music should subsequently cultivate his great talents under the auspices of the aged *maestro*. Haydn writes as follows to his friend in Vienna:—

51.

To Frau v. Genzinger.

Highly honoured Lady,

A violent storm, and an incessant pour of rain prevented our arriving at Calais till this evening (where I am now writing to you), and to-morrow at seven in the morning we cross the sea to London. I promised to write from Brussels, but we could only stay there an hour. I am very well, thank God! although somewhat thinner, owing to fatigue, irregular sleep, and eating and drinking so many different things.

A few days hence, I will describe the rest of my journey, but I must beg you to excuse me for to-day. I hope to heaven that you and your husband and children are all well. I am, with high esteem, &c. yours,

HAYDN.

52.

To Frau v. Genzinger.

London, Jan. 8, 1791.

I thought that you had received my last letter from Calais. I ought indeed, according to my promise, to have sent you some tidings of myself when I arrived in London, but I preferred waiting a few days, that I might detail various incidents to you. I must now tell you that on New Year's Day, after attending early mass, I took ship at half past seven o'clock A.M. and at five o'clock in the afternoon arrived safe and well at Dover, for which Heaven be praised! During the first four hours, there was scarcely any wind, and the vessel made so little way that in that time we only went one English mile, there being twenty-four between Calais and Dover. The ship's captain, in the worst possible humour, said that, if the wind did not change, we should be at sea all night. Fortunately, however, towards half past eleven o'clock such a favourable breeze began to blow that by four o'clock we had come twenty-two miles. As the ebb of the tide prevented our large vessel making the pier, two small boats were rowed out to meet us, into which we and our luggage were transferred, and at last we landed safely, though exposed to a sharp gale. The large vessel stood out to sea five hours longer, till the tide carried it into the harbour. Some of the passengers, being afraid to trust themselves in the small boats, stayed on board, but I followed the example of the greater number. I remained on deck during the whole passage, in order to gaze my fill at that huge monster, the Ocean. So long as there was a calm, I had no fears, but when at length a violent wind began to blow, rising every minute, and I saw the boisterous high waves rushing on, I was seized with a little alarm, and a little indisposition likewise. But I overcame it all, and arrived safely in harbour, without being actually sick. Most of the passengers were ill, and looked like ghosts. I did not feel the fatigue of the journey till I arrived in London, but it took two days before I could recover from it. But now I am quite fresh and well, and occupied in looking at this mighty and vast town of London, its various beauties and marvels causing me the most profound astonishment. I immediately paid the necessary visits, such as to the Neapolitan Minister and to our own. Both called on me in return two days afterwards, and a few days ago I dined with the former—*nota bene*, at six o'clock in the evening, which is the fashion here.

My arrival caused a great sensation through the whole city, and I went the round of all the newspapers for three successive days. Everyone seems anxious to know me. I have already dined out six times, and could be invited every day if I chose; but I must in the first place consider my health, and in the next my work. Except the nobility, I admit no visitors till two o'clock in the afternoon, and at four o'clock, I dine at home with Salomon. I have a neat comfortable lodging, but very dear. My landlord is an Italian, and likewise a cook, who gives us four excellent dishes; we each pay one florin thirty kreuzers a day, exclusive of wine and beer, but everything is terribly dear here. I was yesterday invited to a grand amateur concert, but as I arrived rather late, when I gave my ticket, they would not let me in, but took me to an ante-room, where I was obliged to remain till the piece which was then being given was over. Then they opened the door, and I was conducted, leaning on the arm of the director, up the centre of the room to the front of the orchestra amid universal clapping of hands, stared at by everyone, and greeted by a number of English compliments. I was assured that such honours had not been conferred on anyone for fifty years. After the concert, I was taken into a very handsome adjoining room, where tables were laid for all the amateurs, to the number of two hundred. It was proposed that I should take a seat near the top, but as it so happened that I had dined out that very day, and eat more than usual, I declined this honour, excusing myself under the pretext of not being very well, but in spite of this, I could not get off drinking the health, in Burgundy, of the harmonious gentlemen present; all responded to it, but at last allowed me to go home. All this, my dear lady, was very flattering to me, still I wish I could fly for a time to Vienna, to have more peace to work, for the noise in the streets, and the cries of the common people selling their wares, is intolerable. I am still working at symphonies, as the libretto of the opera is not yet decided on, but in order to be more quiet, I intend to engage an apartment some little way out of town. I would gladly write more at length, but I fear losing this opportunity. With kindest regards to your husband, Fräulein Pepi, and all the rest, I am, with sincere esteem, &c.

HAYDN.

P.S.—I have a request to make. I think I must have left my symphony in E flat, that you returned to me, in my room at home, or mislaid it on the journey. I missed it yesterday, and being in pressing need of it, I beg you urgently to procure it for me, through my kind friend, Herr v. Kees. Pray have it copied out in your own house, and send it by post as soon as possible. If Herr v. Kees hesitates about this, which I don't think likely, pray send him this letter. My address is, M. Haydn, 18, Great Pulteney Street, London.

53.

To Frau v. Genzinger.

London, Sept. 17, 1791.

My highly esteemed Friend,

I have received no reply to my two letters of July 3, entrusted to the care of a composer, Herr Diettenhofer, by whom I likewise sent the pianoforte arrangement of an andante in one of my new symphonies. Nor have I any answer either about the symphony in E flat, that I wished to get; I can now no longer delay enquiring after your own health, as well as that of your husband, and all your dear family. Is that odious proverb, 'Out of sight, out of mind,' to prove true everywhere? Oh no! urgent affairs, or the loss of my letter and the symphony, are, no doubt, the cause of your silence. I feel assured of Herr von Kees' willingness to send the symphony, as he said he would do so in his letter; so it seems we shall both have to deplore a loss, and must trust to Providence. I flatter myself I shall receive a short answer to this. Now, my dear good kind lady, what is your piano about? Is a thought of Haydn sometimes recalled by your fair hand? Does my sweet Fräulein Pepi ever sing poor Ariadne? Oh yes! I seem to hear it even here, especially during the last two months, when I have been residing in the country, amid lovely scenery, with a banker, whose heart and family resemble the Genzingers, and where I live as if I were in a monastery. God be praised! I am in good health, with the exception of my usual rheumatic state. I work hard, and in the spring mornings, when I walk in the wood alone with my English grammar, I think of my Creator, of my family, and of all the friends I have left—and of these you are the most valued of all.

I had hoped, indeed, sooner to have enjoyed the felicity of seeing you again; but my circumstances, in short, fate so wills it that I must remain eight or ten months longer in London. Oh, my dear good lady, how sweet is some degree of liberty! I had a kind Prince, but was obliged at times to be dependent on base souls. I often sighed for release, and now I have it in some measure. I am quite sensible of this benefit, though my mind is burdened with more work. The consciousness of being no longer a bond-servant sweetens all my toils. But, dear as liberty is to me, I do hope on my return again to enter the service of Prince Esterhazy, solely for the sake of my poor family. I doubt much whether I shall find this desire realised, for in his letter my Prince complains of my long absence, and exacts my speedy return in the most absolute terms; which, however, I cannot comply with, owing to a new contract I have entered into here. I, alas! expect my dismissal; but I hope even in that case that God will be gracious to me, and enable me in some degree to remedy the loss by my own industry. Meanwhile I console myself by the hope of soon hearing from you. You shall receive my promised new symphony two months hence; but in order to inspire me with good ideas, I beg you will write to me, and a long letter too.

Yours, &c.

HAYDN.

54.

To Frau v. Genzinger.

London, Oct. 13, 1791.

take the liberty of earnestly entreating you to advance 150 florins for a short time to my wife, provided you do not imagine that since my journey I have become a bad manager. No, my kind good friend, God blesses my efforts. Three circumstances are alone to blame. In the first place, since I have been here, I have repaid my Prince the 450 florins he advanced for my journey; secondly, I can demand no interest from my bank obligations, having placed them under your care, and not being able to remember either the names or the numbers, so I cannot write a receipt; thirdly, I cannot yet apply for the 5,883 florins (1,000 of which I recently placed in my Prince's hands, and the rest with the Count v. Fries), especially because it is English money. You will, therefore, see that I am no spendthrift. This leads me to hope that you will not refuse my present request, to lend my wife 150 florins. This letter must be your security, and would be valid in any court. I will repay the interest of the money with a thousand thanks on my return.

I am, &c.

HAYDN.

As I do not remember the first adagio at the beginning of the symphony in E minor, I take the liberty to mark down the allegro that follows:

Shall I be so fortunate as to receive this symphony by the end of January 1792! Oh yes, I flatter myself that I shall. But how strangely things sometimes come to pass; I believe you received my letter the very same day that I was reading your cruel reproach that Haydn was capable of forgetting his friend and benefactress. Oh! how often do I long to be beside you at the piano, even for a quarter of an hour, and then to have some good German soup. But we cannot have everything in this world. May God only vouchsafe to grant me the health that I have hitherto enjoyed, and may I preserve it by good conduct and out of gratitude to the Almighty. That you are well is to me the most delightful of all news. May Providence long watch over you. I hope to see you in the course of six months, when I shall, indeed, have much to tell you. Good night! it is time to go to bed; it is half past eleven o'clock. One thing more.

To ensure the safety of the money, Herr Hamberger, a good friend of mine, a man of tall stature, our landlord, will bring you this letter himself, and you can with impunity entrust him with the money; but I beg you will take a receipt both from him and from my wife.

Among other things, Herr v. Kees writes to me that he should like to know my position in London, as there are so many different reports about me in Vienna. From my youth upwards I have been exposed to envy, so it does not surprise me when any attempt is made wholly to crush my poor talents; but the Almighty above is my support. My wife wrote to me that Mozart depreciates me very much, but this I will never believe. If true, I forgive him. There is no doubt that I find many who are envious of me in London also, and I know them almost all. Most of them are Italians. But they can do me no harm, for my credit with this nation has been firmly established for too many years. Rest assured that, if I had not met with a kind reception, I would long since have gone back to Vienna. I am beloved and esteemed by everyone, except, indeed, professors [of music]. As for my remuneration, Mozart can apply to Count Fries for information, in whose hands I placed 500*l.*, and 1,000 guilders in those of my Prince, making together nearly 6,000 florins. I daily thank my Creator for this boon, and I have good hope that I may bring home a couple of thousands besides, notwithstanding my great outlay and the cost of the journey. I will now no longer intrude on your time. How badly this is written. What is Pater —— doing? My compliments to him.

Yours, &c.

HAYDN.

55.

To Frau v. Genzinger.

London, Nov. 17, 1791.

I write in the greatest haste, to request that you will send the accompanying packet, addressed to you, to Herr v. Kees, as it contains the two new symphonies I promised. I waited for a good opportunity, but could hear of none; I have therefore been obliged to send them after all by post. I beg you will ask Herr v. Kees to have a rehearsal of both these symphonies, as they are very delicate, particularly the last movement in D, which I recommend to be given as *pianissimo* as possible, and the *tempo* very quick. I will write to you again in a few days. *Nota bene,* I was obliged to enclose both the symphonies to you, not knowing the address of Herr v. Kees.

I am, &c.

HAYDN.

P.S.—I only returned here to-day from the country. I have been staying with a *mylord* for the last fortnight, 100 miles from London.

We already know that Haydn kept a diary of all that he did and saw in London, but it is far from being complete, and in fact treats of few things of general interest, or that everyone might not learn as well, or better, from any popular book of travels. We shall, however, give an extract as a specimen, from the original of Herr Schmidtler. It portrays the simple German citizen of that day, and one who had seen but little of the world. We rarely find an original remark, or even any very close observation of the country or its people. It is, however, characteristic of the old 'papa,' that he only notices anything peculiar or remarkable. It is solely on subjects connected with his profession that he displays enlarged views; there he is quite at home, as we learn from many anecdotes related by Dies and Griesinger.

56.

Diary.

I was invited to the Lord Mayor's banquet on November 5. At the first table, No. 1, the new Lord Mayor and his wife dined, the Lord Chancellor, the two sheriffs, the Duke of Lids [Leeds], the minister Pitt, and others of the highest rank in the Cabinet. I was seated at No. 2, with Mr. Sylvester, the most celebrated advocate and first King's counsel in London. In this hall, called the Geld Hall [Guildhall], were six tables, besides others in the adjoining room. About twelve hundred persons altogether dined, and everything was in the greatest splendour. The dishes were very nice and well dressed. Wines of every kind in abundance. We sat down to dinner at six o'clock and rose from table at eight. The guests accompanied the Lord Mayor both before and after dinner in their order of precedence. There were various ceremonies, sword bearing, and a kind of golden crown, all attended by a band of wind instruments. After dinner, the whole of the aristocratic guests of No. 1 withdrew into a private room prepared for them, to have tea and coffee, while the rest of the company were conducted into another room. At nine o'clock No. 1 repaired to a small saloon, when the ball began. There was a raised platform in this room, reserved for the highest nobility, where the Lord Mayor and his wife were seated on a throne. Dancing then commenced in due order of precedence, but only one couple at a time, just as on January 6, the King's birthday. There were raised benches on both sides of this room with four steps, where the fair sex chiefly prevailed. Nothing but minuets were danced in this saloon, but I could only remain for a quarter of an hour, first because the heat of so many people assembled in such a narrow space was so oppressive, and, secondly, on account of the bad music for dancing, the whole orchestra consisting of two violins and a violoncello; the minuets were more in the Polish style than in our own, or that of the Italians. I proceeded into another room, which really was more like a subterranean cave than anything else; they were dancing English dances, and the music here was a degree better, as a drum was played by one of the violinists!* I went on to the large hall, where we had dined, and there the orchestra was more numerous, and the music more tolerable. They were also dancing English dances, but only opposite the raised platform where the four first sets had dined with the Lord Mayor. The other tables were all filled afresh with gentlemen, who as usual drank freely the whole night. The strangest thing of all was that one part of the company went on dancing without hearing a single note of the music, for first at one table, and then at another, songs were shouted, or toasts given, amidst the most crazy uproar and clinking of glasses and hurrahs. This hall and all the other rooms were lighted with lamps, of which the effluvia was most disagreeable, especially in the small ball-room. It was remarkable that the Lord Mayor had no need of a carving-knife, as a man in the centre of the table carved everything for him. One man stood before the Lord Mayor, and another behind him, shouting out vociferously all the toasts in their order according to etiquette, and after each toast came a flourish of kettledrums and trumpets. No health was more applauded than that of Mr. Pitt.

* This might be effected by the violin player having the drumstick tied to his right foot, which is sometimes done.

There seemed to be no order. The dinner cost 6,000*l.*, one-half of which is paid by the Lord Mayor, and the other half by the two sheriffs.

His letters to his dear friend are far more interesting and instructive, another of which now follows :—

57.

To Frau v. Genzinger.

London, Dec. 20, 1791.

I am much surprised that you did not get my letter at the same time as the two symphonies, having put them myself into the post here, and given every direction about them. My mistake was not having enclosed the letter in the packet. This is what often happens, dear lady, with those who have too much head work. I trust, however, that the letter reached you soon afterwards, but in case it did not, I must here explain that both symphonies were intended for Herr v. Kees, but with the stipulation that, after being copied by his order, the scores were to be given up to you, so that you may prepare a pianoforte arrangement of them, if you are so disposed. The particular symphony intended for you will be finished by the end of February at latest. I regret much having been obliged to forward the heavy packet to you, from not knowing Herr v. Kees' address; but he will, of course, repay you the cost of postage, and also, I hope, hand you over seven ducats. May I, therefore, ask you to employ a portion of that sum in copying on small paper my often applied for symphony in E minor, of which I sent you the theme in my last letter, and forward it to me by post as soon as possible, for it may perhaps be six months before a courier is despatched from Vienna, and I am in urgent need of the symphony. Further I must plague you once more by asking you to buy at Artaria's, my last pianoforte sonata in A flat, that is, with 4 B flat minor, with violin and violoncello, and also another piece, the fantasia in C, without accompaniment, for these pieces are not yet published in London; but be so good as not to mention this to Herr Artaria, or he might anticipate the sale in England. I beg you will deduct the price from the seven ducats. To return to the aforesaid symphonies, I must tell you that I sent you a pianoforte arrangement of the andante in C minor by Herr Diettenhofer. It is reported here, however, that he either died on the journey, or met with some serious accident; you had better look over both pieces at your leisure. The principal part of the letter I entrusted to Herr Diettenhofer was the description of a doctor's degree being conferred on me at Oxford, and all the honours I then received. I must take this opportunity of mentioning that three weeks ago the Prince of Wales (George IV.) invited me to his brother's (the Duke of York's) country seat. The Prince presented me to the Duchess (a daughter of the King of Prussia), who received me very graciously, and said many flattering things. She is the most charming lady in the world, possesses much intelligence, plays the piano, and sings very pleasingly. I stayed two days there, because on the first day a slight indisposition prevented her having any music; on the second day, however, she remained beside me from 10 o'clock at night, when the music began, till two hours after midnight. No compositions played but Haydn's. I directed the symphonies at the piano. The sweet little lady sat close beside me at my left hand, and hummed all the pieces from memory, having heard them so repeatedly in Berlin. The Prince of Wales sat on my right hand, and accompanied me very tolerably on the violoncello. They made me sing too. The Prince of Wales is having me painted just now, and the portrait is to be hung up in his private sitting-room. The Prince of Wales is the handsomest man on God's earth; he has an extraordinary love of music, and a great deal of feeling, but very little money. *Nota bene*, this is *entre nous*. His kindness gratifies me far more than any self-interest; on the third day, as I could not get any post-horses, the Duke of York sent me two stages with his own.

Now, dear lady, I should like to reproach you a little for believing that I prefer London to Vienna, and find my residence here more agreeable than in my fatherland. I am far from hating London, but I could not reconcile myself to spend my life there; no, not even to amass millions; my reasons I will tell you when we meet. I think of my home, and embracing once more all my old friends, with the delight of a child; only I deeply lament that the great Mozart will not be of the number, if it be true, which I trust it is not, that he is dead. Posterity will not see such talent as his for the next hundred years!* I am happy to hear that you and yours are all so well. I, too, have hitherto been in excellent health, till eight days since, when I was attacked by English rheumatism, and so severely that sometimes I could not help crying out aloud; but I hope soon to get quit of it, as I have adopted the usual custom here, and have wrapped myself up from head to foot in flannel. Pray excuse my bad writing. In the hope of soon being gratified by a letter, and with all esteem for yourself, and best regards to your husband, my dear Fräulein Pepi, and the others,

I am, &c.

HAYDN.

P.S.—Pray give my respects to Herr v. Kreybich [chamber music director to Joseph II.].

We now, for a change, give another extract from his London Diary.

* The 'Vienna Zeitung' relates, 'When Haydn, on Dec. 31, 1807, received congratulations on the New Year from some musical friends, and the conversation turned on Mozart, Haydn said, bursting into tears, "Forgive me; I must ever, ever weep at the name of my Mozart."'

58.

Diary.

To-day, January 14, 1792, the life of Mrs. Bellington (the celebrated singer) was published, all particulars of which are laid open in the most shameless manner. The editor, it appears, having got possession of her own original letters, offered to give them back to her for ten guineas, otherwise it was his intention to publish them. She was not, however, disposed to spend her ten guineas, and prosecuted him to get back her letters, but was nonsuited; on which she appealed, but failed again; and though she then offered her adversary 500*l.* for them, he published her precious correspondence to-day, and by 3 o'clock in the afternoon not a copy was to be had. It is said that her character is anything but good, but in spite of this she is a great genius, though hated by all the women, because she is so handsome. It appears that all these infamous letters, with details of her amours, are addressed to her mother. She is herself an illegitimate child. Scandals of this kind are common in London; the husband too often ignoring the affair, in order to profit by it, and get 1,000*l.* damages or more.

59.

To Frau v. Genzinger.

London, Jan. 17, 1792.

Dearest and kindest Lady,

I must ask your forgiveness a thousand times; and I own and bemoan that I have been too dilatory in the performance of my promise, but if you could only see how I am importuned to attend private concerts, causing me great loss of time, and the mass of work with which I am burdened, you would indeed, dear lady, feel the utmost compassion for me. Never in my life did I write so much in one year as during the last, which has indeed utterly exhausted me, and it will do me good to be able to take a little rest when I return home. At present I am working for Salomon's concerts, and feel bound to take all possible trouble, for our rivals of the professional society have sent for my pupil Pleyel from Strassburg, to direct their concerts. So a bloody harmonious war will now commence between master and scholar. All the newspapers have begun to discuss the subject, but I think an alliance will soon ensue, my reputation here being so firmly established. Pleyel, on his arrival, displayed so much modesty towards me, that he gained my goodwill afresh. We are very often together, which is much to his credit, and he knows how to appreciate his 'father;' we will share our laurels fairly, and each go home satisfied.* Professional Concerts met with a great misfortune on the 14th of this month, by the Pantheon being entirely burned down, a theatre only built last year. It was the work of an incendiary, and the damage is estimated at more than a hundred thousand pounds sterling; so there is not a single Italian theatre in London at this moment. Now, my dear angelic lady, I have a little fault to find with you. How often have I reiterated my request to have my symphony in E minor, of which I sent you the theme, copied out on small paper, and sent to me by post? Long have I sighed for it, and if I do not get it by the end of next month, I shall lose twenty guineas. Herr v. Kees writes that the copy may possibly arrive in London three months hence, or three years, for there is no chance of a courier being sent off at present. I also told Herr v. Kees in the same letter to take charge of this, and if he could not do so, I ventured to transfer the commission to you, flattering myself that my urgent request would certainly be fulfilled by your kindness. I also desired Herr v. Kees to repay you the cost of the postage you paid for his packet. Kindest and most charming Frau v. Genzinger, I once more beg you to see to this matter, for it is really a work of mercy, and when we meet, I will explain my reasons, respectfully kiss your fair hands, and repay my debt with gratitude.

* We find in his diary, 'Pleyel came to London on Dec. 23, and I dined with him on the 24th.'

The celebration you mention in honour of my poor abilities touched me deeply, but still not so profoundly as if you had considered it more perfect. Perhaps I may supply this imperfection by another symphony which I will shortly send you; I say, *perhaps*, because I (or rather my brain) am in truth weary. Providence alone can repair the deficiency in my powers, and to Him I daily pray for aid, for without His support I should indeed be a poor creature! And now, my kind and dear friend, I venture to hope for your indulgence. Oh yes! your portrait is at this moment before me, and I hear it say, 'Well, for this time, you odious Haydn, I will forgive you, but—but!' No, no, I mean henceforth strictly to fulfil my duties. I must conclude for to-day, by saying that now, as ever, I am with the highest esteem, yours, &c.

HAYDN.

60.

To Frau v. Genzinger.

London, Feb. 2, 1792.

I have to-day received your kind letter, and also the fantasia, and sonata *a tre*. I was, however, rather vexed, on opening the packet, not to find the long looked for symphony in E minor, which I had fully hoped for, and expected. Dear lady, I entreat you to send it at once, written on small post paper, and I will gladly pay all expenses, for Heaven alone can tell when the symphonies from Brussels may arrive here.. I cannot dispense with this one, without incurring great loss. Pray forgive my plaguing you so often on the subject, but I shall indeed be truly grateful if you will send it. Being overwhelmed with work at present, I cannot as yet write to Herr v. Kees. Pray, then, apply to him yourself for the said symphony. With my kind respects, I am, yours, &c.

HAYDN..

You shall have a good portion of the sewing needles.

61.

To Frau v. Genzinger.

London, March 2, 1792.

Yesterday morning I received your valued letter, and also the long looked for symphony. I humbly kiss your hands for sending it so safely and quickly. I had indeed received it six days previously from Brussels, through Herr v. Kees; but the score was more useful, as a good deal must be altered in it to suit the English taste. I only regret that I must trouble you so frequently with my commissions, especially as at present I cannot adequately testify my gratitude. I do positively assure and declare to you that this causes me great embarrassment, and indeed often makes me feel very sad; the more so that, owing to various urgent causes, I am unable to send you as yet the new symphony dedicated to you.

First, because I wish to alter and embellish the last movement, which is too feeble when compared with the first. I felt this conviction myself quite as much as the public, when it was performed for the first time last Friday; notwithstanding which, it made the most profound impression on the audience. The second reason is that I really dread the risk of its falling into other hands. I was not a little startled when I read the unpleasant intelligence about the sonata. By Heavens! I would rather have lost twenty-five ducats than have suffered such a theft, and the only one who can have done this is my own copyist; but I fervently hope to supply the loss through Madame Tost, for I do not wish to incur any reproaches from her. You must therefore, dear lady, be indulgent towards me, until I can towards the end of July myself have the pleasure of placing in your hands the sonata, as well as the symphony. *Nota bene*, the symphony to be given by myself, but the sonata by Madame Tost. It is equally impossible for me to send Herr v. Kees the promised symphonies at present, for here too there is a great want of faithful copyists. If I had time, I would write them out myself, but no day, not a single one, am I free from work, and I shall thank the good Lord when I can leave London; the sooner the better. My labours are augmented by the arrival of my pupil Pleyel, who has been summoned here by the Professional Society to direct their concerts. He brought with him a number of new compositions, which were, however, written long ago! He accordingly promised to give a new piece every evening. On seeing this, I could easily perceive that there was a dead set against me, so I also announced publicly that I would likewise give twelve different new pieces; so in order to keep my promise, and to support poor Salomon, I must be the victim, and work perpetually. I do feel it, however, very much. My eyes suffer most, and my nights are very sleepless, but with God's help I will overcome it all. The Professors wished to put a spoke in my wheel because I did not join their concerts, but the public is just. Last year I received great applause, but this year still more. Pleyel's presumption is everywhere criticised, and yet I love him, and have gone to his concert each time, and been the first to applaud him. I sincerely rejoice that you and yours are well. My kind regards to all. The time draws near to put my trunks in travelling order. Oh! how delighted shall I be to see you again, and to show personally all the esteem that I felt for you in absence, and that I ever shall feel for you.

Yours, &c.

HAYDN.

P.S.—Please apologise to Herr v. Kees for want of time preventing my sending him the new symphonies. I hope to have the honour of directing them myself in your house, at our next Christmas music.

62.

To Frau v. Genzinger.

London, April 24, 1792.

I yesterday evening received with much pleasure your last letter of 5 April, with the extract from the newspaper, extolling my poor talents to the Viennese. I must confess that I have gained considerable credit with the English in vocal music, by this little chorus, my first attempt with English words. It is only to be regretted that, during my stay here, I have not been able to write more pieces of a similar nature, but we could not find any boys to sing at our concerts, they having been already engaged for a year past to sing at other concerts, of which there are a vast number. In spite of the great opposition of my musical enemies, who are so bitter against me, more especially leaving nothing undone with my pupil Pleyel this winter to humble me, still, thank God! I may say that I have kept the upper hand. I must, however, admit that I am quite wearied and worn out with so much work, and look forward with eager longing to the repose which will soon take pity on me. I thank you, dear lady, for your kind solicitude about me. Just as you thought, I do not require to go to Paris at present, from a variety of reasons, which I will tell you when we meet. I am in daily expectation of an order from my Prince, to whom I wrote lately, to tell me where I am to go. It is possible that he may summon me to Frankfort;* if not, I intend (*entre nous*) to go by Holland to the King of Prussia at Berlin, thence to Leipzig, Dresden, Prague, and last of all to Vienna, where I hope to embrace all my friends.

Ever, with high esteem, &c.

HAYDN.

We find also in the diary of this journey rather an interesting sketch. No further letter seems to be addressed to Frau v. Genzinger.

63.

Diary.

On June 19 [1792], I went from Windsor to Dr. Herschel's, where I saw the great telescope. It is forty feet long, and five feet in diameter; the machine is very large, but so cleverly constructed that one man can with ease set the whole in motion. There are two smaller ones (one twenty-two feet), and which magnify 6,000 times. The King ordered two for himself, each twelve feet. He paid a thousand guineas for them. Dr. Herschel was an oboe-player in the Prussian service in his youth, during the Seven Years' War. He came with his brother to England, where he maintained himself for many years by music, became an organist at Bath, but chiefly devoted himself to astronomy.

* To the coronation of the Emperor Francis II.

After procuring the necessary instruments, he left Bath, hired a room near Windsor, and studied day and night; his landlady became a widow, fell in love with him, and married him, bringing him a marriage portion of 100,000 florins; in addition to which he has a pension of 500*l.* a year for life from the King, and his wife, at the age of five-and-forty, had a son this year [1792]. Ten years ago, he sent for his sister to live with him, who is of the most essential service to him in his observations. He often sits out of doors in the most intense cold for five or six hours at a time.

On his journey homewards, Haydn again visited Bonn, and as the Elector was absent, the court musicians gave him a breakfast at Godesberg, where Maximilian Franz had built a charming Kurhaus. It was on that occasion that the youthful Beethoven showed him a cantata on the death of Leopold II., probably the very one that has never yet been discovered, to which we are told, 'Haydn paid particular attention, encouraging its author to assiduous study.' Beethoven's name is not to be found in any of Haydn's letters. It is true that towards the close of the year 1792 this rising genius was for a considerable period the pupil of the venerable master, but Haydn, in enumerating his pupils to his friend Dies, never once alludes to Beethoven.

The master, richly endowed with the favours of

fortune, now established himself in a small house of his own in Vienna, where he enjoyed the most agreeable existence, continuing to write and to work: universally revered, he now began fully to enjoy life in his fatherland, where a circle of friends took the most lasting and profound interest in his artistic creations. Frau v. Genzinger, of course, again assumed the first place among these. Shortly after his arrival in Vienna, Haydn writes as follows:—

64.

To Frau v. Genzinger.

Vom Haus, Vienna, Aug. 4.

Dear Lady,

As Herr v. Kees has asked me to dine with him today, I shall have an opportunity of giving his wife the promised needles. If you will therefore be so good as to send me some, I shall be able to keep my word, and am, &c.

HAYDN.

We find the last note we can discover of this intimate correspondence, dated November 3, written in the same familiar terms.

65.

Nov. 3.

Dear Lady,

Allow me to wish you good morning, and to beg that you will give the bearer of this the last grand aria of my opera, which I must have copied out for my Princess. I will bring it back to you in two days at furthest. I take the liberty to invite myself to dine with you to-day, when I shall have the opportunity of kissing your hands in return.

Haydn's letters from this time forth are again as unconnected as before in their contents, so we must be satisfied with giving explanatory notes to each letter. The next, which is in the possession of Major-General Leopold Ritter von Weigl, in Venice, is addressed to his father, Joseph Weigl, celebrated at a later period as the composer of the 'Schweizer-Familie.'

66.

To Herr Joseph Weigl.

Vom Haus, Vienna, Jan. 11, 1794.

Dear Godson,

When I took you in my arms shortly after your birth, and had the pleasure of becoming your godfather, I implored Omnipotent Providence to endow you with the highest degree of musical talent. My fervent prayer has been heard. It is long since I have felt such enthusiasm for any music as yesterday, on hearing your 'Principessa d' Amalfi.' It abounds with novel ideas, it is sublime, expressive, in short, a masterpiece. I felt the warmest sympathy with the well merited applause bestowed on it. Persevere, my dear godson, in this genuine style, that you may again show foreigners what a German can accomplish. Keep a place in your memory withal for an old boy like myself. I love you cordially, and am, dearest Weigl,

Your sincere friend and servant,

JOSEPH HAYDN.

Eight days afterwards (January 19, 1794), Haydn set off on his second journey to London, where he remained till August 15, 1795. On this occasion, also, unconnected sketches appear in his diary, some of which are given by Griesinger and Dies, but they seem to me not to possess much interest for us. On the other hand, of the many notices of that period, we insert an extract from a London letter of March 25, 1794, 'On the Present State and Fashion of Music in England' (which appeared, July 1794, in the 'Journal of Luxury and Fashion,' in Weimar), as many may not have met with it. The writer, after speaking of Salomon's proceedings, and particularly of the praise due to him for his performance of the quartetts of 'our old favourite Haydn,' goes on thus:—'But what would you now say to his new symphonies composed expressly for these concerts, and directed by himself at the piano. It is truly wonderful what sublime and august thoughts this master weaves into his works. Passages often occur which render it impossible to listen to them without becoming excited; we are altogether carried away by admiration, and forced to applaud with hand and mouth. This is especially the case with Frenchmen, of whom we have so many here that all public places are filled with them. You know that they have great sensibility, and cannot restrain their transports, so that in the midst of the finest passages in soft adagios they clap their hands in loud applause, and thus mar the effect. In every symphony of Haydn, the adagio or andante is sure to be repeated each time, after the most vehement encores. The worthy Haydn, whose personal acquaintance I highly value, conducts himself on these occasions in the most modest manner. He is indeed a good-hearted, candid, honest man, esteemed and beloved by all.'

The following letter is addressed to the treasurer of Prince Esterhazy's household, an ancient copy of which I found at Rath Schmidtler's, in Vienna. The date is January, 1795. It is written during his stay in London, and is another proof of Haydn's astonishing good-nature, having evidently become security for the profligate major domo, who not being able to pay the money, the debt falls on Haydn. In his will, to be hereafter given, Haydn himself declares that he had paid more than 6,000 gulden for Lungmayer. On this occasion, in spite of his evident annoyance, a kind of grim humour is betrayed, a smile on a sour face, in Haydn's answer, on finding himself condemned to pay the debts of other people. He again realised a handsome sum in London, and it would appear that he paid Lungmayer's liabilities to the Hofkanzlei immediately on his return.

67.

To the Managers of Prince Esterhazy's Estate.

1795.

Gentlemen,

I see by the legal papers forwarded to me, and the enclosure of His Highness the Prince Esterhazy's Office of Management, that, in consequence of Lungmayer's *inability* to pay his debt, I am condemned to do so; pray, why? Because I am supposed to be *able* to pay. Would to God this were the case. But I swear by the *Kyrie-eleison,* which I am at this moment composing for my fourth Prince, that since the death of my second Prince, of blessed memory, I have fallen into the same state of inability as Lungmayer himself, only with this difference, that he has descended from a horse to the back of an ass, whereas I have remained on the horse, but without saddle or bridle. I beg therefore, gentlemen, you will at least have patience till I have finished the *Dona nobis pacem,* and till the Prince's major domo Lungmayer shall have ceased to receive his salary from the poorly paid music director Haydn (who has spent twenty-six years in the Prince's service), and shall begin to receive the salary justly due to him from his most gracious Prince. For surely nothing can be more sad or incongruous than that one servant should pay another servant, that is, the Capellmeister pay the major domo. If I should presently, by my own efforts (*for flatter or beg I cannot*), or by the voluntary impulse of my gracious Prince, be placed in a *better* position, I will not fail to comply with the above demand.

Yours, &c.

HAYDN.

68.

To Messrs. Breitkopf.

Dear Sir,

I ask your pardon a thousand times for having been so long in answering your repeated letters. Do not on that account be displeased with a man who can never be ungrateful to you; have only a little patience, and you shall receive both the money and the music. This is as certain as that I ever am, with high esteem,

Yours, &c.

J. HAYDN.

69.

To Count Saurau.

1797.

Your Excellency,

Such a surprise and such a mark of favour, especially as regards the portrait of my beloved monarch, I never before received in acknowledgment of my poor talents. I thank your Excellency from my heart, and am always respectfully at your command. I will bring the copy at eleven o'clock.

I am, with deep respect, your Excellency's obedient humble servant,

JOSEPH HAYDN.

Count Saurau, Imperial High Chancellor and Minister of the Interior, sent the above letter, and the hymn 'God preserve the Emperor,' in 1820, to Count Moritz Dietrichstein; the originals of both are now in the Imperial Library at Vienna. He writes:—'I often regretted that we had not, like the English, a national air, calculated to display to all the world the loyal devotion of our people to the kind and upright ruler of our fatherland, and to awaken within the hearts of all good Austrians that noble national pride, so indispensable to the energetic fulfilment of all the beneficial measures of the sovereign. This seemed to me more urgent at a period when the French revolution was raging most furiously, and when the Jacobins cherished the idle hope of finding, among the worthy Viennese, partizans and participators in their criminal designs. I caused that meritorious poet Haschka, to write the words, and applied to our immortal countryman Haydn, to set them to music, for I considered him alone capable of writing anything approaching in merit to the English "God save the King." Such was the origin of our national hymn. Haydn, in the original letter, I now enclose, thanks me for a gold box, adorned with a portrait of the Emperor, that I had sent him.'

According to A. Schmid's 'Joseph Haydn and Niccolo Zingarelli' (Vienna, 1847), the date of this letter is 1797. The scandalous Jacobin persecutions and executions in Austria and Hungary took place in 1796.

We learn from Griesinger (Biographical Notice, page 90), how much Haydn himself loved this national air. 'As often as the warm weather and his strength permitted, during the last few years of his life, he used to be led into his back room, that he might play on the piano his hymn "God preserve the Emperor Francis."' Dies, also, in his 'Biography' (p. 192), relates that, during the bombardment of Vienna in May 1809, Haydn seated himself at his instrument every forenoon to give forth the sounds of his favourite song. Indeed, on May 26, only five days before his death, he played it over three times in succession, and 'with a degree of expression that astonished himself.'

70.

To Artaria.

Vom Haus, Jan. 10, 1799.

I had hoped to have an early visit from you yesterday, to show you various pieces of music, but as press of business prevented your coming, I must now let you know that this very morning I had a letter from Mr. Bland, in London, requesting me to write some pianoforte sonatas for him, with violin and violoncello ; I, however, give you the preference on this occasion, and at the same time inform you that the first sonata can be had when you please, the second a fortnight hence, and the third by the end of the Carnival ; ten ducats each, as usual. Be so good, then, as to send me a line early to-morrow, to say what you decide on. I shall expect the money for each of these sonatas on delivery. On the other hand to liquidate my debt, I hope you will also agree to take the twelve new and very charming minuets and trios, for the sum of twelve ducats. In the hope of a favourable answer,

I am, &c.

HAYDN.

On June 12th, 1799, Haydn sent to Breitkopf and Härtel, in Leipzig, his subsequently far-famed 'Creation,' accompanied by the following letter, published by the above firm in Griesinger's 'Biographical Notices of Haydn,' in 1810.

71.

To Messrs. Breitkopf & Härtel.

June 12, 1799.

My business unhappily multiplies with my years, and yet it almost seems as if with the decrease of my mental powers, my inclination and impulse to work increase.

Oh God! how much yet remains to be done in this splendid art, even by a man like myself! The world, indeed, daily pays me many compliments, even on the fire of my last works; but no one could believe the strain and effort it costs me to produce these, inasmuch as many a day my feeble memory, and the unstrung state of my nerves, so completely crush me to the earth, that I fall into the most melancholy condition, so much so that for days afterwards I am incapable of finding one single idea, till at length my heart is revived by Providence, when I seat myself at the piano, and begin once more to hammer away at it. Then all goes well again, God be praised!

I yesterday received another packet of musical newspapers. The mode in which this work is published does you infinite credit, &c. &c. As for myself, now an old man, I only wish and hope that the critics may not handle my 'Creation' with too great severity, and be too hard on it. They may possibly find the musical orthography faulty in various passages, and perhaps other things also, which I have for so many years been accustomed to consider as minor points; but the genuine *connoisseur* will see the real cause as readily as I do, and willingly cast aside such stumbling-blocks. This, however, is entirely *inter nos*; or I might be accused of conceit and arrogance, from which, however, my heavenly Father has preserved me all my life long.

HAYDN

72.

To Artaria & Co.

Eisenstadt, Aug. 15, 1799.

Messieurs,

I take the liberty of sending you the enclosed from Frankfort, begging you to let me know how and in what way I am to act as to the request of these two gentlemen, Herr Gagl and Hedler, never having been engaged in any transaction of the kind. I am well aware that every publisher attends to his own interests in this respect; whether, however, so much ready money be given for each copy, or the thirteenth copy deducted from each dozen sold, are points on which I should be glad to have your candid opinion. I think, however, that neither the one nor the other is the case, because the application has come to me direct from another country, and I have already had experience of that sort of thing, having had letters from Berlin, Danzig, Leipzig, Regensburg, &c. &c.; in spite of which, however, I await your opinion, and shall certainly feel most grateful to you for your trouble. I should like to have handed over to you the third quartett, had I not been withheld by certain doubts, having hitherto received no reply about the three last quartetts I sent to London, and I fear that those gentlemen may publish the six quartetts together, instead of separately, but they probably have not yet appeared. Your edition (in

Vienna) and publication may precede that in London, though it is difficult to think so, when I sent off the three first quartetts on March 27th, and the three last on June 15th. If the publication in Vienna should be earlier than that in London (which I do not expect), and these gentlemen were to declare that they received the quartett direct from myself, it would be a loss to me of seventy-five pounds, a serious matter. Pray, therefore, endeavour quietly to ascertain whether the three first are already published, and also about what time the three last are likely to appear, that I may not at all events have a double fine imposed on me. I will send you the third quartett at once; you must, however, delay its publication until we are satisfied that it is published in London. I rely on your integrity in this matter, and shall always strive to be

Your obliging and obedient,

J. HAYDN.

73.

To Artaria & Co.

Eisenstadt, Aug. 22, 1800.

Messieurs,

I was surprised to receive yesterday a letter from Herr Clementi, in London, of July 16, stating that the copies of my 'Creation' had never arrived there! I earnestly request you to enquire who is to blame, as they were sent off more than three months ago. By this delay I am in danger of losing 2,000 gulden, as Herr Clementi is about to publish the work on his own account.*

Write to me if you have received any tidings of its arrival in London.

I am, &c.

HAYDN.

74.

To Artaria & Co.

Eisenstadt, Sept. 3, 1800.

Messieurs,

Forgive me for again plaguing you. By the enclosed letter from my pupil Pleyel, you will see that I cannot procure for him the passport he desires under such critical circumstances from the Stadkanzlei, as the nameday of my Princess renders it impossible for me to go at present even to Vienna, far less to Dresden; but as I wish to oblige him about my portrait, I must request you, gentlemen, to send him an impression in my name to Dresden. I thought the likeness very good when I was last with you, and it is, no doubt, now finished. Pleyel intends to publish it in a reduced size with the quartetts; I will pay the cost on the first op-

* Clementi had set up a music establishment in London.

portunity. In the hope of your complying with this request,

I am, &c.

HAYDN.

P.S.—Two days after your last letter, I heard from Herr Clementi that at length the first hundred copies of the 'Creation' had arrived in London.

N.B.—If you are able and willing to obtain the passport for Herr Pleyel, that he is so anxious to procure, you will exceedingly oblige us both. I hope for a few lines in reply. One thing more. My Princess, who has just arrived from Vienna, tells me that Lady Hamilton is coming to Eisenstadt on the 6th of this month, when she wishes to sing my cantata 'Ariadne a Naxos,' but I have not got it; so I beg you will send it to me here as soon as possible.

The following letter is in the Imperial Library in Vienna. It is addressed to Wranitzky, the most highly esteemed and productive composer of operas and *burlettas* of that day, to whom we know that Göthe applied with regard to the composition of a second part to the 'Zauberflöte.' It requires no further explanation of its benevolent contents.

75.

M. Paul Wranitzky,

Maître de Musique très-celèbre, à Vienne.

(With ten florins.)

Eisenstadt, Sept. 3, 1800.

Dearest and most esteemed Friend,

Willingly as I have endeavoured all my life to assist everyone, I must on this occasion reluctantly decline giving my consent to your proposal, as a work of the kind is not suitable to the place. Your own penetration will lead you to excuse me in this matter; still poor Naucharz would be somewhat benefited, if all the musical body of artists in Vienna were to combine in giving him some assistance; as I cannot, however, myself be present at that time, I take the liberty of enclosing a bank-note of ten florins for him, and am ever, my excellent friend,

Yours, &c.

HAYDN.

76.

To the Parisian Artists.

Gentlemen,

It is the peculiar privilege of great artists to confer renown, and who can have greater claims to such a noble prerogative than you, who combine the most solid and profound theory, with the most skilful and finished execution, casting a veil over the deficiencies of the composer, and often bringing to light beauties in his works unsuspected by himself! In this way, by the embellishment of the 'Creation,' you have earned the right to share in the applause the composition has called forth. The just tribute that I thus offer, the public will also award you! Their appreciation of your talents is so great, that your approbation ensures theirs; thus your favourable verdict is, for those on whom it is conferred, in some degree a foretaste of the anticipated fame of posterity. I have often doubted whether my name would survive me, but your goodness inspires me with confidence, and the token of esteem with which you have honoured me perhaps justifies my hope that I shall not wholly die. Yes, gentlemen, you have crowned my grey hairs, and strewed flowers on the brink of my grave. My heart cannot express what it feels, nor can I write to you all my profound gratitude and devotion. You will yourselves know how to estimate these feelings; you, gentlemen, who cultivate the arts from enthusiasm, and not from self-interest, and who regard the gifts of fortune as nothing, but fame as everything.

HAYDN.

The origin of the above letter is related by Dies, who first published it in his 'Biographical Notice' (p. 174):

—'Copies of the "Creation" were soon circulated all over Europe. Paris strove to surpass all other cities in doing homage to it, and in fact the first performance took place there, though with some alterations. The applause was so great that the *virtuosi* engaged in it, in a fit of ardent enthusiasm, and to show their veneration for Haydn, resolved to present him with a large gold medal, adorned on one side with a likeness of Haydn, and on the other an upright lyre, over which a burning flame flickers in the midst of a circle of stars. The inscription is *Hommage à Haydn, par les Musiciens qui ont exécuté l'Oratorio de la 'Création du Monde,' au Théâtre des Arts, l'an* IX *de la République Française.* MDCCC.'

The following is a draft of Haydn's will; the much corrected original being in the Court Library at Vienna. It is now for the first time published in its integrity. We have seen various traits of his benevolence of heart in his different letters, but this, his last will and testament, seems to combine the whole in one pleasing union. Dies says: 'Six weeks before his death, in April 1809, he read over his will to his servants in the presence of witnesses, and asked them whether they were satisfied with its provisions or not? The good people were quite taken by surprise at the kindness of their master's heart, seeing themselves thus provided for in time to come, and they thanked him with tears in their eyes.' The extracts given by Dies from the will vary in some particulars from the one now before us, in numbers, and a few other particulars. His final testamentary dispositions were therefore evidently made at a later date. Still it is not the legal, but the moral, aspect of the affair that interests us, we shall therefore here proceed to give at full length Haydn's first draft of his last will and testament.

77.

Haydn's Last Will and Testament.

		Florins
1.	For holy Masses	12
2.	To the Norman School	5
3.	To the poor-house	5
4.	To the executor of my will	200
	And also the small portrait of Grassi.	
5.	To the pastor	10
6.	Expenses of my funeral, first class	200
7.	To my dear brother Michael, in Salzburg	4,000
8.	To my brother Johann, in Eisenstadt	4,000
9.	To my sister in Rosnau [erased, and written underneath:] 'God have mercy on her soul!—To the three children of my sister'	2,000
10.	To the workwoman in Esterhazy, Anna Maria Moser, née Fröhlichin	500
11.	To the workwoman in Rosnau, Elisabeth, née Böhme	500
12.	To the two workwomen there [erased, and replaced by:] 'To the shoemaker, Anna Loder, in Vienna'	200
	Should she presume to make any written claims, I declare them to be null and void, having already paid for her and her profligate husband, Joseph Lungmayer, more than 6,000 gulden.	
13.	To the shoemaker in Garhaus, Theresa Hammer	500
14.	To her son, the blacksmith, Matthias Fröhlich	500
15. 16.	To the eldest child of my deceased sister, Anna Wimmer, and her husband, at Meolo, in Hungary	500

		Florins
17.	To her married daughter at Kaposwar	100
18.	To the other three children [erased]	300
19.	To the married Düsse, née Scheeger	300
20.	To her imbecile brother Joseph [erased]	100
21.	To her brother, Karl Scheeger, silversmith, and his wife	900
22.	To the son of Frau von Koller	300
23.	To his son [erased]	100
24.	To the sister of my late wife [erased].	
25.	To my servant, Johann Elsler	2,500
	Also one year's wages, likewise a coat, waistcoat, and a pair of trousers. [According to Griesinger, Haydn bequeathed a capital of 6,000 florins to this faithful servant and copyist.]	
26.	To Rosalia Weber, formerly in my service	300
	(She has a written certificate of this from me.)	
27.	To my present maid-servant, Anna Kremnitzer	1,000
	And a year's wages in addition	40
	Also her bed and bedding, and two pairs of linen sheets; also four chairs, a table, a chest of drawers, the watch, the clock, and the picture of the Blessed Virgin, in her room, a flat-iron, kitchen utensils, and crockery, one water-pail, and other trifles.	
28.	To my housekeeper, Theresia Meyer	500
	And one year's wages	20
29.	To the old gardener, Michel	24
30.	To the Prince's choir for my obsequies, to share alike [erased]	100
31.	To the priest [erased]	12
32.	To the pastor in Eisenstadt for a solemn Mass	5
33.	To his clerk	2
34.	To the beneficiary	2
35.	To pastor von Nollendorf	2
36.	To pastor von St. Georg	2
37.	To the sexton [erased from 33]	1
38.	To the organ-bellows blower	1
39.	To the singer, Babett	50
40.	To my cousin, the saddler's wife, in Eisenstadt	50
	To her daughter	300
41.	To Mesdemoiselles Anna and Josepha Dillin	100
42.	To the blind daughter of Herr Graus, leader of the choir in Eisenstadt [erased]	100

		Florins
43.	To the four sisters Sommerfeld, daughters of the wig-maker, in Presburg	200
44.	To Nannerl, daughter of Herr Weissgerb, my neighbour [erased]	50
45.	To Herr Art, merchant, in the kleine Steingasse	50
46.	To the pastor in Rosnau	12
47.	To the schoolmaster in Rosnau	6
48.	To the school children	3
49.	To Herr Wamerl, formerly with Count v. Harrach	50
50.	To his present cashier	50
51.	To Count v. Harrach for the purpose of defraying the bequests Nos. 51 and 52, I bequeath an obligation of 6,000 florins at 5 per cent., the interest to be disposed of as follows:—	
	To the widow Aloysia Polzelli, formerly singer at Prince Nikolaus Esterhazy's, payable in ready money, six weeks after my death	100
	And each year, from the date of my death, for her life, the interest of the above capital	150

After her death, her son, Anton Polzelli, to receive 150 florins for one year, having always been a good son to his mother, and a grateful pupil to me. N.B.—I hereby revoke the obligation in Italian, signed by me, which may be produced by Mdme. Polzelli; otherwise so many of my poor relations, with greater claims, would receive too little. Finally, Mdme. Polzelli must be satisfied with the annuity of 150 florins. After her death, the half of the above capital, viz. 3,000 florins, to be divided into two shares: one-half (1,500) to devolve on the Rosnau family, for the purpose of keeping in good order the monument erected to me by Count von Harrach, and also that of my deceased father at the door of the sacristy.* The other half to be held in trust by the Count, and the annual interest of the sum, namely, forty-five florins, to be divided between any two orphans in Rosnau.

---

* The inscriptions, written by the Abbé Denis, are as follows:—'Sacred to the memory of Joseph Haydn, immortal master of the science of music, doing homage equally to the ear and to the heart. Erected by Karl Leopold Count v. Harrach, 1793.' 'He was born in Rosnau, in 1732, April 1 [March 31]. On May 31, 1809, admired by all Europe, he entered the realm of everlasting harmony.'

	Florins
52. To my niece, Anna Lungmayer, payable six weeks after my death	100
Likewise a yearly annuity to her husband and herself of .	150

All these legacies and obligations, and also the proceeds of the sale of my house * and legal costs, to be paid within one year of my death; all the other expenses to be deducted from the sum of ready money in the hands of the executors, who must account to the heir for the same. On their demise, this annuity to go to their children until they come of age, and after that period the capital to be equally divided among them. Of the remaining 950 florins, 500 to become the property of my beloved Count v. Harrach, as the depositary of my last will and testament, and 300 I bequeath to the agent for his trouble. The residue of 150 florins to go to my step-mother, and, if she be no longer living, to her children. N.B.—Should Mdme. Lungmayer or her husband produce any document signed by me for a larger sum, I wish it to be understood, as in the case of Mdme. Polzelli, that it is to be considered null and void, as both Mdme. Lungmayer and her husband, owing to my great kindness, lavished more than 6,000 florins of mine during my life, which my own brother, and the citizens in Oedenberg and Eisenstadt, can testify.

[From No. 51 is repeatedly and thickly scored out.]

53. To the widow Theresia Eder and her two daughters, lace-makers	150
54. To my pupil Anton Polzelli	100
55. To poor blind Adam in Eisenstadt	24
56. To my gracious Prince, my gold Parisian medal, and the letter that accompanied it, with a humble request to grant them a place in the museum at Forstentein.	
57. To Mdlle. C. Czeck, waiting-woman to Princess Graschalkowitz [erased]	1,000
58. To Fräulein Anna Buchholz	100

Inasmuch as in my youth her grandfather lent me 150 florins, when I greatly needed them, which, however, I repaid fifty years ago.

---

* After his first journey to London, Haydn bought a small house and garden, in the Vorstadt Gumpendorf, kleine Steingasse No. 73.

		Florins
59.	To the daughter of the book-keeper Kandler, my piano, by the organ-builder Schanz.	
60.	The small Parisian medal to Count v. Harrach, and also the bust *à l'antique* of Herr Grassi.	
61.	To the widow Wallnerin in Schottenhof	100
62.	To Father Prior Leo, in Eisenstadt, of the 'Brothers of Mercy'	50
63.	To the Hospital for the Poor in Eisenstadt [erased] . .	75

For the ratification of this my last will and testament, I have written it entirely in my own hand, and earnestly beg the authorities to consider it, even if not strictly or properly legal, in the light at least of a codicil, and to do all in their power to make it valid and binding.

JOSEPH HAYDN.

May 5, 1801.

Should God call me away suddenly, this my last will and testament, though not written on stamped paper, to be considered valid in law, and the stamps to be repaid tenfold to my sovereign.

In the name of the Holy Trinity. The uncertainty of the period when it may please my Creator, in His infinite wisdom, to call me from time into eternity, has caused me, being in sound health, to make my last will with regard to my little remaining property. I commend my soul to my all merciful Creator; my body I wish to be interred according to the Roman Catholic forms, in consecrated ground. A first-class funeral. For my soul I bequeath No. 1.

JOSEPH HAYDN.

Vienna, Dec. 6, 1801.

78.

To Chorus Director Stoll, Baden.

Vienna, July 30, 1802.

My dear Friend,

I yesterday evening had the pleasure of seeing my Prince in my cottage, when he requested me to go next week to Eisenstadt, in order to rehearse under my direction various pieces of music, and among others two vespers and a mass of Albrechtsberger, and a vesper by Fuchs. I therefore regret that I cannot at present visit Baden; moreover, I am expecting the installation of a vice-capellmeister in the place of my brother. The name is as yet unknown to me. I thank you heartily all the same for your kind offer to receive me into your house, and with a hearty kiss to your wife, I am, my dearest friend, yours sincerely,

JOSEPH HAYDN.

P.S.—Herr v. Albrechtsberger received a princely remuneration for his composition, which caused me great pleasure.

The Leipzig 'Allgemeine musikalische Zeitung,' of 1844, records the following letter, and also gives its origin thus:—

'At the beginning of the century, a kind of musical union had been formed in the small town of Bergen, in

Rügen, in the house of the assessor Dr. K., under the direction of Cantor D., and on the 'Creation' being performed there for the first time, even with their weak orchestra, and accompanied by an ancient flute pianoforte, the effect was so extraordinary, that the enthusiastic K. called for a bumper to the health of the composer, in gratitude for such an enjoyment. The most hearty and unanimous applause ensued, on which K. proposed to write a simple and faithful description of their overflowing sentiments of sincere thanksgiving to the great man. The letter was written on the spot, and signed and forwarded by the two founders of the musical union, in the name of the whole society.'

This is related by the son of one of the subscribers, to whom his father made a present of Haydn's letter, which has been carefully preserved for nearly half a century, in the same ancient flute pianoforte.

79.

To the Members of the Musical Union in Bergen.

Vienna, Sept. 22, 1802.

Gentlemen,

It was indeed a most pleasing surprise to me to receive such a flattering letter from a place, where I could have no idea that the fruits of my poor talents were known. When I now, however, see that not only is my name familiar to you, but that my compositions are performed by you with approval and satisfaction, the warmest wishes of my heart are thus fulfilled; and these are, to be considered by every nation where my works penetrate, as a not wholly unworthy priest of this sacred art. You tranquillise me on the point so far as regards your fatherland, and, still further, you give me the pleasing conviction (which cannot fail to be the most fruitful consolation of my declining years) that I am often the enviable source from which you, and so many families susceptible of true feeling, derive pleasure and enjoyment in domestic life. What happiness this thought causes me! Often, when contending with the obstacles of every sort opposed to my works, often when my powers both of body and mind failed, and I felt it a hard matter to persevere in the course I had entered on, a secret feeling within me whispered, 'There are but few contented and happy men here below; everywhere grief and care prevail; perhaps your labours may one day be the source from which the weary and worn, or the man burdened with affairs, may derive a few moments' rest and refreshment.' What a powerful motive to press onwards! and this is why I now look back with heartfelt cheerful satisfaction on the works to which I have devoted such a long succession of years, and such persevering efforts and exertions. And now I thank you in the fulness of my heart for your kindly thoughts of me, and beg you to forgive my answer having been somewhat delayed. Feeble health, the inseparable companion of the grey-haired man of seventy, and likewise pressing business, deprived me till now of this pleasure. Perhaps nature may yet accord me the gratification of composing a little memorial of myself to send to you, from which you may gather the feelings of a gradually decaying veteran, who would fain even after death survive in the charming circle of which you draw so pleasing a picture.

I have the honour to be, with highest consideration,

Your obedient servant,

JOSEPH HAYDN.

The following letter is an answer from Haydn to the city magistrates of Vienna, who, on May 10, 1803, bestowed on him the golden burgher medal, 'as a small token of gratitude for the benefit derived through him by the poor citizens of St. Marc.' In the following year, the grand civic diploma of honour was also conferred on Haydn. The first performance alone of the 'Creation' brought 4,162 florins, and that of the 'Seasons' 3,209 florins. The letter quoted by Dies is as follows:—

80.

To the Vienna Magistracy.

Respected Magistrates and honourable Gentlemen,

In endeavouring to contribute by my acquirements in the art of music, to the support of old and impoverished citizens, I esteemed myself very fortunate, in having thus fulfilled one of my most agreeable duties, and could not flatter myself that the Honourable and Imperial Magistracy of His Majesty's capital, would deign to bestow on me in return for my exertions so distinguished a mark of their consideration.

It is not the gift alone, gentlemen, highly as I shall prize it as a mark of your goodness, during the remaining days Providence may yet have allotted to me, but even more highly do I value your kind letter, a thorough transcript of your noble mode of thinking; my deeply affected heart being uncertain whether most to admire your gratifying conduct towards myself, or the benevolent care you bestow on your impoverished citizens.

While expressing my sincere gratitude for both, in the name of the poor citizens, as well as in my own, permit me, gentlemen, to conclude by the fervent wish that Providence may long preserve, for the benefit of this imperial city, so humane a magistracy. I am, with deep respect, gentlemen,

Your obedient servant,

JOSEPH HAYDN.

The next letter, to Zelter, is from a draft in the Imperial Library at Vienna. Written outside, we find, 'Vienna, February 25, 1804. Highly honoured lady, there was a time.' On the back of the same page, there is a sketch of a letter from Haydn to his 'gracious

Prince,' in which a petition of the tenor, Joseph Richter, is strongly urged; and also a letter, 'stimatissimo amico mio,' in which Haydn promises soon to send his 'brutto ritratto,' to his personally unknown friend. Fasch's biography of Zelter appeared in 1801. The date, however, of the following letter, as may be seen from Zelter's answer, is 1804.

81.

To Zelter.

Feb. 25, 1804.

My highly respected Friend,

My very great weakness will not permit me to write you more than a few words, but they are words from my heart. You are a rare example of gratitude, which is proved by the biography of your teacher Fasch. You are a man with a deep and thorough knowledge of the science of music, which is evident from your faithful analysis of my 'Chaos,' for you both could and would have composed it just as Haydn has done. I thank you truly for sending it to me, but you will receive far more gratitude from posterity, for striving by your musical institute once more to elevate the now degenerate art of singing. May God preserve you for many years to come.

Yours, with high esteem. [No signature.]

P.S.—I am also much obliged for the portrait. I

may as well mention one slight mistake. I was born in 1732, not 1733 ; so I am a year older, but it matters little.

Again, I wish that my dear Zelter would take the trouble to arrange the 'Even Song' from my quartett for voices, 'Der du mir das Leben,' &c. for the whole of his chorus singers; four solo parts to alternate with semi-chorus, and with full chorus. N.B.—In which case it must positively be accompanied by the pianoforte, just as I have arranged it.

Zelter's answer is given in Dies' 'Biography' and well deserves a place here.

Berlin, March 16, 1804.

Revered Master,

I have not words to express the joy I felt on receiving your charming letter of February 25, which I intend to bequeath as a relic, and a patent of nobility, to my eleven children. I know that I ought to ascribe such praise, rather to your own kindness of heart than to my merits, but praise from you is so precious, that I will anxiously and earnestly strive to deserve it.

You are aware that the analysis of your masterly work is written by me, and that I have long sincerely revered you, but to write the work as you have done, great master, I never could. Your spirit has entered within the sanctuary of godlike wisdom; you have brought down fire from heaven to warm and to illuminate our earthly hearts, and to lead them to a sense of the Infinite. The utmost we can do is only to give thanks and praise to the Almighty, for having sent you to us, that we may discern the miracles which He has revealed in art through you.

What I wished to have from you, my dear friend, for my singing academy, now consisting of 200 sonorous voices (160 of which may be pronounced both vigorous and useful), is some sacred composition, which has long been my cherished wish; but fifteen years elapsed before the funds of the institution were in a condition to afford the outlay for such a masterwork. I feel only too well how small is the sum we offer for a work of yours, which indeed no money can repay, and therefore I rely more on your love of art, and the glory of God, than on our paltry money. I beg you then, if your bodily strength admits of it, to undertake this work, that your great name may resound in our circle to the honour of God and of art; its exclusive purpose being to preserve and to revive church and sacred music, too long neglected.

In order to possess at least something of yours, I took the liberty to arrange for our choir the two Gellert songs, 'Herr, der Du mir das Leben,' and 'Du bist's, dem Ruhm und Ehre gebühret.' Your wish has therefore been fulfilled for more than seven months past; whether I have done them properly, you will be able to judge from the accompanying scores, and I earnestly entreat you to let me know any improvements you may suggest. I wish I could procure you the delight of hearing your choruses sung here, and gladden your heart by the repose, piety, purity, and reverence, with which your beautiful chorus, 'Du bist's, dem,' &c. is given. The best and most accomplished of the Berlin youths assemble here with their parents, like heaven filled with angels, celebrating in praise and joy the glory of Almighty God, and practising the works of the greatest master the world has yet seen. Oh, come to us! come! You shall be received like a deity among mortals. We will sing a *gloria* in your praise, and your venerable grey hairs be thus transformed into a laurel crown, for our master Fasch has taught us how to honour great men.

Farewell, dear and beloved master. May God long preserve you! No work you have hitherto produced shows any symptoms of advanced age. Your 'Seasons' display youthful vigour and mature mastership. I commend you to God.

Yours,

ZELTER.

The 'Société académique des Enfants d'Apollon,' established in Paris in 1740, had appointed Haydn a member of their society, by a letter of December 30, 1807, and likewise sent him their gold medal. His reply is as follows:—

82.

To the Members of the 'Children of Apollo,' in Paris.

April 7, 1808.

Messieurs,

The resolution of the 'Société académique des Enfants d'Apollon,' to inscribe my name on the list of its members, is highly flattering to me, and touches me profoundly.

I beg to assure the society through you, that they could not have conferred that distinction on anyone more fitted to appreciate their esteem, or to feel the value of the honour bestowed on me. I beg, gentlemen, that my sentiments may be permitted to be the transcript of your own, and at the same time the interpreters of my gratitude, for the distinguished token of approbation that you have transmitted to me, by sending me a copy of your statutes and regulations, accompanied by a gold medal. You have thus, gentlemen, scattered some flowers on the path of life that yet remains for me to traverse. I am profoundly affected by it, and I keenly feel that, though old age may weaken the faculties, it does not diminish sensibility of heart, which makes me regret that my great age prevents my having any hope of ever seeing myself among you, to share in your labours, and to co-operate in the culture of an art which forms the charm of society, and to participate in the celebrity which the academy enjoys by so many dear and precious titles.

This is a consolation which my infirmities force me to renounce, and my regrets are as lively as my gratitude is profound. Pray receive this assurance, as well as the expression of my most sincere esteem, and the distinguished consideration with which I have the honour to be, gentlemen, &c.

JOSEPH HAYDN..

One year later, May 31st, 1809, the energetic life of the celebrated master came to a close.

CARL MARIA VON WEBER.

BORN 1786; DIED 1826.

WEBER'S LETTERS.

1.

To Artaria.

Freyberg, in the Saxon Mountains,
Dec. 9, 1800.

SIR,

I BELIEVE that I shall not make your celebrated firm, as music and printsellers, an unwelcome offer and proposal, if I submit for your acceptance the hereafter described *arcanum,* being an apparatus highly to be recommended, on account of the rapidity with which it works, combined with a *small outlay,* and which shall become your sole property on the subjoined conditions :—

1. I can engrave music on stone in a manner not to be surpassed by the finest English engraving, which the accompanying specimen testifies.

2. A workman in winter is able to complete two or three plates, and in the long summer days three or four.

3. A plate of this kind can be used afresh thirty times, that is, polished up.

4. Two men can in one week print off as many thousand sheets as can be printed with ordinary type.

5. The whole stock of the machinery does not ex-

ceed 100 dollars. I await your reply to the enclosed address.

Further, of the musical works I completed while studying under Michael Haydn, I can offer you :—

Three easy trios for violin, viola, and violoncello, for dilettanti ;

Six variations for the pianoforte;

Six ditto ;

Three ditto, pianoforte sonatas;

Six ditto, variations on the song 'Lieber Augustin.'

I ask six copies of each work and a moderate sum, which I leave you to propose with your usual fairness. In the expectation of a favourable answer on both points, I am, &c.

CARL MARIA V. WEBER,
Composer.

2.

To Hans Georg Nägeli.

Mannheim, May 1, 1810.

As my circumstances are altered, and I have once more devoted myself entirely to art, I take advantage of the first moment of time that offers, to renew the connection already established between us by Herr v. Wangenheim, and likewise to thank you for your favourable opinion of my compositions. But I cannot refrain from touching on a point too important for me to be passed over in silence. You seem from my quartett and caprice to discover in me an imitator of Beethoven, and flattering as this might appear to many, it is far from agreeable to me. In the first place, I hate everything that bears the stamp of imitation, and, secondly, my views differ far too much from those of Beethoven ever to come into contact with him. The fiery, nay, almost incredible, inventive faculty which inspires him, is attended by so many complications in the arrangement of his ideas, that it is only his earlier compositions that interest me; the later ones, on the contrary, appear to me only a confused chaos, an unintelligible struggle after novelty, from which occasional heavenly flashes of genius dart forth, showing how great he might be, if he chose to control his luxuriant fancy. Though I certainly cannot boast of the great genius of Beethoven, still I think I can vindicate both the logic and the phraseology of my music, each individual piece causing a definite impression. For it appears to me that the aim of an artistic composition is to deduce the character of the whole from individual thoughts, and that, amidst the greatest diversity, still unity, displayed by the first principle or theme, should always shine forth. An amusing article on this subject is given in the 'Morgenblatt,' No. 309, published December 27, 1809, which may serve further to illustrate my views.* It so happened that, besides the quartett I had the honour to send you, nothing but the

* The 'Fragment of a Musical Tour which may perhaps be published sharply criticises the 'B flat major Symphony,' and the 'Eroica.'

caprice was written out, whence you probably concluded that all my compositions bear the stamp of the *bizarre*. I hope, however, that, when I have the pleasure of sending you some of my other works, you will not fail to perceive at least my efforts to attain clearness, harmony, and feeling.

As you declined publishing the quartett, I sold it to Herr Simrock, and therefore request you to return it to me as soon as possible, to my address, C. M. v. Weber, Darmstadt, at Herr Kammerrath Hoffmann's. Herr von Wangenheim told me that you wished to have something from me for your 'Pianoforte-Repertorium,' and I beg you will decide in what style it is to be. I should very much like to see a work of mine published by your respected firm, and as I have a store of compositions of every kind, I beg you will write to me, and say what would best suit you.

I must press for a speedy answer, for, being about to undertake a distant journey, I cannot stay much longer in these parts. I trust you will have no cause to regret having entered into nearer connection with me, and begging you to excuse this scrawl, I have the honour to be, &c.

C. M. v. WEBER.

The greater part of the contents of the following letters of Weber to the Tyrolese, Johann Gänsbacher (the originals of which are in the hands of his son,

Dr. Gänsbacher, in Vienna), have been already made use of in Weber's biography. They commence on May 13, 1810, when Weber writes from Auersbach to his 'dearest friend and colleague,' at Darmstadt. Both had been pupils at the same time with Meyerbeer, of Abbé Vogler, whom Weber in his letter calls 'our dear teacher,' but usually 'papa,' or 'grandpapa.' The details of the circumstances of both can be gathered in the course of the correspondence, the second letter of which (Frankfort, July 1, 1810), after all kinds of business commissions and playful witticisms, closes with these words, 'Think for some years to come of your desperately loving *ami* Weber.' The following letter, of September 24, 1810, written after Gänsbacher's leaving Darmstadt, proves the great intimacy between the two men, who were destined to remain friends through life.

3.

To Gänsbacher.

Darmstadt, Sept. 24, 1810.

Dearest and best Friend and Brother in Harmony,

I ought long ago to have given you news of myself, for you, of all others, certainly take the deepest interest in my welfare, but I was too unsettled, and, besides, I wished to await the performance of my opera [' Silvana.'] This has now taken place, and I am living quietly with 'grandpapa' in humdrum Darmstadt, and mean to devote the whole forenoon to you, that I may relate, by the aid of my diary, all that has occurred from the moment of our separation.

I set off on July 14, and arrived safely in Mannheim on the 15th, where I was received with the usual love and cordiality. I went straight to Berger,* to ascertain from him whether he meant to accompany me to Baden, according to our previous agreement, but to my great regret I found that he could not travel with me at that time, on account of the illness of the other tenor, Decker. You can easily imagine how vexatious this was to me, as I had built so many hopes on this expedition. Having come so far, however, I did not choose to retrace my steps; so I resolved to undertake the journey alone. G. Weber and his wife and Dusch† said that, if I would wait a few days, they would come with me; who more willing than I? and then I received your letter of the 18th, with the announcement of your departure.

Why should I attempt to express in words the melancholy feelings this news gave rise to in our whole circle, and especially in myself? On the 19th, Weber and his wife, Dusch and I set off, and arrived in Carlsruhe the same evening; the journey was one of the

* An actor in Mannheim.

† Gottfried Weber, well known as a solid musical theorist and critic, at that time a lawyer in Mannheim. Alexander von Dusch; subsequently minister for Baden, also in the law.

most agreeable of my life; you were thought of times innumerable, and we were heartily provoked that the 'young bird should so soon take wing from its nest.' 'Really,' said Weber, 'it is too bad of the fellow to take himself off like that!' At last, on the 20th, we arrived in Baden, which was so full that it was with difficulty we could at last get quarters in the house of some friends. I found numerous acquaintances from every part of the world, and expected to do good business there. Weber and Co. departed on the 22nd; so I was left to my fate all alone. I delivered Nägeli's letter to the Crown Prince of Bavaria, by whom I was graciously received; I fixed the probable date of my concert, and anxiously awaited the arrival of Berger, and the music that Archer was to send, for an orchestra was out of the question; so I was obliged to do my best with the slender means at my command. But neither music nor Berger arrived, and to complete my annoyance, neither in Baden nor in its environs could I find a piano that it was possible to play on. I was told of one in Rastadt; so I went off there, and arrived just as the owner of the instrument had left the place. Meanwhile time passed, Princess Stephanie went on a journey, the Crown Prince talked of leaving; so I became provoked, and gave it up altogether. I recognised in all this my evil genius, who had too long allowed things to go on pleasantly not to play me some vile prank on this occasion. My stay and my journey cost me ten carolins, which vexed me exceedingly; still I made many interesting acquaintances, who may be very useful to me hereafter. The Crown Prince of Prussia often went about with me for whole nights when I was giving serenades. I also met the far-famed poet Tieck, and a number of my friends from Stuttgart, which helped to make many a moment pass agreeably. The most gratifying of all to me was meeting my friend Cotta, the well-known great bookseller from Tübingen, who asked me to write something about Baden for his 'Morgenblatt' (which I did under the name of Herr Melos), and to whom I offered 'The History of my Artistic Life' for publication. To my great joy he accepted it, and it is to appear at the next Easter fair, with some engravings. His firm enjoys such a distinguished literary reputation, that through that alone the success and the value of my work will be already half-secured in the eyes of the world.

I set off again on August 2, and arrived in Mannheim on the 3rd, when I was instantly summoned to the Museum, where I played on the 4th. On this occasion I stayed with Weber, and began to work at my opera of 'Abu Hassan.' People would let me have no rest till I arranged a musical *soirée* in Heidelberg, consisting only of quartetts and singing. I gave this concert on the 13th, and, in spite of the beauty of the weather and the consecration of a neighbouring church, there was a numerous and indulgent audience. Just as the concert began, I was exceedingly surprised, and much touched, by the sudden appearance of the Hertling family, &c.; in short, twenty in number of my friends had come from Mannheim, expressly to attend my concert, and were to drive back afterwards. These are among the few happy moments of life that outweigh years of chagrin, through the feeling of having acquired the love and esteem of worthy men. I returned on the 15th to Mannheim, and left it again on the 18th, with a heavy heart, having no hope of seeing my dear friends again, and with Darmstadt in prospect, but without *you*. Here I received your kind letter of July 28 from Franzensbrunn, and learned from it that you had arrived safely at home. I honour and love your noble patrons * for your sake, as those who attach you so strongly, and with whom you are so happy, must be good people; and if I ever find it possible to come to Prague, I shall certainly do so; but I am only the ball of Fate, who rolls me about the world according to her will and pleasure. Your canon pleased me exceedingly, and recalled many gay and happy hours passed together when 'L'Amerò' resounded. What is to be done about your music? I went to Frankfort on the 27th, to attend a rehearsal of my 'Silvana,' made every arrangement with the Music Director Schmitt, and then hurried back. I composed the first allegro for my concerto, with which 'papa' is

* His Excellency Count Firmian, in Prague, as Weber always addresses to him.

highly pleased, and rewrote the fugue on the first theme, taking as a counter subject—

which delighted papa so much that I can't tell you all he said about it. Thus time passed, and on September 6, I at length took leave of our kind hostess, who spoke of you every day, and proceeded to Frankfort, where I was plagued the whole day with rehearsals, visits, &c. till at last on the 16th my opera was brought to light. The rehearsals and all else went on so well, and everyone worked for me with such goodwill that I began to think I was for once to see something of mine succeed without any obstacles; but no such good luck was to be mine. Mademoiselle Blanchard chose to fix the same day for her balloon ascent, and the moment of the ascent being postponed till half-past seven o'clock, caused such restlessness and distraction in the public and in the theatre, that I became very uneasy about my bantling. But after all the birth was propitious, and it was received with great applause; one aria was encored, and at the conclusion Silvana and I were called before the curtain. She appeared, but I did not, of course. The day after to-morrow, the 26th, is the second representation, and I am to return there to see how it goes off.

I gave your songs to André with my arrangement.

Simrock sends you his kind regards. 'Papa' is not well, and suffering from hæmorrhage; he, however, sends you his blessing and best wishes; he is not allowed to sit up much, but will write to you soon. [Meyer] Beer, my sole refuge at this moment, sends you his love. Beer, G. Weber, and I have entered into a *harmonious alliance*, to which you also belong; in my next letter I will give you more minute details of its laws; it is of great moment both to art and to ourselves. The two others have in the meantime elected me director, if you are satisfied. I do not close my letter, in case anything may occur to me, and now I am going upstairs to see 'papa.'

Here follows your 'song with piano,' which papa revised, and presented in your name to the Grand Duchess on her birthday.

Kühnel [partner in the 'Bureau de Musique,' in Leipzig] had the impertinence to offer only four Friedrichsd'or for the chorals. 'Grandpapa' was highly indignant, but I persuaded him to treat the matter *en bagatelle*; on which I wrote to Kühnel to say that he might engrave them at once, as both Nägeli and I considered it quite beneath us to bargain further on the subject. Publishers seem all to be shabby dogs, and though every second word with them is art! art! they ought to say money! money! [My ever beloved friend, although it is my intention to write you a very long letter by the next post, still I cannot allow this opportunity to pass without some friendly words from me, and embracing you in my thoughts. Ever yours, J. M. Beer.] Now, dear Jörgel,* write soon. I expect a long, long letter; remember that such a letter, in my solitude, would be balsam to my wounds; I shall count the days till I can hear from you. Till then, farewell! and continue to love your friend, as he will ever continue to love and esteem you.

CARL MARIA V. WEBER.

4.

To Gänsbacher.

Darmstadt, October 9, 1810.

Dearest Friend,

I take up the pen in 'papa's' name to answer your letter of October 3, and to scold you soundly in my own for abusing me. Did I not on September 24 write you a letter an ell in length to Hagensdorf? I cannot at all understand why you have not yet received it, and could I possibly write until my opera had been given? Eh?!! It was performed for the second time on the 26th with great applause, and so admirably executed that it left me very little to desire. If you find anything about it in the 'Morgenblatt,' pray see that an extract from it is inserted into one of your papers. How does your opera get on? Have you composed any-

* Tyrolese for Johann.

thing new besides the chorus? If the Vienna papers contain a notice of you, send it here at once, that the Alliance may circulate it. The bill of exchange arrived safely, and 'papa' sent it to Herr Bauscher, in Frankfort, to be cashed, but has received no account of it as yet; he has no doubt that the sum will just balance. He says you need not trouble yourself about the other one, as he is quite willing to wait for it till May. 'Papa' wished to write to you himself, but he is so much occupied with a new treatise on Hebrew rhythm that it is impossible for him to do so. I am to give a concert at Frankfort the end of October, and my present plan is then to proceed to Munich, Berlin, Hamburg, &c. &c. Meanwhile I work like a horse; six small sonatas for André are sadly in my way, but three of them are now finished. I also work hard at the 'Artistic Life,' and papa's biography. The latter is indeed a work, the completion of which at present is out of the question, but I do as much of it as I possibly can. What would I give to be able to fly to you in my beloved Vienna! Weber writes to me regularly from Mannheim, and often mentions you. His wife expects her confinement in a few weeks. I have heard nothing of Berger, since he went to Stuttgart; in fact, he is too lazy to write. Our delightful Heidelberg circle is entirely broken up, most of them having left the place, and settled elsewhere. Schleifer, Loyzow, the two Starkloffs, Schweitzer, among others, and some whose names I cannot recall, have all left Heidelberg. As my pianoforte concerto is now finished, I should like very much to play it in Mannheim, but I do not think that circumstances will admit of my returning there at present; when once I have left dismal Darmstadt, I trust I shall get on more briskly. The day before yesterday I paid a visit to our old landlady, who enquired after you, and I promised to give you her remembrances. Our little maid-servant—the ugly creature—is actually going to be married to a chancery clerk, who is certainly rather addicted to drinking, but in other respects an excellent fellow. Herr Reiner still makes witty remarks; Therese still sings out of tune; our *colleague* the Bear writes canzonets and psalms; the old woman takes snuff; Marianne still whines, Bärbel cooks, and the family is increased by a wretched black poodle, that Beer's servant thrashes, and his master caresses, and now you have all the last news of our household. I shall expect a tremendously long letter from you, and am, ever, your most faithful brother in harmony,

WEBER—MELOS.

Apropos, Weber's signature henceforth is *G. Giusto.* Address your letter to me to 'papa's' care, who sends his kind regards to Fräulein Paradies [a blind pianiste], and I send mine also.

5.

To Gänsbacher.

Mannheim, Dec. 7, 1810.

Beloved Brother,

Your letter from Salzburg of October 17th, I duly received in Darmstadt on November 1. My not having written to you for so long did not proceed from laziness, but because the enclosed was not settled, and I was also anxious to await the issue of an important event in my fate; but now to give you details as usual.

I at last completed the six sonatas for André, and sent them and the concerto to him on October 18th. I long delayed the concert I intended to give at Frankfort, waiting till the colder season set in, when at last a favourable time arrived; my acquaintances and also the circumstance that no concert had been given there for a very long period, all seemed to promise me good receipts on the 22nd; therefore I drove off from Darmstadt to Frankfort; but imagine my horror when the French entered the town at the same moment with myself, and confiscated all English wares and groceries in the town for their own use. The alarm and universal lamentations were so great, that it was utterly useless to think of giving a concert. I remained some days in Frankfort, to see if the matter might not take another turn, but as there seemed no likelihood of this, I returned on the 30th to Darmstadt. I had gone previously to André, in Offenbach, and was very angry at his sending me back my sonatas, because they were too good; he showed me some of Demars, &c. and said that was what they ought to be; I explained to him that I neither could nor would write such miserable trash, and demanded payment, on which he only gave me one-half of the sum, and said it was his custom not to pay the other half till the work was published. As for your songs, they are in course of publication; but he only gave me eleven florins, saying that he understood from what you had written to him the ten copies were to be deducted; I was too angry to waste another word on him, and came away.

I had the joy of receiving your letter on November 1st, on the very day that your mass was performed in Leipzig to the great delight of 'papa' and brother Beer. Herr Hofkammerrath Hoffmann persuaded me to go with him to Mannheim, and, tired of so many disagreeables, I was glad to devote some days entirely to my friends and to recreation. I, therefore, set off with him on the 8th, and took my dear Mannheimers by surprise. I need not tell you how I get on here; it is like paradise, everyone thinking of you with love and friendship, particularly the whole Salomé family, the Hertlings, Edel, but above all the brothers Weber and Dusch; Frey too sends you his regards.

On the 19th, there was a *museum*, where one of my

overtures, one of Beer's psalms, and my concerto were given. Princess Stephanie was present, and quite enchanted, and begged me to sing some little songs to the guitar, and took such a fancy to me that she proposed on the spot that I should remain in Mannheim. Everyone congratulated me, and seemed delighted to keep me with them, and I can with truth say that the prospect of living and working among such kind people was very welcome to me. The affair was now daily spoken of, the Oberhofmeisterin of the Princess arranged the whole, and I was offered at once 1,000 florins, lodging and firewood, and the thing was considered settled, when one day (after I had been repeatedly with the Duchess, singing and playing) the Oberhofmeisterin informed me the Princess had spoken to her treasurer, and she regretted much that the state of her finances would not admit of her engaging me at present. I was not told this till after I had been paraded about for a fortnight, having lost much precious time, and not even received a present. As I am working hard at my little opera 'Abu Hassan,' I resolved to finish it here, which I have done, with the exception of the instrumentation of three pieces. I am now starting in God's name for Munich, Berlin, Hamburg, and Copenhagen. I was at Heidelberg the day before yesterday, where all your acquaintances sent you their remembrances.

I am much distressed to hear that your opera does

not get on better; why not send it to *Giusto?* Perhaps we might make it more known.

Do try to get us some good correspondents in Vienna, for Weber and I will probably publish a musical paper, of which you shall have the prospectus in my next letter, and you must endeavour to procure subscribers for us. Above all, write regularly to the *Centrum* about every novelty, and the various concerts, operas, &c. in Vienna, that we may furnish the information in our paper. Strive to acquire some influence with any important journal in Vienna; for instance, the one that Schlegel edits; these are all positive duties. Now pray answer me at once, and I will write to you from Darmstadt. My respectful compliments to your noble house; and always think with affection of your faithful friend and brother,

MELOS.*

6.

Harmonic Society.†

The perpetual one-sided verdicts and party feeling connected with art, the work of men bribed by pub-

* Two whole pages follow by Brother Giusto, who details more minutely to Jörgel the prospectus of the paper they are about to establish.

† This interesting document, the original of which is written (the latter half) by Gottfried Weber's own hand, has been repeatedly published; but it must not be omitted here, otherwise many of Weber's following letters would be quite unintelligible.

lishers to praise everything they publish, and the difficulty of procuring for what is truly good (unless a great name is attached to it) distinction and a place in the world, have induced Carl Maria v. Weber, Gottfried Weber, and Alexander v. Dusch, to form a Harmonic Society, which, by mutual and energetic support, may act and work for the benefit of art. The fundamental principles of the union are the same zeal for art, the same views on the subject, and especially a perception of the necessity of more closely cultivating the æsthetics of art. Fate does not permit all the members to work together in one place; thus we deem it indispensable to prepare and settle a prospectus, for the effectual working of the whole. The truly irreproachable object of this society must be pre-supposed by each member, and as many distorted views and misinterpretations, and many obstacles, may have to be overcome, we have chosen for our motto 'Perseverance reaches the goal.' The society is justly entitled to be called the Harmonic Society, as all are animated by the same zeal, the same views, and the same feelings, even on the most disputed points.

1. The strictest secresy as to the existence of the union is a duty which springs from the very nature of the case. All its good effects would be rendered null and void were it to be made known; for the public would scarcely give credit to such a union for impartiality and truth.

2. The management of the whole to be entrusted to Carl Maria v. Weber, as director.

3. Mannheim is fixed on for the central point. Gottfried Weber, as secretary of the union, takes charge of the archives and the cash accounts, and will enter in a book the receipts and payments, the articles communicated, and, above all, every legal document, marked and arranged so that the progress of the work may be at once ascertained.

4. All letters to the director to be sent open to the address of Herr Licentiat Weber, in Mannheim, who, being in constant communication with the director, will forward them to him at once.

5. As, in any event, considerable expense in postage, &c., must be incurred, a certain sum is to be hereafter appropriated for this purpose.

6. Regularly appointed members to consist of those only who are both composers and authors, and, above all, whose characters are not likely to debase the true object of the society.

7. In addition, literary brothers may also be included, that is, those who, without being composers, combine knowledge of music with literary talent, and by their poems, and other literary works, are useful to the science of music. These brothers to enjoy precisely the same rights and privileges as the others.

8. The greatest caution must be observed in the choice of new brothers. No member, therefore, can be

admitted, for whom the proposer does not become strictly responsible.

9. On a new member being proposed to the director, a close analysis of his views on life and art must be subjoined, to be laid before the other brothers, by the director, for their opinion.

10. It is, of course, understood that the proposed candidate must know nothing of the existence of such a union; thus abuses will be prevented, and men of talent by no means excluded from the beneficial working of the society.

11. Each brother to select a signature for himself, with which he will subscribe his criticisms, &c., when he does not sign his own. All possible collisions will thus be averted, as each brother will at once recognise their mutual writings.

12. Should any brother find it necessary to make use of several names or signatures, or to adopt a new one, he must at once declare it to the central bureau, when his wish will be submitted to the other members.

13. Two months after admission (i. e. always providing that the union shall at that time have been already formed two months), each brother is bound to send in his biography to the archives, in which his progress in art must chiefly be treated of, and, at the close of each year, punctually deliver a continuation of the same. It will be the office of the central secretary to remind dilatory members of this duty.

14. The chief object of the society, and consequently the chief duty of each brother, is to promote and bring to light what is good, *wherever it is to be met with*, and particular regard to be paid in this respect to youthful rising talent.

15. On the other hand, as the world is deluded by so many bad productions, which are often extolled only by patronage, and by unprincipled critics, it is equally a duty to expose and to warn the public against these wherever they are to be met with. But we hope that a depreciating tone in criticism may be carefully avoided.

16. The circulation and due praise of the works of the brothers will form an agreeable duty.

17. Every work proceeding from the pen of a brother to be at once submitted, on publication, to the director by the author, by which means he can observe the individual tendencies of his works. The director will then transfer them to another brother, to be reviewed in a particular paper, and notify the same to the author.

18. The author of every review, &c., must supply the archives with a closely written copy of the same in octavo, by which the working and the progress of the archives can be seen, and which will be instructive and welcome to each member.

19. All party feeling to be strictly avoided, and fair censure in criticism not to be exceeded; and in any

case to be adjudged with due modesty, and not in the biting malicious spirit of our modern critics.

20. If one of the brothers should compose something really bad (an occurrence by no means probable), the director must tell him so candidly, and persuade him to take back his composition. If the author objects to the verdict of the director, the latter must then appeal to the judgment of two brothers; and if one of the two concurs with the director, and advises the composer to withdraw his work, and yet the latter still objects to do so, then rule 15 is to be put in force against him.

21. Though the tendency of the society is in no wise to be a measure of policy, yet it is taken for granted that each brother will, with all his powers, serve another, wherever he may meet with him, and thus prove that he is elevated far above the too common and petty envy of artists.

Central Archive, November 30, 1810.

7.

To Gänsbacher.

Darmstadt, January 13, 1811.

My good Brother,

I have got from Beer your letter of December 12th last, and hope you have received mine of December 7th, from Mannheim, with its important enclosure; for Giusto and I are anxiously expecting your reply. Things appear to be going badly at worthy Salzburg; all seems in a state of decay, and your description quite carried me back to the days of my youth. I wish I could at this moment be by your side there, and point out to you many a favourite spot of mine.*

Will you speak to Liebich† about my 'Silvana'? I shall be glad if you do; you have only to write to Geh. Secretary Hiemer, in Stuttgart, who has taken charge of forwarding the opera. He is a poet, and will be glad to hear from you, for he knows you already by my letters, and I will previously apprise him that you are to write to him. It is in one sense disagreeable that there is no Austrian newspaper in which you can be employed, but on the other hand not so, as then our fame will come to us from other countries. Let me know at once what are the most popular and independent papers in Vienna. God grant that your opera may soon be given, and received by the public as it deserves; you have my most cordial good wishes. I have sent an article to the 'Elegante Zeitung,' as to what you wrote to me about the 'Vestale' [Spontini's]. You must, however, yourself enter into direct communication with the 'Morgenblatt' and the 'Elegante Zeitung.' Your other articles to be forwarded to the central point, where they will be attended to.

I have answered your letter, so I resume my own history.

* Weber had been there with his father, who had undertaken the Salzburg theatre; he received instruction at that time from Michael Haydn.

† Director of the theatre in Prague.

I wrote to you on December 7th, and, on the 8th, I set to music a splendid farewell song, written for me by Dusch; it is admirable, and the music for it came from my soul. Countess Benzl (the wife of the well-known author of the 'Golden Calf'), a most charming person, persuaded me to go to Carlsruhe, as the Queen of Bavaria was there at that time; so I made up my mind quickly, and, laden with letters, set off on the 12th. I was received with great distinction, but could scarcely find a day to give a concert, as, owing to the presence of the Queen, something was going on every day. I did not therefore play before the Queen, but she desired me to be told that she rejoiced at the thought of hearing me in Munich, which was very gratifying to me, and at last the Museum gave me up a ball day, thus enabling me to arrange a concert for the 21st, which went off famously, and I was overwhelmed with applause. On the 23rd, I returned to Mannheim, and was there so besieged to give another concert that I at last resolved to do so. I requested the co-operation of the musicians, which they all promised. I advertised the concert, had a capital subscription, and every prospect of first-rate receipts, when the orchestra all of a sudden changed their minds (owing to a cabal of Herr Ritter), and informed me in writing that, so long as their own concerts were going on, they had a law which prohibited their assisting foreign artists. I did not let the matter rest, but inserted in the papers a delicate hint that the gentlemen in question had broken their promise, which caused a great sensation; but what good did that do me? I was cheated of good profits. A couple of days afterwards, Herr Kreuzer and Herr Leppich arrived with their 'Panmelodicon,' and lo! and behold! they gave a concert. You may be very sure that I do not intend to keep silence on the subject, which will probably give rise to a little angry discussion. On the 31st, I played again in the Museum, and on January 6th, I returned to Darmstadt, after bidding a sorrowful farewell to Mannheim. We spoke daily of you. Pray do write to Giusto. I have quite completed my opera of 'Abu Hassan' here, and mean to present it to-morrow to the Grand Duke, to whom it is dedicated. I will give one more concert, and then away into the wide world. 'Papa' is indeed very unwilling to allow me to go, but I cannot thus continue to dream away the best days of my life. He is also composing a little opera, the subject a very inferior one, given by the Grand Duke, and I think it will be finished in a few days. He sends you his kind regards. The chorals are come at last, and very beautifully engraved. I have also received what Kühnel published of yours, and already sent it off to be reviewed. Farewell! Ever your most faithful friend,

MELOS.

P.S.—Write soon, and send the letters to Giusto.

8.

*A Rêverie.**

January 18, 1811—11 o'clock P.M.

Escaped from the social circle, I take refuge in my quiet retired chamber, the solitude of which acts with soothing influence on my feelings, and at least enables me to cast aside self-imposed restraint, and to exclude the world from my inmost thoughts. Weighed down by struggling against adverse circumstances [?], I have attained so much apparent calmness that few, under my cheerful, nay even gay, exterior, are likely to discover the grief that consumes me, oppressing and irritating both body and soul.

Does the wave rise only under pressure? Only under pressure does the steel spring show its elasticity? And have unfavourable circumstances and conditions alone given birth to great men? In that case the anticipation of a great destiny, and a great aim, ought to be firmly rooted within me, for never could any poor mortal boast of circumstances more adverse, and oppressive, or more unpropitious to all talent, than

* From the autograph of five detached folio pages in the Imperial Library at Vienna (see Weber's posthumous writings). It is inserted in the first volume of the romance 'Künstlerleben,' to which it evidently does not belong. It is manifestly the spontaneous effusion of momentary excitement, and has little or nothing in common with æsthetical views.

myself. In the most trivial as well as in the most important undertakings of my life, fate has always cast obstacles in my path, and even, if I succeeded in anything, difficulties were to be surmounted, hindrances beyond belief to be overcome, till all my enjoyment was embittered. Dogged obtuseness to all the strokes of fate is the only resource, which, however, entails on me the crushing feeling that joy itself can no longer bring brightness from without, because, hand in hand with her, comes before me, like a spectre, the sure conviction that my happiness is to be poisoned. From the hour of my birth, the path of my life assumed a very different aspect from that of other men; I cannot revel in the remembrance of a gay frolicsome childhood; no uncontrolled youth gladdened me; still young in years, I am old in experience; all comes through myself, and from myself, and nothing from others. I have never loved, for reason always too quickly showed me, that all those by whom I foolishly fancied I was beloved, were only trifling with me from the most pitiful motives. One coquetted with me because, perhaps, I was the only man in —— under forty years of age; another was attracted by my uniform; a third, perhaps, thought she loved me, because it was a necessity for her to have a love affair, and chance brought me into her domestic circle. My faith in womankind, of whom I cherish a high ideal within my heart, is gone for ever, and with it a large share of my pretensions to human happiness.

If I could only hereafter find one who would at least take the trouble to deceive me so cleverly that I might believe in her, how grateful should I be even in awaking from my dream! I feel that I must love; I adore woman, and yet I hate and despise her. I never knew the tender ties of fraternal affection; my mother died early; my father cherished me but too fondly, and in spite of all the love and esteem I bear him, this deprived him of my confidence, for I often felt how weak he was towards me, and love of this kind is seldom forgiven. I thought I had found friends. The familiarity of daily intercourse had linked them to me; we parted, and I—was forgotten. I threw myself into the arms of art, worshipped great artists with idolatry, and at length, after attaining the intimacy I sought, found them, with all their godlike qualities, nearly on as low a level as myself.* The masters being inconsistent, what could the pupil be? If there had not existed within thee, godlike art, the means of grasping thee, I must have been lost, and yet thou, my sole resource, my all, even thou canst stand in hostility before me, and while I passionately embrace thee, though conscious of my nothingness, thou, even thou, canst strike me to the earth at thy feet. The overwhelming force of events—the Hercules garment of humanity—it is ye who estrange me from my beloved art, and from God! While yielding to your power, I

* See in this respect letter No. 2, and the criticism of Beethoven.

destroy myself; while I laugh, I perish, and in a *bon mot* pronounce my own death-warrant.

In short, misery is the lot of man; never attaining to perfection, always discontented, at war with himself, he is yearning personified, unstable, yet ever moving on, devoid of strength, volition, or repose, the fleeting impressions on his mind vanishing as soon as made, and even these utterances from the depths of my heart are proofs of this.

9.

To Gänsbacher.

Würzburg, Feb. 27, 1811.

Dear Gänsbacher,

I had much pleasure in reading your letter with the description of your charming reception by Esterhazy. But you make no allusion to a topic, most interesting to me, your opera. How does it get on? I have at last, by a strong effort, got away from Darmstadt, and left our good old teacher; I really felt it deeply, but I knew it must be done at last, and in fact I had already lingered too long.

To continue my usual custom, I must now tell you everything in detail: my last letter but one carried my story on to January 13th, and was sent to Prague. On the 14th, I despatched 'Abu Hassan' to the Grand Duke, but for some days I heard not a word about it; at last, Mangold told me the Grand Duke liked it very much, and now there was no doubt that my concert would go off well, and so it did; for though it was still delayed, at length it took place on February 6th, and was astonishingly brilliant and crowded, for Darmstadt. I composed a little duet for Madame Schönberger and Mangold's daughter, who has a splendid contralto voice; it pleased exceedingly, and was encored. The Grand Duke took 120 tickets, besides making me a present of 40 carolins for the opera. But only imagine! on the day of the concert, just as I was going to dress, the door opened, and who should walk in but Weber and Dusch from Mannheim. You can easily imagine my delight at this surprise, which was further increased by these worthy youths staying on till the 10th, when we were obliged to separate, and, Beer too went off to Mannheim on the 12th, to meet the professor, who had been staying with his sister. So I was then left all alone with papa. On the 13th, I sent you a letter through Fräulein v. Paradies, and, on the 14th, I tore myself away from all I loved and valued, and found myself once more among strangers. I passed a few days in Frankfort, and proceeded on the 18th to Giessen, a university eighteen hours from Frankfort. There I was surprisingly well received and regarded as a prodigy; all were very hospitable and most friendly. On the 22nd, I gave my concert, which was so full that no one in Giessen can remember anything like it, and which brought me about eighty-two florins. Every day being now precious to me, I left on the 23rd, in spite of all the entreaties of my friends, for Hanau, saw a bad theatre there, went on the 24th to Aschaffenburg, and the 25th arrived here (Würzburg). Yesterday I went about making a round of visits. I may be mistaken, but I scarcely think there is much to be done here. The Grand Duke hears no one who is not recommended to him, and the concert master Krise, an Italian, is a false *canaille*, who is glad to turn over everything on other people's shoulders. I shall see to-day what is to be done, that at least I may not be long detained here, and spend money for nothing. Yesterday evening I learned that a little Frenchman is here, a violinist, and likewise Madlle. Weber the harpist. It is really confoundedly unlucky coming into collision with so many, and I must now wait to see which of us is to keep the field, I or they. From here I go to Bamberg, Augsburg, and Munich, and thence by Leipzig, Berlin, and Hamburg, to Copenhagen. God knows how it may turn out! I am often obliged to call reason to the rescue, to prevent my becoming careless and morose; for can anything be more wretched than to run about from one stranger to another, and to play by snatches to each in turn, just to show one can do something, and, out of thirty, scarcely to light upon one who feels either sympathy or zeal in your cause? I seem, however, to have found one such person here, in the Music Director Fröhlich; at least he went about everywhere with me yesterday in search of a piano. I have just heard that nothing is to be done here; a young Frenchman, Delain, a pianist, has already permission to give a concert; so I should have to remain a fortnight longer, which would not do at all. I therefore leave this the day after to-morrow. I went early to-day to the Grand Duke, wishing to present my opera to him, but the hour of audience was past, so I must see what to do about this in the course of to-day or to-morrow. Farewell, dear brother. My compliments to your noble patrons, though still unknown to them, and write soon to

Your busy and loving brother,

C. M. v. WEBER.

Immediately underneath Beer writes:—

10.

Dear Brother Triole,

An oratorio,* the words of which I got a short time ago from Professor Schreiber, of Heidelberg, soon to be performed in Berlin, entails so much work on me that, alas! I dare not think at all of letter writing. Meanwhile I may at least tell you that I have reviewed your Kühnel songs in the 'Morgenblatt,' and also said something of your Augsburg works [?] in the 'Freimüthigen.' Write soon to your hard-working brother,

MEYERBEER.

You must return the enclosed circular to Mannheim.

* 'Gott und die Natur.'

11.

To Gänsbacher.

Munich, June 27, 1811.

I cannot understand, my dear brother, why you have never written me a single line for so long, as I am persuaded that you have not forgotten me, and you are also aware that I am in Munich. I wrote to you on February 27th, from Würzburg, and gave you my usual report,* and you have not yet answered me. To show, however, that I bear you no malice on that account, I write again, and urgently entreat you to reply soon to my letter. You are in the midst of your family, I am quite alone, so remember how welcome and cheering every word of yours would be to me. I must now give you a brief account of myself. I could do nothing either in Würzburg, Bamberg, Nürnberg, or Augsburg; I confined myself therefore to Munich, where I arrived on March 14th. I was admirably received by everyone, and the whole orchestra in particular treated me with the highest consideration. After a thousand difficulties, I succeeded in giving a concert in the theatre on April 5th, which was one of the most crowded that had been seen for a long time,

* At the end of February, he had again written to the Triole, urging them to take active steps about the affairs of the 'Union,' and particularly to establish a connection with Austrian newspapers, through such men as Treitschke, Kanne, and Castelli. The short letter contains nothing further of importance.

and I was gladdened by the most enthusiastic applause. I forthwith had so many applications and commissions to compose concertos, &c., that, as this was an unfavourable summer for travelling, I resolved to remain here, as I could easily defray the expenses of my stay by my compositions, and subsequently, provided with fresh recommendations, steer my course further. I have as yet followed this plan, and have been rather industrious, and also put my 'Abu Hassan' on the stage here (of which I enclose a play-bill); it was given twice with great applause. I pass my time agreeably enough, at least in so far as it is possible without the companionship of anyone of my own friends. In the beginning of August, I have some thoughts of making an excursion into Switzerland, and returning here in September, for the purpose of giving another concert, and then, if God wills, to take up my pilgrim's staff and proceed to Berlin, &c. I heard from Weber yesterday, who tells me that he is going to Darmstadt on the 21st, where 'Samori' [composed by Vogler for Vienna] is to be given; I shall be rather curious to hear the result; no one can deny that they have at all events studied it long enough, having had the trifling average of about 1,000 rehearsals!

I have my fears about 'Samori,' for my last information was that Mangold and the whole orchestra were far from working at it *con amore*, and you know what a difference that makes. How does your own little opera get on? What have you lately written? can I be of any use here, by your sending me your opera, or by performing a mass of yours? The latter might be more difficult than the former, as the envious Winter* stands in the way of everything of the kind. For some time past I have taken a good deal of trouble about a mass of Weber's, and hope I shall at last succeed in having it performed. There are no court musicians at present in the church, as the court is not here. You have, no doubt, seen my review of your variations *à quatre mains*, in the 'Musikalische Zeitung.' It is quite inconceivable to me why André has not yet brought out your songs; have you sent nothing in the meantime to Kühnel? Don't forget to advertise any new work. I have been chiefly engaged lately in composing clarionet concertos for the inimitable Bärmann; he played a concertino at my concert, which pleased exceedingly, and a concerto (in F minor, C major, and F major) with the Mechanikus Kauffmann, from Dresden, who played it at his concert on his newly invented harmonichord, and for which I also wrote an adagio and rondo with full orchestra. The latter especially was deemed hard work, writing for an instrument the tone of which is so odd and strange that it requires the most lively imagination to make it harmonise with the other instruments. It is

* Johann Peter Winter, composer of 'Das unterbrochene Opferfest,' was at that period Court-Capellmeister in Munich. His envious malicious nature is fully exhibited in 'Mozart's Letters.'

own brother to the harmonicon, and has one special peculiarity, which is that the octaves are prominent in each sustained passage, owing to the contact of wooden pegs, for by these again the strings are once more set in motion. Both compositions pleased exceedingly throughout. I am eagerly longing for a good new libretto, for when I have no opera in hand, I never feel quite happy. It is long since Papa Vogler wrote to me, but I have no doubt he is much occupied with 'Samori.' I beg you will take charge of the enclosed letter, which was sent to me yesterday, and in order not to delay it, I will now break off my twaddle. Farewell, dearest and best of friends. I trust you will soon by a few lines gladden the heart of your attached and faithful brother,

MELOS.

12.

To Gänsbacher.

Bern, Sept. 22, 1811.

You must think, dearest brother, that I am taking my revenge, and have delayed writing to you as long as you did to me, but, by Heavens! this is not the case; it is merely because till to-day I could not find a moment to write you a satisfactory letter, and now I have so much and so many things to write about that I don't know where to begin. First of all, I must reply to your welcome letter of July 25th, which I received on the 31st at Munich. Yes, indeed, you are right, the letters of those whom I love are my only comfort and compensation for many a vexation, and the thought that we are pressing forward together to one great aim, which is, to become one day more worthy supports of art, alone sustains me, while the bond that unites us becomes daily stronger and more practical. Your peaceful agreeable existence rejoices my heart for your own sake, but as an artist I often wish I could hunt you out of your repose, and plunge you into the vortex of the world. Contact with the powers of others calls forth new ones in ourselves, but your fiery zeal comforts me under these reflections. The pleasant though distant hope you hold out of my embracing you next year in Salzburg will probably remain a bright dream. I return to Munich in a fortnight, give another concert there, and then hasten on to Leipzig, Dresden, Berlin, &c., to make use of the winter. My Swiss excursion has considerably reduced my cash, and my poor pittance of hard-earned money is again all spent. Still I do not lose courage; God has so often helped me that He will not allow me to sink this time either. I am by no means pleased to hear that the performance of your opera is so long delayed; at any rate, inform the Centrum at once if you wish to dispose of it otherwise, and I will give preparatory notice in Munich. I should like to hear your 'Requiem,' and should feel particular interest in hearing it sung by your peasants, for if you were satisfied with its performance, it certainly must have gone off well. I will try to make it known wherever I can. If you went to Eisenstadt, write to me forthwith every detail of how you got on, to give me an opportunity of again making public mention of you. When I passed through Augsburg, I talked of you with Gombart,* and he was then quite satisfied with the terms; so if he now complains, or makes any difficulties, it is only the usual way of publishers. They are all the same, even the very best. André and Simrock treat me as they do you; for I hear nothing either of your works or of my own; I lately wrote again to both; so as soon as anything is ready, I shall get it, and will attend to the advertisement. As director, dear brother, I devolve on you the duty of establishing a connection with some popular paper in Vienna, which is necessary, as we have as yet obtained no influence there. You cannot be at a loss for materials; extracts from our letters, notices, &c. I will refer you to some in our next circular.

But to return to myself. My last letter was up to June 27th. On July 7th I got a letter from Weber, who writes that they wish to engage me in Wiesbaden as director of a newly built theatre there, with a salary of 1,600 florins; I was much surprised, and did not know what resolution to form. How could I give up a

* A music publisher in Augsburg.

journey so propitiously begun, and leave the path of fame to bury myself in such a hole? I thought, however, I would wait. So I wrote on the 19th to the intendant to ascertain the real state of the case. I received a very polite answer on August 3rd, to say that they should esteem themselves fortunate if I would come, but could only offer me 1,000 florins, a sum I at once declined to accept. I should have thought it my duty to take the 1,600, but I can, as it is, earn 1,000 florins, and acquire honour and fame besides. There was a concert on the 7th in Nymphenburg, where Bärmann played my concerto in F minor splendidly, and the King and Queen were much pleased with it. On the 9th I left for Augsburg, and arrived on the 11th in Ravensberg, a small town in Würtemberg, where I had some difficulties about my passport, and was obliged to remain there three days, till it was brought back from Stuttgart by a courier; then I got a chill, which nearly ended in inflammation. I left again on the 15th, paid a visit to Baron Hoggner, a distinguished musical amateur, at his property, Wolfberg, on the Bodensee. I spent a few agreeable days there, and arrived on the 19th at Schaffhausen (where the great 'Helvetian Musical Society' assembled this year), for the purpose of giving a grand concert. The society gave me an agreeable surprise by politely appointing me an honorary member; so I was enabled to attend all their *séances*, which I found very interesting. On the

22nd, in the midst of the concert, some one suddenly embraced me, and who should it be but our dear brother Beer! You may imagine our mutual joy; his parents had gone to fetch him from Darmstadt, to go with him to Strasburg. The time during which we were together was, alas! but too short. On the 24th we both left, I to go to Winterthur, and he to Constanz. I met him again in Winterthur for a few hours, and how often we talked of you, you may easily imagine; your ears must have tingled, worthy member of the Trias. I gave a concert on the 28th, which brought me a great deal of applause, but very little money. After deducting the expenses, I got—16 florins. On the 29th I set off for Zürich, where I renewed the acquaintance with Nägeli, which I had already made in Schaffhausen. I also spoke to him of you, and he seems much inclined to publish something of yours hereafter; but more of this and other things of importance in my next circular. On September 3rd I gave a concert, when my profits were —8 florins. You must admit, my dear brother, that such things may well cause a man to feel depressed, especially as nowhere is travelling more expensive than in Switzerland. Early on the morning of the 6th I went, accompanied by the pianist Liszt, on foot to ascend the Rigi, and to visit various classical spots. I saw Tell's chapel, and the defile where he shot Gessler, &c. and reached Lucerne on the 7th. There also nothing was to be done. On the 9th I went to Solothurn, where the

Diet was assembled; so there seemed to be some hope, but this, too, was a failure, and after a stay of four days, I took myself off to Bern, where I resolved not at least to have come to Switzerland for nothing, and at all events to visit its beautiful scenery on foot. I only returned yesterday from this excursion; I have climbed over glaciers, traversed lakes, crept through chasms, and as I made the whole journey alone, with only a guide, I thought of you times without number; what happiness it would have been could we only have enjoyed these glorious scenes together. But fate will not have it so, and drives one to the South, and the other to the North. Perhaps you could come to Dresden when I am there. It is not so very far from Prague; what say you? I intend to leave this to-morrow, for Aarau, where I mean to engage in our interests a very popular paper, 'Miscellany of the Latest News,' and on to Basle, where I hope to Heavens I may make something, and then return to Munich.

An idea occurred to me in Munich to write a 'Handbook for Travelling Artists,' to serve also as a contribution to the history of art at the present time. The general tendency of the work is to enable travelling musicians at once to learn all the musical relations of every town, to whom to apply, and, in short, to place before them, at a glance, and distinctly, the proper mode of proceeding, without which they must waste no end of time and money. Above all, the work is to include Germany, in the widest sense of the word, and I propose also to supply a general survey of the state of art in every country, and in every city. I send you a prospectus in the shape of questions, and beg you to reply to these in detail as regards Prague; and if you know anyone in Vienna, I shall be glad if you will do the same there. I may rely on you, dear brother, for Prague at all events; may I not? I have already secured a publisher, the celebrated Orelli and Fuessli, booksellers in Zürich.

1. *Arrangements for a Concert.*—Permission for the same. The usual localities, or any others. Mode of advertising. Subscriptions or none. What sort. Newspaper announcements. Bills, &c.

2. *The Concert itself.*—Director. Strength of orchestra. Class of music preferred. Parts to be filled. What singers and instrumentalists to be had, and which of these most popular. Time the concerts begin. Arrangement of the pieces of music. What number of pieces given, and where the best piano is to be met with. What instrument most liked, and least often heard.

3. *Finance.*—Best season of the year. Best day of the week. Statement of the theatre days. Expenses in detail. Concert service. Usual prices of admittance. Receipts good, indifferent, or very large. How much time required to arrange a concert.

4. *General Remarks.*—General condition of music.

Names of amateurs. Names of families interested in music. Notice of dilettanti and of established concerts, &c. If possible, a list of the artists who have given concerts within the last few years.

I do beg that, if you see any objections to this plan, you will let me know them at once. You need be in no hurry in your enquiries; if I receive your report two or three months hence, it will be time enough. I hope it may prove an interesting little work. Now, dear brother, don't let me wait long for an answer, and write to me to Munich, care of Heinrich Bärmann, where I shall be certain to receive your letter safely. I have not heard a syllable from Papa Vogler for a very long time, although I have frequently written to him. Are you happy? Farewell, most beloved brother; do not forget your most loving and attached brother,

WEBER.

13.

To Gänsbacher.

Munich, Nov. 13, 1811.

Dear Friend and Brother,

I can only write you a few lines; but I hope they will give you more pleasure than ten letters. I received your letter of October 28th on November 4th. I spoke to Bärmann, the clarionet-player, a truly great artist, and admirable man, and we have determined to embrace you in Prague the beginning of December; so pray make every preparation, and let it be publicly known. You will see from the accompanying newspaper the result of my concert here; I beg you will insert an extract from it in the Prague journals.

A certain Herr C. R. André edits a weekly paper in Prague—the 'Hesperus;' apply to him also. Oh! I have so much, so much, to tell you that I grudge every syllable I write to you. Answer this at once, and I shall have time to get your letter.

My heart is too full, I can write no more. Beer and also Vogler come here in ten days, and I leave this at latest on December 3rd.

Farewell, my dearest brother; soon will your most faithful brother embrace you.

WEBER.

Set everything in motion to secure us a good concert.

14.

To Gänsbacher.

Leipzig, Dec. 31, 1811.

Dear Brother,

Do not be angry that I have not yet written to you, but it was almost impossible to find a moment's leisure; besides, I was anxious to write you something decided. On the 14th, by truly miserable roads, and half dead from the stormy weather, we arrived in Dresden. My first step was to enquire about Mieksch [teacher of singing in Dresden], and I learned that the court was not to return till January 6th, when of course, even then, just at first, much could not be done. We, however, quickly resolved to make use of the intermediate time to kill off Leipzig, Gotha, and Weimar. So we only delivered the letter from Wrtby to Abbé O'Kelly and poor Count Morzin, and set off to Leipzig on the 26th, where we arrived safely at an early hour on the 27th. As you may imagine, for a few days we had scarcely time to draw breath, till we had delivered all our letters to those tiresome shopkeepers. Our concert here is now fixed for the 14th, as it so happens that the devil prompted a whelp of a pianist, a young lad from Brunswick, of the name of Mühlenfeldt, to come here, and his concert takes place on the 7th. I have spoken to Kühnel, who sends you his regards; he will find out where the copies were sent to, for he thought they had been forwarded to yourself. He was particularly glad to hear something of our friend, Dr. Lang, to whom I beg you will give the enclosed few lines, with my kind remembrances. Kühnel asked me to give him something of mine to publish; perhaps he may engrave the delicate overture in D minor. I wrote to-day to the Centrum, giving a report of you, and also mentioning your 'Requiem.' Here, too, I have made cabals against you, and spoken ill of you! Above all, take care that I receive without loss of time the score of 'Silvana,' and the librettos of both operas. We stay till the 16th; so you can send your answer here. I lodge with Herr Küstner, in the Hôtel de Bavière. You can easily conceive what a striking contrast our visit to dull Leipzig forms to our dear, cordial, hospitable Prague, and every hour our thoughts return to you. My consolation is that I shall have ample time here to write letters too long delayed, treatises, &c. &c. Did you forward those I sent you? Let me have three copies of any Prague newspaper that gives a report of our concert. Best regards to all acquaintances, but especially remember us to your noble patrons, whose friendly reception of us we can never forget; your devotion to them I can now fully understand. Kind regards also to Liebig, Count Pachta, the Clams, &c. &c. Farewell; write soon and often. From here we go to Gotha and on to Weimar. *Vale et me amas.* Ever yours,

WEBER.

Zounds! Jörgl, I had almost forgotten,

A happy New Year!!!!!!

Canone à 4 voci.

Canone in infinitum sempre dacapo.

No change in us!!

And here is a hearty kiss. O

15.

To Günsbacher.

Weimar, Jan. 28, 1812.

My dearest Brother,

I received to-day your kind letter of the 24th, and hasten to send you a few lines in reply, for as I wrote to you on the 20th from Gotha,* I have little more to say. Our stay in Gotha was beyond measure agreeable. Prince Friedrich and the reigning Duke treated us most kindly, and invited us to spend a couple of months with him next summer; indeed, the Duke seems strongly disposed to appoint me director of a theatre now being built there, but this must remain *entre nous*. Our receipts at court consisted of thirty ducats and a couple of handsome antique rings. The concert in the town just sufficed to cover the expenses of our stay; so we came off very well. We received besides a letter of introduction to the Grand Duke and Duchess here. We are to play before the latter to-morrow in her private apartments. No concert can be given here at present, as some birthdays intervene, which are celebrated every day by fêtes. We hope to arrive in Dresden on the 2nd or 3rd, and thence go on to Berlin, where I beg you will write to me poste restante.

May good fortune attend you, dear brother; you are

* This letter has not been found.

right to set sail gallantly at once. I only wish that I could be with you in dear Vienna. May God grant you every success! You see I contrived to make the 'Musikalische Zeitung'* in Leipzig very complaisant. Now, pray, don't be lazy. Above all, I solemnly charge you not to forget my little book of reference. You have the best opportunity in Vienna of collecting notices for it, and as I lay great stress on good and correct information about the music in that capital, pray do not delay anything connected with the subject. You might possibly find some one to assist you in the matter. If you can discover a certain youth from Lucerne, Xaver Schnyder by name,† do pay him a visit; he is now in Vienna, studying composition, and I have talked much of you to him. Ask Treitschke, when you have an opportunity, about my 'Silvana' and 'Abu Hassan,' which have been a long time in Vienna. Now farewell; write and let me know how long you mean to remain in Vienna; a long letter above all. May God grant you health and happiness!

Ever your brother,

WEBER.

* 'Allgemeine musikalische Zeitung,' edited by Rochlitz.

† Schnyder von Wartensee, now above eighty years of age, is a composer and theorist in Frankfort-on-the-Main. He had letters of introduction to Beethoven in Vienna, from Nägeli, and also from Dr. Troxler, an intimate friend of the great master, who lately died at Bern, at the age of eighty-four. Beethoven, however, was not to be persuaded into giving the young man instruction, who then went to Baden, and pursued his studies there.

16.

To Gänsbacher.

Berlin, March 20, 1812.

*As to the little 'Handbook,' you may be quite at ease. I wonder how you could think of it with so little spare time; the measures you have taken to procure me notices are excellent. Perhaps I may go to Vienna myself next winter, as my journey to Petersburg seems nearly at an end. Oh, my poor Jörgel! that was indeed an unlucky expedition; the times become daily worse, and men likewise, which is the greatest evil of all. You cannot really think how indignant I felt on reading your letter about the capellmeister, secretary, prince, &c. Take comfort, however, for, at all events, you have heard your work given, and no doubt learnt something from it. Is Müller no longer with Esterhazy? I thought he had only gone to Munich on leave. My 'Silvana' seems unlucky everywhere, and, from what Treitschke says, it will not be given at all in Vienna. I do not think that 'Abu Hassan' is yet in Vienna; so offer it to Treitschke in my name for five gold carolins (I don't know your rate of exchange at present), order a copy, and pay for it out of that sum. On your opera, also, a curse seems to rest; we must try to remove it in Mann-

* A corner is torn off this page; hence the letter is rather fragmentary, and difficult to understand.

heim. I have long known that Salieri, like the rest, is a shabby dog, and I make Master Weigl heartily welcome to the downfall of his opera.

Oh, noble soul! let me embrace you. So you thought of my welfare when you made the engagement with that pretty girl? You deserve to be well rewarded. By-the-bye, as we are on a subject of this kind, greet my dear Jung for me 1,000,000 times.

I resume my own history. We got on very well indeed at Weimar, and played twice before the Grand Duchess, and a court concert was on one occasion arranged on our account, which had never before been done. We arrived in Dresden on February 5th, I miserably ill, having caught cold, and rheumatism likewise attacked my chest. A few days in bed cured me. After thousands and millions of obstacles, we gave our concert on the 14th, which turned out very indifferently, in spite of the enormous number of letters of introduction we brought with us. The people here are far too poor and sordid. The most agreeable house is Neumann's, for whose acquaintance I have to thank Jung. On the 18th, we were promoted to the high honour of playing before the King in his private apartments, a thing quite unexampled, and in return we were treated to a couple of pretty little gold boxes. On the 19th, we left for Berlin, where we arrived safely on the 20th. On the 22nd, Bärmann set off to join his parents at Stettin, our concert having been adjourned. . . . . .

I proceed to Gotha and to Prague, if I can manage it, in the autumn. It is too late for me to go to Hamburg, nor indeed would it be advisable to undertake anything there at present, as summer is so close at hand. I can live for nothing in Gotha and work hard.

'Silvana' was rehearsed here some months ago, under Righini, but it went so confusedly that they all pronounced it to be crazy stuff. I laughed at this, and now that my concert is over, the whole orchestra are prostrate at my feet. But such is everywhere the case unless either yourself or a friend are present. I live most agreeably with Beer's parents, but, on the whole, I do not like this place. The people are cold, full of talk, but devoid of heart, regular reviewer souls, carping at everything.

I send you a circular from Billig. Meyerbeer is in Würzburg, and expected in Munich a few days hence, for the purpose of putting his opera 'Jephtha' on the stage there. I was on the point of having rather an angry discussion with that worthy youth; he is dilatory and indolent about writing, and pretty much the same in business matters. So I wrote him a few sharp words of remonstrance, which the young gentleman chose to take amiss, but I hope now all is once more on its former footing. . . . . .

Write to me if you still intend to leave Prague next summer. My best regards to your amiable patrons and to Count Clam, to whom you may say that his spectacles have never quitted my nose since I left Prague. Also to Count Pachta and Tomaschek, &c. I regret much that Madlle. Breda is going to Vienna. My compliments to her and to Madlle. Löran. I have not forgotten about Munich, and now I have done. I have written enough. Write soon, and do not forget your ever loving

WEBER.

17.

To Gänsbacher.

Berlin, April 25, 1812.

Dearest Brother,

Your long silence makes me very uneasy. You no doubt received my letter of March 20th, and the circular. On April 3rd, too, I wrote to Liebich, acknowledging the receipt of 'Silvana,' but have as yet got no reply. A melancholy duty compels me now to take up my pen, and to repose my grief in the breast of a friend. The day before yesterday, through Gottfried Weber, I received the intelligence that my beloved old father died peacefully on November 16th, and even in his last moments thought of me. Long prepared, as I must have been, for such an event, occurring to an aged man of seventy-eight, still it has most deeply affected me; so if I write to you to-day in an incoherent and disconnected manner, you must forgive me.

Let me know who paid for the copying, and draw a bill on me for the amount; or shall I send you the sum in banknotes? I should also be glad to know whether the twenty-eight florins are in Einlösungsschein. In any case, copying is cheaper in Prague than here, and as I have sold both my operas to Dresden, be so good as to have them copied out again, and likewise the texts. Now to my own doings.

We gave our second concert in Berlin, on March 25th; the last we gave together. It was a failure, and only cleared the expenses, but this arose from untoward circumstances. French troops were announced on the day previous, two millions demanded from the merchants, and we had the most detestable weather on the evening of the concert itself. On the 28th, I went with Bärmann to Potsdam, and the same evening I parted with deep regret from that excellent man, with whom I have lived under the same roof for nearly a year. Since then I have been wandering about here and there. Bärmann arrived in Munich on April 2nd, and the King and Queen immediately enquired about me. My stay here seems likely to be protracted, as I am determined not to go till my 'Silvana' has been given. I have also written to Gotha, but have as yet got no answer; all the world owes me answers. Beer is to arrive in Munich about this time. Vogler has detained him till now in Würzburg, where he gave three organ concerts. My residence in the house of his parents is very pleasant; indeed, everyone strives to make Berlin agreeable to me. My music, too, seems coming quite into fashion.

Weber writes that he intends shortly to give the 'Requiem.' Are you working at anything new? I am on the look out for an opera text. I have written to Liebich about a new opera I am to write, and said I would come in the autumn, when we could strike a bargain; try to find out how matters stand, and give me a clear and sensible report on the subject. Do not let me wait so long this time for an answer, but dispel my anxiety, if you can; I stand so alone in the world, and have nothing but my friends. Say all that is kind from me to the Firmians, Jung, Clam, Pachta, &c.

Ever your most faithful brother,

WEBER.

18.

To Gänsbacher.

Berlin, May 16, 1812.

Dearest Brother,

I received your welcome letter of the 8th on the 13th, to my great joy, for your long silence had led me to fear there was something wrong. Your letter was true balsam to me, and I eagerly drank in the heartfelt love that shone forth in it.

That my answer may still find you in Prague, I write only a few lines to-day. Yes, dear brother, we do indeed stand alone; let us heartily clasp hands, and form an enduring bond. Your love affair causes me great anxiety. Receive my cordial congratulations on your birthday, and explain to me what it was that so embittered the day to you; sympathy soothes grief, and mine will certainly not fail you, therefore I shall expect the promised letter about this affair.

I am glad that Liebich still wishes me to come in the autumn, but he has not yet answered my letter. Give me some kind of idea *au fait*, as to what I ought properly to ask for an opera in Einlösungsschein, as circumstances are now so altered. I could not in any event come before October. What a glorious prospect you hold out to me, in the hope of passing part of next winter with you; do endeavour to realise this; how we shall talk and work together!

I thank you for the notices of Vienna; they are indeed very imperfect, but as I am going there myself, I can then complete them. I am charmed beyond measure to learn that the overture to your opera has been successful, for these base creatures will now see that we can put forward our man everywhere. I highly commend your activity in circulating your works. Yesterday at 9 o'clock I put up an ejaculatory prayer for you to Heaven! Write me every particular of the performance, and I will then put a notice into the papers. Do not forget to keep up your connection with the 'Elegante,' &c. My kind regards to Tomaschek, and tell Wittasch that I have not forgotten him, and he may soon expect something from me. The prospects of your compositions at Würzburg are very good; they pay well there, and ready money is a very fine thing. I receive the most delightful letters from Gotha, where I am anxiously expected, and I mean to go there as soon as my 'Silvana' has been given, which, however, seems rather a distant prospect. I think I already told you that Righini makes cabals, inasmuch as he formerly laid aside my opera, declaring that it could not be performed. At length, on the 11th of this month, there was a grand rehearsal, which I directed myself; the orchestra have a real love for me, and all went off as admirably as if we had already rehearsed it ten times; everyone was astonished, and scarcely recognised the music again; so I trust there will now be no further hindrance to its performance. You may well believe how much I am embittered by the treatment I have received, and I intend soon to give them a bit of my mind on the subject. I like very much being here, and everyone shows me much esteem. Pray send me something from your masses to be sung by four voices to the piano, so that I may properly trumpet forth your merits. Several of Gottfried's quartetts have been already sung here. The day after to-morrow is old Beer's birthday, for which I have written a trifle. Now farewell, dear brother. My best regards to all, all, especially to Jung, and your patrons, and write soon to your loving brother,

WEBER.

19.

To Gänsbacher.

Berlin, July 14, 1812.

Beloved Brother,

You must not be angry that I have not written to you for so long, but the rehearsals of my opera absorbed every moment of my time; besides, I was anxious to let you know the result at once, which was as brilliant as any man could desire; it secured for me the utmost possible triumph over all cabals, &c. &c. It was given for the first time on the 10th, and is to be repeated to-day. I directed myself, and besides the applause given to the music, after each act there were loud cries of 'Bravo, Weber!' It did indeed go off admirably, and the singers and the orchestra vied with each other.

In reply to your letters, I must tell you that I got yours of June 12th on the 18th, and that of July 2nd on the 9th. I gave the list of your compositions to Schnabel;* he has returned to Breslau by way of Leipzig, Dresden, &c. and is to consult his superiors about the purchase, and then write to me what his wishes are. But how does it happen, dear brother, that you have overlooked the most important point in my letter about Berner,† and have written me nothing on the

* Capellmeister of the cathedral at Breslau.

† 'My old and intimate friend, who is distinguished both as a com-

subject? The votes being unanimous, he is now one of us, and is called Ernst. He will also do his best for your compositions in Breslau. He is an excellent man, and a very fine artist. Your loving confidence touches me to the heart. Yes, by Heavens! you are not mistaken in me, and the breast which has already withstood so many conflicts, will gladly also bear the sorrows of a friend.

I have had letters from Liebich and Victorine, and am now resolved to pass August and September in Gotha, and to go to Prague in October. How I rejoice at the happy prospect of embracing you, and our spending a couple of months together! What do you say to coming to Gotha to fetch me? How delighted Bärmann would be to see you in Munich. Vogler and Beer will probably stay there for three or four months yet. Beer has played twice before the Queen, and his opera will certainly be performed. Our Union, thank God! is in splendid bloom, and promises rich fruits. I will attend to the advertisement of your 'Requiem' in the 'Elegante' here, &c., but how shall I manage to give you any tidings of it, when you are on your journey? You can always address your letters to me here, as, even if I had left, I shall receive them safely. Write to me by return of post, to say how long you are to remain in Salzburg, and, above all, let me know as minutely as possible your plans, and say if I can do any-

poser and pianist, and writes well too,' says Weber himself of Berner, in a note written on May 23rd of this year to Gänsbacher thing for you in Munich; though, to be sure, Bärmann and Vogler being there, you are certain of all you want. If you can find an opportunity in Salzburg to converse with an old friend of mine, Susann, an actuary, in Teisendorf, pray take advantage of it, and write to me to say how he is; perhaps he may be of use; you may remember that I showed you some of his letters. I leave Berlin the beginning of August at the latest, in order to work in peace in Gotha. I have got a beautiful text for a cantata from Rochlitz, which I intend to compose, and to give in Leipzig, for the first time, at the New Year. I must now conclude with compliments to your excellent patrons, and begging you will not forget your ever faithful brother,

WEBER.

20.

To Gänsbacher.

Gotha, Oct. 12, 1812.

Dear Brother,

This letter is in fact no letter at all, but merely for the purpose of presenting to you Herr Spohr and his wife. In the one I mean to write two days hence, and which you will receive before this, you will find all particulars. I now, therefore, only cordially recommend to you good honest Spohr. Strive to do all you can for him. I have given him letters to Jung, Liebich, and Victorine, and also to your patrons. Introduce him everywhere. Farewell. You shall soon be embraced by your attached brother,

WEBER.

21.

To Gänsbacher.

Gotha, Nov. 25, 1812.

Dearest Brother,

I answer your welcome letter of the 17th, in great haste and briefly, though it caused me the utmost joy. I have at length got from Berlin your letter of October 25th, from Brunnersdorf. No doubt you have meanwhile received one from me written on November 11th, with an enclosure to Spohr. So the preparations for my entry into Prague are all made! I prohibit illuminations, fireworks, and other expensive doings. It really is a confounded business that I cannot manage to get away from here. Prince Friedrich has also arrived; so I have been obliged to promise first him, and then the Duke, to stay a week longer. But I will make all possible haste, for I yearn quite as much as you do once more to rest on the breast of a friend. From here I go by Weimar and Leipzig. I have this moment written the last note of Rochlitz's hymn, which will, I hope, please you; there is a little fugue at the close. The portrait painter remains here. What a foolish affair of

Victorine; that girl never seems to be at rest; she ought not to sacrifice so agreeable an existence to a mere whim; besides, I do not like to interfere in theatrical matters. No doubt it will soon be all arranged. I entirely subscribe to your opinion of Spohr. My kind regards to Madame Schönberg, and say that to my great joy I got her portrait from Bertuch. Yesterday a pupil of Spohr's gave a concert, in which Madlle. Schlick, my pupil, played my concerto in C exceedingly well. If I can discover a good subject for your stage, I will not fail to secure it. It is not likely that Madlle. Harlas will come to please Bärmann, but probably she will appear in starring parts. I don't envy you the correction of the 'Requiem;' I have had the same trial, and have it still. It is at all events a good thing that the expenses are covered, and that we may now talk about it. Adieu! you can write once more to me here. My regards to all friends.

Ever your most faithful brother,

WEBER.

I will tell you about Beer when we meet.

22.

To Gänsbacher.

Vienna, April 2, 1813.

Dearest Brother,

I write you only a few hasty lines. I arrived all right in Vienna early on Monday, at half-past eight o'clock, looked up Papa Vogler, but did not find him till Wednesday; he was in great delight, and greets you cordially. To-morrow I dine with him, and bring him the money. He got your letter, but you must have missed one of his, for he maintains that he wrote to you to pay the money to some one in Prague, but he is quite as well pleased as it is. You can figure to yourself the joy of Bärmann and Madlle. Harlas, and that we immediately began to talk of you. With Beer the matter stands thus: I met him with all the old love and cordiality, and made no allusion to what had passed, and he too has not as yet taken any notice of our difference; on the surface, we appear to be just as we were, but my implicit trust in him is at an end. Bärmann, and still more Vogler, complain of him, amazed by his pride and insatiable vanity and his touchiness, all equally great, and which must repel everyone.* He declares that he never received the letter I sent him by Weber; it may be so, but I believe he intends to ignore it, even when he does get it.

Of course, I have done nothing in the way of business during these last three days; time will be required for that. I am everywhere well received, and have not yet delivered one-fourth part of my letters, nor yet spoken to Haas or Treitschke. I miss you at every turn. Each time that the door opens, I think you

* Meyerbeer had at that time the most brilliant success as a pianist in Vienna.

must come in, and every moment there is something I should like to ask you. Write soon and often; remember me kindly to your excellent patrons, and to Count Clam. The carriage conducted itself admirably, and nothing was broken except one screw of a trunk. I intended to have written a few lines to my good Victorine, but I have been so besieged by visitors that I cannot manage to write to-day. Say all that is kind to her from me, and beg her to let me know what day she means to arrive here, and I will write where she ought to come to, for as yet I have found nothing suitable. Pray take some charge of her, dear brother. A thousand greetings to Jung, and ask him why he did not send me what I expected? My concert is likely to be considerably delayed. How gets on your overture? I heard 'Figaro' here An der Wien, the 'Vestale' at the Kärnthner, and 'Orfeo' at the Kasperl. I liked the first the best, except the *tempi*, which were all too much hurried. Now adieu, my dear brother. I embrace you cordially in thought, and am your faithful brother,

WEBER.

23.

To Gänsbacher.

Vienna, April 16, 1813.

Dearest Brother,

I have received your welcome letters of April 1st and April 8th. I should like to write to you much and often, but cannot manage to do so. A thousand times at least have I wished the good town of Vienna to be swept from the face of the earth. I have so much to do in running about myself, and being overrun with visitors, that I really cannot collect my thoughts, and can enjoy nothing in Vienna, except spending my money freely. I have scarcely been able as yet to deliver one-half of my letters. I have spoken with Haas once or twice, but he gave me no commission for you, as he returns soon himself, but I am by no means done with him yet. I will enquire about the aria in the 'Vestalin.'

It is now high time that *C minor* should arrive. Good luck, dear brother, and success! The criticism of my concert made me laugh heartily. Hauptmann * sends you his regards, and he is not engaged for Spohr's orchestra, having prospects in Dresden, which, indeed, are rather dim at present. 'Papa' sends you a thousand greetings; he wished to add a few lines to this letter, and also to acknowledge the receipt of the forty florins, but you know there is no getting hold of him, especially here. He goes to the country for some time to-morrow. The Stephen tower thanked me very politely when I gave him the compliments of your *cara*, so he requested me to place him at her feet, which, however, I declined, as it would be such hard work to lift him up again! on the other hand, I beg you will place

* Now Cantor at the Thomas School in Leipzig; at that time he lived in Vienna.

me at her feet, with my cordial regards. I cannot bear the thought that on my return I shall no longer find you in Prague, and yet so it must be if your departure is still fixed for the 20th. My concert is on the 25th, in which Madlle. Harlas and Bärmann sing and pipe, and I propose leaving this about May 2nd or 3rd. If it be at all possible, pray arrange that we may still meet. I congratulate you on the completion of your overture, and anticipate much pleasure from hearing it. That I am to meet *D minor* is capital, for it ensures my having some one with whom I can frequently speak of you; only pray make her acquainted with my peculiarities, and that I look as gloomy, and growl as fiercely, as an approaching thunderstorm. I grieve to hear that the 'Seven Words' [Haydn's] did not go divinely. I would give a good deal to be with you to assist in modulating such different keys as *F major*, *C minor*, and *D minor*. Only beware of unresolved discords. Rhode* is here, and will be in Prague in a few days. I must own that I don't care much as yet about being here, not one of the whole lot to whom I brought introductions take the slightest trouble about me, and you know I don't like paying many visits. I am only anxious to discover what the result of my concert is likely to be; the day was one of the best I could get hold of. I have only hitherto played once in society,

* That celebrated violinist had returned from Russia the previous autumn.

and then merely the variations with Bärmann, which made their proper effect, but what is that? You are curious about my diary? Alas! its contents are very meagre, and I can almost tell you in three words what goes on from day to day. From 7 till 11 o'clock my room is like a dove-cot, in and out perpetually; then I pay visits till 2, dine at four, visit again; and then either to the theatre, a party, or home to write. I find almost everything beneath my expectations; the great lights appear so little when seen closely. Moscheles, Hummel, Kruft, &c., are all only stars of good but common magnitude.* What I have hitherto seen and heard are Mayseder's concerto on the 4th, excellent, but it left one cold. The 6th, 'Titus;' Madlle. Harlas sang the part of Sixtus admirably, as usual. The 8th, 'David,' a new opera of Liverati, a hanger-on of Spontini, who started in life as a trombone-player; the 1st act tolerable, the 2nd very dull; however, it pleased much. The 9th, 'Papa's' organ concert, which Beer and I managed; much that was glorious, and much that might have been omitted. The audience consisted of 300 paying people at 3 florins; the applause—so, so. He intends to give some more; he is in all respects just what he was, and Herr Steiner [music publisher] also. The 10th, I

* Beethoven does not seem to me to have come into contact with Weber at that time. Perhaps he was partly withheld from this by his teacher Vogler, who was not well disposed towards Beethoven, and partly perhaps by his own shyness on account of the criticism in the 'Morgenblatt.'

spoke to Palffy,* who received me with extreme politeness, and made me promise to send all that I write for the theatre first to him. The 12th, 'The Seasons,' in the Kärnthner Theatre with 200 musicians, but it produced no great effect. The 13th, Bärmann's birthday, when you were often thought of. Beer and I each surprised him with a quartett, and we dined in Schönbrunn. Went in the evening to Clement's concert, in the Leopoldstadt; crowded, and he played right well; old school, but correct. The 14th, made the acquaintance of Herr Mosel, and heard his wife play. The 15th, at last, had an interview with Prince Lobkowitz; and, finally, the 'Seven Words' were given to-day in St. Peter's Church, and in the evening, at Professor Zizius's; we are to have Pergolesi's 'Stabat mater.' Your fair friend, the revered countess, I have not yet spoken to; there lies quite a curse on me, I never find anyone at home.

I have bought two splendid instruments, one from Streicher, and the other from Brodmann. In the course of one day, I saw at least fifty different ones, of Schanz, Walter, Wachtl, &c., not one being worth a charge of powder, compared to either of those I got.† I spoke to Treitschke about your opera, and

* Count Palffy shared the direction of the theatre with Esterhazy and Lobkowitz, since the year 1807.

† J. F. Reichardt, in his 'Vertraute Briefe,' relates that, as early as the year 1808, Streicher had improved his instruments very carefully, according to the suggestions and demands of Beethoven.

he says he would give it at once, if he could see any possibility of a good cast for it, without which it would make no effect. Bärmann has made a note about Mitterdorfer, and Vogler the same about Holzmann. I had a considerable alarm lately. Only imagine! I received a letter from *C major*, in L. (enclosed to me by Liebich), and open, which was done by Frau Johanna in a fit of absence, as it came along with other letters for her husband. Luckily, it might have been read with impunity by anyone, but that was only a chance! I still feel the effects of my terror in every limb. I see and hear nothing of Gottfried, and yet he had a great many important things to write to me about. I am apparently on the old footing with Beer, but pure and entire trust can never return; to this a thousand other causes also contribute, too numerous to write about.

Is it long since you were at the Wenzels'? Did you make my excuses for not taking leave of them, and do you know anything of *C major*? The editors of the newspapers now sprawl at my feet, and I hope that, in spite of my short stay here, much has been done to make me known in Austria. I have nothing new to write about politics; besides, you are nearer everything of the kind than we are. I expect Victorine on Monday; I shall make her tell me a great deal about you.

My engagements for the opera go on very slowly, as

I cannot spend much money on salaries, and the people here have too many resources. Still I hope to pick up something. I shall not be able to do any business with publishers till after my concert. It is unlucky that I must then hurry home at once. Madlle. Harlas has prolonged her contract for a month, till the middle of May.

I have now scribbled enough, and can scarcely see any longer. Farewell, my most dear and faithful brother; write to me soon and often. My kind regards to all my friends, particularly to the charming Clam family (I could not find Countess Rastory), and continue your regard for your unchangeable brother,

WEBER.

24.

To Gänsbacher.

Vienna, April 22, 1813.

Dear Brother,

I write you a few lines in the greatest haste to bid you a loving farewell from a distance.

You, no doubt, got my letter of the 16th. Victorine arrived on the 18th, and brought me yours of the 12th, and I have just received the one written on Easter Sunday, mentioning the completion of your overture. May good fortune attend you, dear brother. I hope to Heavens that it has pleased everyone, and am only vexed that I could not be present. I thank you a thousand times for your good report of yourself, which amused me exceedingly. Beer sends his regards; he has at last got your letter from Gottfried, from whom I also received a letter for you, with the enclosed play bill. The arrangements for my concert swallow up all my time. To-day, Victorine set off for Graz, and sent her best regards to all. On the 18th, there was a concert here for the benefit of the poor, where Bärmann fired off the concerto in E flat, and Moscheles played a heavy concerto of Hummel. On the same day, I got thirteen letters at once from Berlin, which had all been delayed. On the 19th, I at last heard 'Salem.'* Admirable ideas, but coldly carried out, and devoid of genius. The 20th, the 'Zauberflöte,' An der Wien. Forti as Sarastro, insignificant. Wild, very good. The 21st, Kanne called on me, and spoke of his operas.† My 'Abu Hassan' is to be given at the 'Wieden' a few

* An oratorio of Ignaz Freiherr von Mosel.

† Friedrich August Kanne, first a theologian, next a doctor, and then a musician, had already made himself favourably known by many instrumental works, and composed twelve operas and vaudevilles on texts written by himself. In June 1808, the Weimar 'Journal des Luxus und der Moden' mentions that Kanne's opera 'Orpheus' had been given eight times in the Kärnthnerthor Theatre, with full houses and much applause. But as these works had no very lasting or brilliant success, Kanne preferred coming forward as a critic. He was, as Schindler says in his 'Biography of Beethoven,' vol. ii. p. 165, a man of universal cultivation, but scepticism personified. He had many a dispute about art with Beethoven (whose intimate associate he was), especially about the signification of the different keys.

weeks hence. Palffy takes a particular charge of me, and has several times enquired whether I had a long engagement at Prague. My opera acquisitions still proceed very slowly. I have again been interrupted. My concert is fixed for the 25th; so hold your thumb for good luck. Forward no more letters to me after the 25th, as I leave this on May 3rd or 4th. I could thrash myself soundly when I think that I shall no longer find you in Prague. How shall I ever be able to bear it? Let me know where to address my next letter. Now farewell, beloved brother. May God grant you health and happiness, and soon restore you to

Your ever attached brother,

WEBER.

Gyrowetz wrote only one aria in the 'Vestalin.' [?]

25.

To Ignaz von Mosel.

Prague, June 3, 1813.

My highly esteemed Friend,

To avoid all appearance even of ingratitude, I employ the pen of another, rather than wait longer to tell you how heartily I rejoiced in your truly friendly remembrance. Herr Meyerbeer must have better tidings of my health than I have myself, for, alas! I am not yet able to undertake the smallest business, as both reading and writing are strictly prohibited. You may imagine how disagreeable this is to a man whose habits are usually so active. How gladly would I have been present at the last performance of 'Salem,' with which you were yourself so well satisfied; meanwhile I hope in some degree to compensate for this, by studying your opera, and enjoying its individual beauties. It is only the tribute due to distinguished genius that prompts the efforts of Herr v. Collin and Frau v. Pichler in your behalf. Any one acquainted with the difficulty of procuring a good opera text may well wish you joy of yours. Your exceedingly kind expressions about 'Abu Hassan' caused me the most extreme pride and pleasure; the applause and enthusiasm of the public at large are no doubt our chief aim, but we are more truly invigorated and rewarded by the genuine approbation of those whose genius we prize, and who can thoroughly understand and appreciate us. Poor Hummel has again been treated *à la Wien*; you really ought not to let this pass unreproved. I beg you will assure Count Moritz Dietrichstein of my sincere esteem, and also thank him for the interest he showed in my work. Our friend Liebich plays to-day for the first time in the 'Essighändler.' Iffland is expected every hour. Music here is still in a dead sleep. At this moment I feel a positive repugnance to it, which probably arises from being constantly occupied with it in the feverish dreams of my delirium.

Pray, once more, my dear friend, receive my heartfelt

thanks for your speedy and minute information, which I doubly value, coming from a man of business, and overwhelmed with work. My best regards to your amiable wife, and to all who care to hear of me, and in conclusion, I beg you will receive the assurance of the distinguished consideration and esteem [from this sentence, written by Weber's own hand] with which I have the honour to be,

Your sincere friend and admirer,

C. M. v. WEBER.

26.

To Gänsbacher.

Prague, July 28, 1813.

Dear old Hans,

I duly received your two letters of May the 8th and 17th, and gave the enclosures to Jung, who promised me to answer you. I cannot manage to see much of him just now, although I call on him every three or four days, for he is so much occupied. I regret extremely that the letter I sent you by Poissl is lost, as there were all sorts of things in it. I lately got two letters from Vogler, in which he asks me to fix the sum for his 'Samori,' &c. and to send it off at once to Vienna. You know this cannot be so quickly done, and how can I fix the sum for it? These are odious commissions; I have written to him to-day. He also insisted on my publishing in the Prague newspapers what you sent to me about his organ concert. I am heartily glad that he has come to a friendly settlement in Munich, and doubt, quite as much as you do, any great sum being given in advance It does distress me to see these blemishes in so great a genius. He is constantly complaining of Beer, who is indeed a careless dog, and respects no obligations.

The members of my orchestra are gradually submitting to the iron sceptre, and knocking under to me.* We shall no doubt lose the two Herr Krals, which will not make me tear my hair. Probably, nothing can be done about your friend Hasslauer, for there are very tolerable violinists here; so if he is not something very remarkable, he must not be allowed to come. You can have no idea of all my business, and all my worries, and I miss you sadly many a time when I would fain pour out my heart to you, for I have not a single soul near me whom I can trust. I own it is rather a godless wish, but I declare I almost pray for a speedy outbreak of war, because then I should get you back here. *D minor* left this on the 15th, which I really regret,

* He had already written from Prague on the 23rd June to his friend, who was still in Salzburg, complaining loudly of his rebellious orchestra, with whom he had been carrying on a regular paper war. 'You may well believe that they reap no great harvest by this; indeed, they are all now quite exhausted, and ready to do whatever I please.' On the 4th of July also he says, 'I have much annoyance from my orchestra,' and on this account Weber had applied to his friend to send him some clever musicians.

for she has a true sense of art. I wish to write to you a great deal on that subject, but I reserve it till we meet; besides, how can one say much about women? It is always the old theme, with trifling variations, and you know what I think of the original melody.

I rejoice to hear that you are working, no matter at what, only always be doing something. The sonata *à quatre pieds* we will slash away at together; what a clever fellow you are with your reminiscences and interweavings.

I need not attempt to think of work at present. In a few days Passi will finish the opera, and then I will seize every minute to work at it, for I feel the most eager wish to do so. My rehearsals too will soon begin. You probably know that Madme. Grünbaum has created quite a furore in Vienna. She returns here on August 9th. Meyerbeer wrote to me that she disliked me very much; how unwise to allow a thing of the sort to be observed; if I were not such a meek animal, I could pay her off for this. Yesterday was the wedding-day of our former landlady, Madme. Hammer, with Count Czernin's stud groom—rather he than I! I am learning Bohemian with a vengeance, and by the time you come, I shall have forgotten all my German.

I took possession of my new quarters on the 8th, and I think you will be much pleased with my pretty little room, which is really most comfortable. I should have liked much to have gone up the Untersberg with you which is an old friend of mine, like all the hills round Salzburg. My canzonets will be ready in a few days, and then I begin my six new songs. Haas will probably publish the pianoforte arrangements of 'Abu Hassan.' Now I have scribbled long enough, and must conclude. Best regards to all my friends. To-day I dine with the Kleinwächters in their garden, where you will certainly be remembered. The Liebichs move today to the Redoutenhaus. I have no more news except that you will find a number of pretty girls in this ballet, and that the poet Tieck is here, whom I have to thank for many a pleasant and instructive hour. I sang for him the song with his words, you know which—that bewitching one—and it pleased him exceedingly; perhaps he may write an opera for me.

My respectful compliments to your estimable *cara*, and pray write soon to your most faithful brother. *Vale et me amas.*

Yours till death,

WEBER.

27.

To Gänsbacher.

Prague, Sept. 7, 1813.

Dear Hans,

I write you these few lines in great haste (your esteemed countess having permitted me to enclose them in her letter), to express my joy at your safe arrival, and to thank you for your letter. You write little of yourself, and I do not as yet clearly understand the nature of your appointment and position; so set me at rest on these points as soon as you can. I get on pretty well. 'Cortez' [Spontini's] was given yesterday for the first time, and went off admirably, and pleased as much as anything can please these cold beings. The orchestra and chorus did all that was possible, and I was very well satisfied. The overture was highly applauded, and at the end of the first act, the same honours were bestowed on myself. How I did miss you yesterday, for then I should have had at least one soul to feel sincere sympathy with me, and to appreciate and understand what was accomplished. Many things went really quite inimitably. On the 14th, I gave a concert for the benefit of the poor invalided soldiers, with whom our city is filled. I hoped thus to give the nobility an opportunity of showing their liberality and benevolence. Write to me as soon as possible. I read over your letter ten times at least; every moment I miss you. It is long since I have felt so entirely alone as I do now. But as God wills! I have strength to endure, and shall plunge into a vortex of work to deaden my feelings. My health is very tolerable, but I am still rather weak. Farewell, dearest brother; may a guardian angel hover near you, and guard your precious life and health!

Your ever faithful and attached brother,

WEBER.

28.

To Mademoiselle Bach,
Actress and Singer in Augsburg.

Prague, Jan. 29, 1814.

Respected young Lady,

I received with much pleasure your esteemed letter of the 19th, and hasten to reply to it.

The directors of the Royal Bohemian States Theatre, at Prague, hereby offer you an engagement for the first vocal and character parts, &c. on annual contract, with the reservation that, if your *début* be attended with entire success, the contract is to be valid for three years; otherwise for one year only, and six months' notice.

They agree to give you an annual salary of 2,000 gulden, payable in monthly instalments, and also guarantee your benefit at 1,000 gulden. The latter invariably exceeds this sum, and the 3,000 florins amount to more than you demanded, and in our present favourable circumstances we may daily hope for improvement in our rate of exchange.

The contract itself, according to our usual custom, will be signed by two members of the States, and therefore prepared here. Till then you may consider this letter as a legal substitute for a contract, and equally valid in our eyes.

Not to delay your departure by superfluous correspondence, the directors transmit you the enclosed bill of exchange, being the 12 carolins you desired for your travelling expenses, and an advance of 12 carolins. Your entire wardrobe, except the usual French dresses, to be furnished by the directors.

The complimentary expressions you do me the honour to apply to me, induce me to hope that you will accede to our proposals; and in return I am fully convinced that not only will you never regret your decision, but that you will no doubt gladly co-operate with an artistic establishment, of which all the members strive in peace and harmony to attain one grand aim, and who, in Herr Liebich, possess a director whose well-known rectitude and cordiality towards his coadjutors, as well as his impartial and unselfish conduct, certainly constitute him the friend and father of the members of his company.

In the hope of a speedy answer, I have the honour to be,

Mademoiselle, your obedient servant,

C. M. von Weber.

29.

To Gänsbacher.

Prague, March 5, 1814.

Most beloved and dear old Hans,

Scold, rage, abuse me, call me a dog, what you will, only spare me one thing: do not think that I could ever for a moment cease to be devoted to you with the heartfelt love of old, for that can only end with my life. The sole cause of my long silence was simply that I had no time to write to you satisfactorily, and I did not wish to put you off with a few lines, and so I delayed writing from day to day. You know the kind of thing. I have followed you in all your undertakings with the greatest sympathy, and sincerely rejoice to hear of your more substantial appointment.* How can you think that I disapprove of your course? Did I not myself urge you to it, though with a heavy heart? I am so entirely alone, and always in a very melancholy mood; so my constant occupation is a real piece of good fortune for me. I have written to Gottfried, and got letters from him in return; he too could not understand my silence. I certainly have become a very dull fellow, so depressed and so isolated. I cannot work as I ought. You will receive with this some old letters that I did not think it right to withhold. I would, moreover, have written to you long since, if F. had not insisted on enclosing my letters in hers. I only got your address three days ago, and at the same time a catalogue of your works, to send to Botzen, which shall be done, as they are written out.

I must now tell you what I have been doing here. I have given the following operas:—1. 'Cortez;' 2.

* Gänsbacher was Oberlieutenant in the Fenner Tyrolese Jägercorps of the Austrian army in Trient.

'Die vornehme Wirthin;' 3. 'Joseph;' 4. 'Vestalin;' 5. 'Wasserträger;' 6. 'Uthal;' 7. 'Faniska;' 8. 'Lotterieloos;' 9. 'Carlo Fioras;' 10. 'Aschenbrödel;' 11. 'Johann von Paris;' 12. 'Don Juan;' 13. 'Die Dorfsängerin;' 14. 'Adolf and Klara;' 15. 'Das Hausgesinde;' 16. 'Die Verwandlungen;' 17. 'Sargines;' 18. 'Titus.' On December 25th, I also gave in the theatre here, for the benefit of the Widows' Society, Meyerbeer's oratorio 'God and Nature.' We rehearsed it like the deuce, and it went off well. My poor worthy tenor Mohrhardt died of nervous fever; so I had your 'Requiem' performed for him on February 25th, at nine o'clock, at St. Galli. It was well executed, and I was with you in spirit; it is an admirable work, dear brother, and I should like to have embraced you for it. On February 28th, we had the 'Creation' for the benefit of poor pensioners. It went famously; indeed, your heart would beat with joy if you could hear my orchestra now. They have such energy, fire, and delicacy, I am very much pleased with them, and in fact this is my sole pleasure. In all other respects I lead the life of a dog; straight home from the theatre, and not a living soul to take any interest in me, or with whom I can talk of art. 'Silvana' was given in Weimar with great applause on February 16th and 19th, in honour of the Grand Duchess's birthday. Now you know all I have to tell you; so I proceed to answer your letter.

We have done with Dölle, he has too long made fools of us, so now we have given him up altogether. Jung has a great deal to do. His wife had a little girl lately, who died three days afterwards, and you may imagine his grief. Everything goes on in the old way at Kleinwächters' and the Liebichs'. I gave 'Don Juan' for my benefit, and realised 1,200 florins, which were sent off instantly to Stuttgart. I hope to get rid of this burden in a year or so, and then to work for myself.

I yesterday received your letter of February 19th, and the chorus. I dine to-day at Firmians', and I will then mention what I think advisable about it. The overture of mine that you heard in Botzen, is no doubt the one in E flat major, dedicated to the then King of Westphalia. I had the Weber 'Te Deum' performed in the Wallenstein Garden in summer. I will transcribe your Kreuzfahrer overture, and send it to Mannheim by the first opportunity. The thought of Jörgl in Paris really delights me. May Providence protect you, and preserve you to me and to art. The chorus is very fine, and I intend to give it soon, if only for my own satisfaction.

D minor is here, and much annoyed about some inheritance; I see her about once a fortnight, as I have no time to go more frequently, so now you will be the order of the day with her; I will give her your address, and she will certainly write to you. You live amid the tumult of war, to which you sacrifice the Muses; I worry myself all day in their service and yet do nothing. I have begun a new sonata in A flat major. Your songs, especially the one in F minor, are truly refreshing, and I know them all by heart. All goes on as usual in the Clam family; I often dine there, when Pepi always inquires eagerly after you. The Schlicks wished me to take your lesson, but I declined at once. I am to give a concert on April 4th, when I intend to introduce nothing but Bohemian composers, and to give something of Tomascheck, Wittasch, and Weber, and intersperse some minor pieces by Vogler and Gluck. Only fancy! Polawsky is to marry Mdlle. Schechtizky. When you return you will find a couple of pretty girls added to our theatre, Mdlle. Brand * and Mdlle. Bach. O brother! I cannot realise all my delight in once more being able to have a right good talk with you, but I must conclude, as it is time for rehearsal. I press you warmly to my heart in thought, and stretch out a brother's hand to you from afar, until fate once more reunites you with your ever loving and unchangeable brother,

WEBER.

I am now rehearsing 'Samori.' What are you doing? Love from all friends.

* Caroline Brand, subsequently Weber's wife.

30.

To Gänsbacher.

Prague, May 13, 1814.

My dear Brother,

It is really not right that you should so totally forget us here, and keep us in such painful uncertainty about your fate. Ever since March 5th, when I sent you a letter to Trient, I have vainly hoped for news from you. So long as the Firmians were here, I at least heard something, but since then, nothing whatever. I despatch these few lines at random into the world, as a most grievous occurrence compels me to do so. The organ-builder, Reiner from Darmstadt, announced to me yesterday, that on the 6th, at half-past 4 o'clock in the morning, our beloved master, Vogler, was suddenly snatched from us by death. I need not attempt to describe my sorrow. Peace be to his ashes. He will ever live in our hearts! I only hope his works may not be scattered, and that he has made one of us heir to them. At all events I shall write at once to Reiner and beg to have his bust. I mean the one to which we added a pedestal. I would gladly write about other things, but my heart is too full. My own health is still very delicate. Six weeks ago I had an attack of ague, so I could not be present at my concert on April 4, and it turned out very badly. I have therefore resolved to take advantage of the leave of absence in my contract, and make an expedition to Gotha, Leipzig, Liebwerda, and Berlin. I promise myself much amusement from this, and hope it may tend to restore my strength and inclination for work. My life here is too miserable, too melancholy, so entirely alone, without one sympathetic soul.

The Jungs beg to be remembered to you; they are well, but abuse you roundly for your silence. On April 30th, being the eve of Jung's nameday, we played your serenade in C, which I heard for the first time, and much admired. You were standing so life-like before my soul, that I was soothed by thus recalling you, and felt how happy I should be were you only here. Set me at rest by a few lines as to your present condition, and your future plans and life. If nothing occurs to detain me, I shall leave this on June 1st, and stay away till the end of August. I beg you will therefore address your answer to the care of Ballabene [banker in Prague] who will forward the letters to me. All our acquaintances are well, and greet you. I see *D minor* very seldom. *C minor* asks after you more frequently than any one, and whenever I dine there, which is very often, you are the subject of conversation. Wittassek has left his count, and is now conductor of the Cathedral Choir; Breda has quitted us. Now I have no more to say, except the old story, which is that I love you truly, and am ever your most attached brother,

WEBER.

31.

To Gänsbacher.

Bad Liebwerda, near Reichenberg,
July 15, 1814.

Beloved Brother,

At length I can manage to answer your welcome letters of May 1st and 31st, which I received in Prague on June 18th; I could not write sooner, owing to my unsettled state and my affairs. Day after day I was on the point of leaving, when something always intervened; at last, after having witnessed the illuminations and the celebration of peace, I started on my journey on the 8th at midnight for this place, where I arrived on the 10th, and where I intend to nurse my health and to enjoy the most entire rest, and once more to work for myself

Madame Liebich and Allram came with me here, and are the only society I have, or wish to have: all the time that I can spare from baths, drinking the waters, and walking, I mean to spend in my quiet little room, at my writing table. Perhaps you will scarcely believe me when I say that I had a heavy heart when I quitted Prague, but the enigma will be quickly solved, when I tell you that I left there a beloved being, who, though not one of the highest class, might make me very joyful and happy, for it really seems to me that she truly loves me. You need not, however, fear that I am on this account blind, and that my previous experiences have not left me timid and distrustful; but I intend to find out what stuff she is made of, and whether the substance will stand wear and tear, and my three months' absence will furnish a good opportunity to put this to the test. But I go on talking at random, and you don't even know to whom I allude. It is Mdlle. Caroline Brand, whom I fervently love, and daily do I pray to God that He will vouchsafe to make her a little better than the rest of her sex.

The food this is for Krähwinkel you can easily imagine. They have married me already at least 50,000 times, but there was no truth in any of these reports. You know my views and principles on this point. It is certainly a hard lot to sacrifice the happiness of the man for the sake of the artist, but—it must be so, for no man can be more than one thing thoroughly, and I hate half measures.

I shall stay here three weeks, and go to Berlin in August, and in September make a tour by Leipzig, Weimar, Gotha, and so home. Address your answer to the care of the banker, Herr Beer. But enough of myself, so to reply to your letter.

I see with pleasure that you begin to live like a man, and no longer cling to a cherished but futile chimera, which can only embitter your existence, and deaden your interest in life, in art, and in your friends. Courage! dear brother, and when you are practising the '*Divertimento à quatre Mains*,' think of me—*à propos*, I suppose you received your works long since. *D minor* gave me back my songs, otherwise I could not have sent them to you; but what would she not do for your sake? I have not forgotten to forward you any note, but conscientiously sent them all. So why do you always tease me about her? She must have written you some curious stuff. She went to the country on June 28th. Angst stands only so so with *F major*; with No: very badly. It was truly diverting to see the forced friendship and cordiality between *D minor* and *F major*. I am on the best possible terms with the latter, so much so, indeed, that she has lent me her pianoforte.

Your determination to remain with your corps fills me with joy. It would be very wrong were you to give up a career so well begun, merely to sink back into an unsettled, vague, and desultory existence. In more peaceful times you will have ample leisure to do homage to art, and, indeed, you declare that you can work now, so stay where you are in God's name; and much as my heart bleeds at the thought of your being wholly lost to me, still your welfare and your honour are dearer than all else to me. I rejoice doubly, too, on account of the assertions in Prague, that you would not have sufficient strength of mind to leave *F major*, and that only the flickering of a momentary flame could detain you from her even for a short time. Your resolution has enabled me to cast the reverse in their teeth. And now I wish you all prosperity and every blessing, and a strong will to persevere; and for myself, the hope to have you with me if possible every year during the one month of your leave, when you must stay with me, and we can dream that the old Darmstadt days have come back again.

I can easily believe that you worked away zealously at the organ in remembrance of our dear old Vogler, and only wish I could have heard you. The remuneration too was not so bad, and I congratulate you on living with men who feel love and enthusiasm for the cause.

I hear nothing whatever of Meyerbeer, and have had no answer to three letters of mine, asking him for his opera. He sent me messages by Clement, who was in Vienna during his holidays. He is writing a new opera, and intends to have it performed there. Some little time ago I received a letter from Gottfried, which caused me so much sorrow that I have not yet been able to make up my mind to answer him. He was very bitter, and said I did nothing for him, and had not even noticed the performance of his 'Te Deum,' &c. I have long owed a report to the 'Musikalische Zeitung,' so now I will prepare it at once. You cannot think what pain a thing of this sort causes me. He certainly did much for us, but we only wanted the opportunity to do the same for him. That a review of his songs has, owing to some negligence, been long omitted, is true enough, but how can I help that? At the close of the letter he once more becomes cordial, and says that if we could only talk it over together, then all would again come right. I think so too, but I do not see the most distant hope of such a thing.

Now farewell, my dear and faithful Hans. Hold fast to your resolution, and continue your regard for your unchanging, affectionate, and faithful friend,

BROTHER WEBER.

Mdlle. Liebich's best regards. Count Clam comes the end of this month. *Addio senza addio.*

32.

To Gänsbacher.

Prague, September 30, 1814.

Dearest Brother,

Do not be angry with me for not having sooner replied to your welcome letter of August 13th, which I received on the 30th at Berlin, and am now answering just one month later, from my head-quarters, Prague. It really was impossible for me to get away sooner, which you will yourself see from the details of my proceedings. After being well soaked with water, outwardly and inwardly, at Liebwerda, I left it on July 31st for Berlin, where I arrived safely on August 2nd, and at once plunged into such a vortex of society and work that I really often scarcely knew whether my head was still on my shoulders. But such lively enthusiasm for art, and so much interest in my compositions, did me good, and revived my pleasure in working; it had also the most beneficial effect on my health, as I entirely got rid of my headaches, and I felt myself thoroughly reinvigorated. There seemed to be a considerable inclination to keep me in Berlin as Capellmeister, but as I never do seek anything, but prefer waiting till an offer is made me, the affair did not progress quickly. I attended all the festivities, and gave a concert on the 26th, which proved most successful in every respect; my share amounting to about 100 ducats. 'Silvana' was given on September 5th, with an overflowing house, and unanimous applause. An hour after the performance was over I started for Leipzig, which I reached on the 7th, but unluckily could do nothing there, as all the rooms were occupied as hospitals for the wounded, &c. I went off, therefore, leisurely to Weimar, and got there just in time to witness the departure of the Grand Duchess, so I once more took up my pilgrim's staff, and arrived in Gotha on the 11th, where I found the Duke at his Château Tonna, and passed some delightful days enjoying his intellectual society.

On the 18th we drove back to Gotha, where I played the same evening in a court concert, and also on the 20th, when I proceeded to Altenburg, where I gave a concert on the 23rd, and at last arrived safely at Prague on the 25th. I would not, in fact, have returned so soon, as my leave extends to October 8th, if Liebich had not moved heaven and earth to get me back on account of the Michaelmas Term, which is of importance in concluding contracts. So out of regard for him and the rest, I sacrificed a concert I was to have given in Leipzig on October 4th, and which would assuredly have been most successful. I doubt very much whether he will ever acknowledge this, but, on the other hand, I have the conviction of having done my duty in its most ample sense. Meanwhile things had been going on very badly here, for though Clement is an admirable violinist, he is a very poor director, and all strongly felt my absence. But this will do no harm eventually, for they had begun to look upon great order and energy as quite the usual routine, and to think that all must now go on well of itself. I need not, however, tell you that I have no chance of peace or comfort at present, but find more than enough to do and to arrange. In every other respect things here are just as they were. All the world either in Vienna or in the country. Countess Pepi came yesterday, and I shall see her either to-day or to-morrow. I know nothing of *D minor.* Angst is well and as usual.

I now refer to your letter. Poor fellow! so your present life no longer contents you? That I can well believe, but tell me any one thing that has not as many drawbacks. Is not an artist the most oppressed and persecuted of human beings? What do you mean to do?—earn your livelihood by your compositions, or become an artistic beast of burden, and daily turn the mill-wheel of children's training, and give lessons? In the former case, what with the bad payment of publishers, and your not choosing to write for them by the ell at random, you would fare badly enough; and in the latter, within a year you would be seized with the same disgust you now feel, and be more dissatisfied than ever. Or do you wish to be replaced in your previous circumstances, and allow yourself to be fed, tormented, and deadened to all active exertion and independence? Reflect well on what you are about to do, dear brother. In your present position you have at your command both time and a sphere for work as a composer, and you are placed in an honourable position in worldly relations. You are not made to dream away your time in a quiet little room in Botzen! you may do so for a few weeks, or even months, but then the spirit of this world will break loose again with threefold vigour, and drive you out into the whirlpool at haphazard. So make your decision deliberately, and weigh it well. Whatever you turn to or engage in, you well know that your faithful brother's hand and heart are equally at your service, and that to his latest breath he will stand by you, and beside you.

Your present residence makes me uneasy about your

health, so I hope you will soon set my mind at rest on the subject. I cannot at all understand why you have not yet got your music, as I sent it off by the post carriage, and took a receipt for it; write to me at once, that I may enquire about it if necessary. I forwarded it to your old address at Trient.

When are we likely to see each other once more? How much have I to say to you that cannot well be confided to paper; besides, it would be too diffuse. I often talked of you in Berlin with Beer's parents; he is still in Vienna, but I hear nothing from him or Gottfried. Bärmann is very flourishing in Munich, and his family increases yearly. Now, dear brother, farewell; I embrace you warmly, and would only be too happy to do so in reality, and to tell you myself how unchangeably you are beloved by your faithful old brother,

WEBER.

33.

To Gänsbacher.

Prague, December 1, 1814.

Beloved Brother,

I send these lines at random into the wide world, for it is indeed distressing to hear nothing of you, and not to know how or where you are. I have been told at tenth hand that you are still at Mantua, so this letter must journey thither. You probably never received the one I wrote you on October 9th, and sent to you *poste restante* to Botzen? So pray write to the postmaster to forward it.

I should like to write you a great deal of news from here, if there were any. All the world are by degrees returning from the country, and the old round is beginning again. I scarcely go anywhere except to our Kleinwächter, and to the Clams. Christel was very ill with inflammation of the throat, and Countess Caroline narrowly escaped being burnt to death, her dress having caught fire. She thought herself lost, and in order to die more quickly she was on the point of throwing herself into the fire, when the steward saved her. The Liebichs have bought a garden at the Ziskaberge; they are well, and send you their regards. That old Don Juan, Bassi, is here just now, and boards with the Liebichs. He acts the Capellmeister in the 'Corsar aus Liebe' capitally. My orchestra daily improves, and I have made a splendid acquisition in a good hautboy player, who plays with soul and skill. On the 21st I gave Beethoven's 'Fidelio,' which went to perfection; what grand things there are in that music, but—they are not understood—it is enough to drive one distracted! 'Kasperl,' that is the thing for the people here! Andreas Romberg was here, and gave a concert without much applause, but good receipts. The tickets five florins each, so he got 1,100 florins.

Bärmann and Madame Harlas come here on February 9th, so you may imagine my delight. All goes on as usual at Jung's. Maldini has married Lotte Vignet, and is very ill; so now you know all that is worth knowing.

I am quite well, and have a great deal of work, and strive to keep my mind in peace, which is, however, impossible when one loves, and the demon of doubt extends its fangs in all directions. Oh that I only had you here, to confide everything in the heart of a friend. Write to me soon, and tell me minutely how you are, and what you are doing, and thus show me that you have not wholly forgotten your truly loving brother,

WEBER.

P.S.—The violoncello is here and much admired.

34.

To Gänsbacher.

Munich, Aug. 11, 1815.

Dear Brother of my heart,

I feel that I am much to blame towards you, and can only appeal to your brotherly love to forgive me for having so long kept silence. But you know that there are times in life when a dark veil seems to overspread everything, and the soul becomes so painfully oppressed that it is impossible to give utterance to your feelings. Ah! if you only could have been near me how would my heart have been soothed! I have become very gloomy and reserved. The first and only being I ever loved has torn herself from me. She has not the courage to love me irrespective of all else, and I have not the courage to make her and myself miserable, after the first few weeks, by marriage without a secure income. I am therefore once more alone, my heart full of love, and shall now cast myself unreservedly into the arms of art, for which I mean exclusively to live, and thus, as a man, renounce all the happiness of life. Here you have a brief picture of my condition. I left Prague in deep sorrow on June 7th, and went to solitary Hradeck, where I was received with cordial and considerate friendliness. I came here on the 18th, and am staying with my good Bärmann. I gave a concert on August 2nd, with the most brilliant success, and one on the 8th in Augsburg, with the same result. On the 10th I received a ring of brilliants from the Viceroy, with his cypher, and I am now settled quietly here till the end of my leave, September 7th, and am working at a grand cantata, 'The Celebration of the Battle of La Belle Alliance.' I shall then pass a melancholy year in Prague, and once more plunge into the great vortex of the world. My reasons for this decision are, first, that one seems buried, as it were, in Prague; secondly, because I have a public for whom I cannot write; thirdly, because I have so many official duties, that it is impossible for me as a composer to accomplish anything; and fourthly, because I can save nothing, and everywhere I can earn a subsistence.

Now, dear brother, you know all, but you alone. To refer to your letters. No 2, from Padua, of February 24th, I received March 10th. You say something in it of Angst's influence in detaining the Firmians in Vienna, but the grounds for this I have in vain tried to discover, and the report seems to me to be without foundation. Your letter No 1 from Padua, of December 27th, 1814, I received on January 10th, 1815. So I have made a confusion between the two letters. What you said of my love affair was the exact counterpart of my own feelings; since then the knot has been loosed, though in another way. Your account of your musical and military relations amused me much, and I heartily thank you for telling me of them. Valoti * was certainly Vogler's teacher, and to him he is indebted for his system.

I have been urging Haas about a settlement of the account, but they are most tiresome people; on my return I will see what can be done. When the Firmians passed through Prague, your sister was with me, and we decided that if Haas did not pay in time to settle the house-steward's claims, you are then to become my debtor, when I will take care to make my profit out of you.

No. 3, from Innsbruck, July 24th, just come; thanks for the surprise. After the first part of my concert, on

* Padre Valoti, in Bologna.

August 2nd, Bärmann came to tell me that an officer in the Harlas box had brought me letters from you; I rushed down, and, behold! it was Colonel Call who had arrived just in time for my concert. You may conceive my delight; next day he called, and brought your welcome letter.

I thank God for having guarded you through every danger so safely and so happily. It is really terrible to be so near, and yet not be able to speak to each other. Call is inexhaustible in your praise; when will Fate once more unite us?

I cannot help laughing at your expressions of jealousy; you may be quite at ease on that point; besides, my visit to *F. major* is at an end, for I do not take Leipzig on my way home, as I had projected, but return direct from here. If my songs arrive, I will send them to you. Write to me again immediately, and say how long you remain in Innsbruck.

Weber is now Tribunalsrath in Mayence; it is long since I have written to him, for my state of depression severs me from everyone. Meyerbeer, when I last heard of him, was in Paris; where he is now to be found, I don't know, but no doubt I can soon find out, and write to you. Farewell, old Hans; I enclose a few lines from Bärmann. Kindest wishes from Madame Harlas, &c.

Ever and ever, your most faithful brother, till death,

WEBER.

35.

To Gänsbacher.

Prague, Jan. 20, 1816.

Dear Friend and Brother,

My first leisure evening belongs to you, to whom I have so long owed tidings of myself, and who have the best right to be very angry, if you did not know that a person may think of a friend with the most devoted attachment, and yet be unable to seize a moment to assure him of this. I am the same as ever, and the pressure of circumstances alone prevented my sooner writing to you, of which you will be best able to judge when I give you every detail of my life since you were here.

On October 6th, you left me, and terrible was the void in my life; you know my outward mood, and how vigorously you upheld me, but scarcely were you gone than I felt disgust at my work; at every bar I wanted to ask your opinion, and I missed you in all things. After a long lapse of time, I received on the 7th a very agreeable letter from Meyerbeer, in which he wrote a great deal about his life and occupations in Paris; no doubt he has done the same to you. The rehearsals of his opera 'Alimelek' were still going on, and many official duties accumulating. He wished me to compose three songs with orchestra for a piece of Gubiz, to perform them here, and send them to Berlin. On the

13th, a novel idea occurred to me to interest the public; so I wrote the accompanying articles, and have continued to do the same with regard to each new opera. On the 22nd, 'Alimelek' was given for the first time with partial success, but repeated on the 24th, and received with enthusiasm, and still more liked at each subsequent performance. You can easily imagine how heartily I rejoiced to see this good fellow's reputation thus vindicated in spite of the Viennese; and all the writing that fell to my share in order to report it to Wohlbrück and his parents. I wrote also an analysis of it in the 'Musikalische Zeitung,' so you see that I have not been idle. Minette came on the 27th, and I went to see her on the 28th. I found her the same kind sensible person as ever, and full of true sympathy. I have dined with her since then, every Monday, otherwise we seldom meet, as my labours seem every day to accumulate. On November 8th, I got your letter of October 27th, which caused me the deepest sorrow, as, from my own experience, I can only too well put myself in your place. I would gladly have expressed to you all my heartfelt sympathy, but, strange to say, I could not find the frame of mind to do so. I frequently seated myself at my desk with the intention of writing to you, and yet I always stared thoughtfully at the paper, till time passed, and some other occupation called me away. Your letter made a great impression on all your friends, but very different in degree. I think M. felt it most of all, then perhaps B., and last of all Angst. I derived some consolation from the happy result of your affairs here, the satisfaction of your superiors, and the occupation and distraction which I saw would accrue from all this. Work and time! What wounds do not these heal? About that period I was very unwell, and dreaded an illness, but, thank God! it passed away. On the 12th, I composed a ballad for a tragedy of Reinbeck, which made considerable effect, and pleased exceedingly. Herr Ehlers sang it beautifully. I have had a good many explanations with him since then in the presence of Liebich, and now the matter is at length set at rest, and we behave with politic civility, detesting each other all the time. He is a low fellow, and is now every day with Mdlle. Böhler: I wish him joy: I had a letter from Liebich on the 13th, in which he says that he had received a remonstrance from the director for nothing having been done during three years for the opera, upon which I wrote a reply that I do wish you could have seen. It brought verbal excuses without end, and 'that I was not the person alluded to,' &c. Is it not cruelly mortifying, in a place for which I have done everything, sacrificing time, brains, and health, to see things so perverted, and indeed to be reproached into the bargain? This put the seal on my resolution, in any event to leave Prague. The concert-givers are beginning to announce themselves, so it struck me that it would be advisable to give my own concert as soon as possible, on November 26th. I came therefore to the weighty conclusion to have my cantata performed on

December 22nd. There was not a minute to lose, for transcribing, rehearsing, &c. take up so much time. I worked away with the utmost vigour every night till two or three o'clock in the morning, with some of my old energy, and was consequently quite ready by December 18th. Considering my numerous official duties and rehearsals, it was really a giant feat, but all else, of course, gave way to this. Your letter of December 10th, which I got on the 16th, shared the same fate, as it arrived just at that time. It did cheer me so much, for in it you kindly yourself make excuses for me, when my cantata prevented my writing to you; only I did feel distressed that you could imagine I was annoyed with you, you stupid,—if so, I would write and abuse you, but not be silent.

How I envy you the pleasure of having had Bärmann and Made. Harlas with you. I knew that they had arrived safely in Venice, but not the result of their *début* there: I almost tremble for them. How did your old 'new cantata' please and turn out? Haas is a low fellow, and no remonstrances seem to be of any avail. Schlesinger at first declined your songs, owing to want of workmen, but in his last letter he promises to take them soon, and then to fix the sum he will give for them; I will urge him forward, and let you know the result. As for your braces, I speak about them often enough, and I believe they really are in progress. On the 22nd, 'Johann von Wieselburg' was given, a parody on 'Johann von Paris.' It was a complete failure, although Herr Ehlers showed himself off in it. Siebert gave a concert on the 30th, and his receipts were from 1,100, to 1,200 florins. Madame Czeka gave one on December 8th, and made as much; Sellner and Janusch also gave theirs on the 15th, and took the same sum. At length, on the 22nd, my concert was given, and turned out badly, considering all the novelties I produced; as I look upon 900 florins for me to be very shabby receipts. I gave Mozart's symphony in G minor, then Madame Grünbaum sang an aria beautifully, then I played a concerto, then came the cantata, which takes three quarters of an hour; it went splendidly, full of fire and life, and to enjoy it to the uttermost nothing was wanting but you. God be praised! I was not mistaken in any of the effects, and I think you would be pleased with the whole, for many happy ideas are introduced into it. At the concluding fugue, you were present with me throughout in my thoughts, and my spirit must certainly have hovered near yours on that evening; at last it seemed to lay hold on the cold audience, and they were forced to break loose, whether they would or not. I certainly have many enemies here, the devil alone can tell why. I only wish to do what is right, and stand in the way of no man, but still I am no sycophant, nor the obsequious servant of anyone. The miserable criticisms on the part of the nobility that I heard through M. are incredible, and all this kind of thing embitters my life. On the 26th, Weigl's opera 'Peter der Grosse' was given, which justly failed from its insipidity. I then fully intended writing to you, when Fränzl arrived to stay with me, on January 1st, and I was obliged to manage entirely for him, to take him everywhere, and to arrange his concert, which took place on the 12th, and on the 15th he left Prague. 'Joconde' was given for the first time on January 11th, for Grünbaum's benefit, and pleased. Judge therefore for yourself how busy I have been, and show some indulgence to your poor harassed brother; and now I must take breath after this long story.

It is really strange sometimes to see how everything seems to occur at the same time; for instance, the theatrical copyist Petrarsk is dying, so he cannot write; and things came to such a pass, that I was obliged to sacrifice a couple of nights to write out myself the parts of the wind instruments in the second act of Joconde, to prevent the performance of the opera being impeded.

As for my own mood, dear brother, it still is the most singular in the world, full of love for a being whom my reason daily tells me that to marry would make us both ultimately miserable. But I have attained so much self-control that I can work and think seriously of the preparation for my journey. Under the seal of the strictest secresy (for no one as yet knows the fact), I may tell you that I have had proposals from Berlin, and yet, can you believe it? they cause me more pain than pleasure. If I secure a permanent livelihood there, and am thus relieved of all difficulty in providing for a wife, and I do not then offer my hand to Lina, I could not but look upon myself as a bad-hearted fellow, although my conscience and my convictions would absolve me. It is an endless labyrinth, so I leave everything to time, and hope it will disentangle the affair better than I can. What I should like best would be a long distant journey, far away into the wide world, to escape, as it were, from myself. Pity and advise me if you can, but, I repeat, no one as yet knows of the affair.

The enclosed letter to P. has been lying here for a fortnight. I give three lessons a day at present to a pupil of the name of Freytag, to Countess Swerts, and to Frau v. Lämel, whom you may perhaps remember as Madlle. Seligmann in Mannheim. I am really very industrious, and that is something. They have a presentiment here that I wish to go away, but no one knows it for a fact, and I shall take care not to announce it before the close of Easter. I hope they will eventually feel my loss; at present they are accustomed to what is good, and think that it cannot be otherwise. Good night, dear brother; Lina [Brand] begs her kind regards: she has the highest opinion of you, and speaks with enthusiasm of your songs. I am going to bed, where I generally lie awake half the night, for the amount of night work I have done has fairly knocked me up. *Item*, write to me soon, and do not have recourse to reprisals. May God grant you health, and me your affection.

Ever and always, your faithful and loving brother,

WEBER.

N.B.—When you have read the newspapers, forward them to G. Weber in Mayence. I have no other copies,* so I referred him to you. Pray don't forget this.

36.

To Gänsbacher.

Prague, March 18, 1816.

Beloved Brother,

I thank you cordially for the warm and heartfelt sympathy expressed in your letter of February 16th, which I received yesterday in the theatre from Captain Rumpelin. I went with the letter to Convalina to hear all about you, and to have a long chat over a glass of wine, but I learned very little; the worst part of the matter is that he sets off to-day at noon, so I cannot fulfil even one of your wishes. I will see, however, what can be done about the 'Miserere,' but I have no concert music that I can send you.

I was just going to write to you, for it is so long

* These were, no doubt, articles on Meyerbeer's 'Alimelek', and the concerts, already alluded to, of different *virtuosi* in Prague.

since you have given any living soul the least token of your existence, that we feared you might be ill; you may therefore believe how doubly welcome is our certainty of the reverse. Your health will be drunk at dinner to-day, and I will likewise deliver your letter to Madlle. P. this forenoon; she has been enquiring about you for some time past, and was displeased at your not answering her letter. The worthy Madlle. M. has been obliged, for the sake of her children, to frequent all the balls and parties, to her great annoyance: a few days hence she returns to Hradeck, which delights her exceedingly; I must therefore take leave of her for a long time, as she will not come in here again, nor I go out there. 'Maria Stuart' has been given three times in Clam's private theatre, with the utmost pomp and splendour, for the benefit of the Brothers of Mercy, who realised 10,000 florins by it. P. was Maria Stuart, Countess Schlick, Elizabeth, and the whole cast was really very good. There was no lack of remarks of every kind, and it was said that these two ladies had undertaken their parts, in which there is so much that is attractive, chiefly to show off their fine dresses; for that was the principal thing!

We have got a new theatrical president in Prince Lobkowitz, who at once began by urging me strongly to remain here.

I must now speak of myself. Oh! dear brother, how needful is your presence to me at this moment, to support and to console me, assailed, as I am, by every kind of distress, but I must bear it all firmly like a man; I am beset on every side, but the most painful of all these trials proceed from Lina and Liebich; the latter probably now begins to see what he is about to lose, and is quite inconsolable, though at the same time he fails in proper attention to me on many points. For instance, on the 14th, I gave Beethoven's 'Fidelio' for my benefit, and had very poor receipts. Thirteen boxes empty, and 140 stalls the same. My benefit is guaranteed at 1,000 florins; the sum total was sent to him, being 538 florins, and yet he does not make up the difference. Yes, indeed, so it is! For some days past I have been so harassed, especially by Lina, that I feel quite ill and exhausted. She seems always to have clung to the secret hope that I would remain here, although I believed that she was as fully convinced as myself of the necessity for my departure. Now I discover, to my exceeding vexation, that her views of high art do not rise beyond the commonplace pitiful conception, that esteems art merely as the means of procuring soup, roast meat, and shirts. But it cannot be helped. I do really believe that the last half-year has cost me so much, that I shall almost give way under it, for such daily worry and annoyance is the hardest of all to bear; still I adhere firmly to my convictions. What you say on the subject is only too true, but even the very thought that it might possibly be otherwise, and a precious heart be broken, fills me with anguish, but I leave it all to time, and to Providence above.

Strangely enough, no answer to my letter has yet come from Berlin. I care not. I will go forth into the world free, leaning on my own strength.

How am I touched by the solicitude and affection, dear brother, with which you endeavour to make my works known; pray receive my heartfelt thanks; such pleasures form the bright moments of my life. Would that I could work for you more efficiently; Schlesinger, in his last letter, again enquires about your works, as he has already received several of them. I wrote to him on the subject at once, and hope at last to see the matter settled.

The bookseller Cramer here is publishing the pianoforte arrangements of my cantata. I enclose an article by me respecting the text of the cantata, and a newspaper; try, if you can, to circulate them.* I am certainly very unlucky, for, only imagine! I have not as yet been able to send off one single copy, for want of copyists; at length, eight days ago one was ready, when, lo and behold! the bookbinder spoiled it; it seems as if I were only to attain my object by the most difficult paths. You will probably again have the pleasure of seeing Bärmann and Mdme. Harlas in passing. Em-

* A review of the cantata 'Kampf und Sieg,' and 'Dramatic and Musical Notices of the Performance of Operas in the Prague Theatre.'

brace them both cordially in my name. In the course of time (who can say when?) I hope to embrace you, dear brother, also. I am at present rehearsing the 'Athalia' of Poissl [theatrical intendant in Munich].

I must conclude, beloved Hansel; do not let me wait too long for an answer, and continue your love for your poor brother, who so greatly needs comfort.

Your ever faithful,

WEBER.

N.B.—Jung has been suffering from his breathing, and confined to his room for a fortnight. The Kleinwächters are well. Liebich, Lina, and all send their remembrances.

37.

To Gänsbacher.

Prague, Aug. 4, 1816.

Dear Friend and Brother,

I am almost disposed to think that you must be dead, at least to everyone but those in Innsbruck. I have not heard a word of you since March 17th, and not a line in reply to the letters I sent you by Rumpel Mayer. Have you really so much to do that you can no longer spare a moment for your best friend, who is quite alone in dull Prague, where no man knows his condition better than you? Well! I know from experience that, even with the best inclinations, it is sometimes not easy to write. I proceed to give you a brief report of what I have been doing.

I began to send off my cantata in April, which has hitherto, however, brought very little; a medal from Prussia, and a gold box from Saxony and the Netherlands; so eleven crowned heads are still in arrear. Our Viceroy sent it to our gracious Emperor, with the most urgent recommendations, but as yet this has produced nothing. The performance of Beethoven's 'Schlacht bei Vittoria' has vividly recalled my cantata. I had a request from Bremen for the score, to be given in honour of the anniversary of the battle, June 18th. This induced me to propose its performance to the King of Prussia. He agreed, and I went to Berlin the beginning of June for the purpose of conducting it myself (you will see all particulars from the enclosed), and it was received with great enthusiasm. Count Brühl apologised to me for having allowed Romberg to be forced on him as Capellmeister, and the whole orchestra gave me the strongest proofs of attachment and esteem. I took the opportunity of speaking to Schlesinger about your four songs, quartetts, and fantasia, and he will give twelve Friederichsd'or for them, but not till December If you are satisfied with this, write to me, that I may send him the pieces in December, and you the money. I left Berlin on July 9th, with Meyerbeer's father, for Leipzig, where I received an offer to undertake the

German opera next year, with a salary of 1,500 dollars. I went on to Carlsbad, where I stayed three days, and met many acquaintances, and at last returned here on the 18th. Liebich is still making every effort to detain me, but, of course, utterly in vain. He has again been very ill, and Jung likewise, who had a seizure which threatened to end in apoplexy; during the last six months, poor Fanny's house has been quite a hospital; but they are all well again, and the whole family going to Carlsbad for three weeks.

I had an offer in Carlsbad to go to Dresden, as royal Capellmeister, and director of the German opera, now being built there. I accepted on certain conditions, but have not since received any written ratification, for I had arranged everything verbally with the intendant, Count Vizthun. So there are plenty of prospects for me! But this is all a secret as yet, known to no one; indeed, I don't place much dependence on it, knowing my star of old. There are many changes here. Herr Bayer's affair with Made. L—ch is at an end, and a miserable end too, for Herr Stöger, our new tenor, supplanted him, and both parties abuse each other shockingly. Made. Grünbaum was at Munich during her leave of absence, and created quite a *furore* there; as for him, he no longer sings, and declares himself that he is quite done up. I pity him from my heart. I gave Poissl's 'Athalia' previous to my visit to Berlin, and it is to be repeated with Herr Häser as our star. A fine work, but the Merry Andrew element is wanting for Prague.

Beer, the father, comes here from Carlsbad, in a few days, and the mother from Berlin, to see Meyerbeer's 'Alimelek;' then they all go together to Munich and Innsbruck, rejoicing at the thoughts of seeing you, and proceed to Italy, where Mdme. Beer intends to take sea-baths in Genoa, having made a *rendezvous* with their son there, who is at present in Naples. They are excellent worthy people, and really loaded me with kindness and attention in Berlin.

Our Herr Siebert has run away, which places me in some embarrassment, for he was engaged in all our operas, glad as I am to get rid of so odious a man. I leave Prague the end of September, you must not therefore let me wait so long as usual for an answer, otherwise your letter will not reach me. As for my health, it is now, thank God! excellent, and my mind also is much more calm and cheerful. Lina conducts herself very well, and shows the most sincere desire to improve. If Providence should bestow on me a permanent situation to ensure me a livelihood, and if Lina about a twelvemonth hence is as reasonable as now, she will then leave the theatre, and become my faithful wife. You shake your head; but a year is a long time, and she who abides that test must certainly be a good woman.

I know nothing whatever of the worthy Minette, except hearing from Vice-president Schüller, that she was in Marienbad with her daughters. I wrote to her some days ago, having shamefully neglected doing so since her departure. Frau von Kleinwächter is as round as a ball, and returned from the baths in perfect health. Your braces are here, and have been finished for a long time, waiting for an opportunity to Innsbruck. Shall I send them with the 'Miserere?' I, too, hear nothing of Bärmann! I owe Gottfried a letter, but I must conclude, being summoned to rehearsal. May God keep you well and happy! Do not be so lazy, and write to me how you are, how you are living and working, and always continue your affection for your ever loving and faithful brother,

WEBER.

38.

To Gänsbacher.

Prague, Sept. 12, 1816.

Beloved Brother of my heart,

Your welcome letters of August 12 and August 29 caused me the utmost joy. I only wish I could once more have a long chat with you; but you can imagine all the work I have to get through, as I propose leaving this early in October; so I have twice as much as usual to regulate; the devil, too, brings on my head just at this moment a number of strangers, who all rely on my obligingness and services, to which at any other time they should be so welcome. The chief object of my letter is your commission about the oboe that Kleinwächter wished me to get for him, as he is in Jublona, and cannot, therefore, give directions about it. I have got a very good instrument from our first oboist Sellmer, which will be forwarded to you by the next post carriage, and only costs 80 florins. It has C, C sharp, D sharp, then the thumb-key to play octaves legato, then G sharp, B flat, F twice, and the low B natural key. An ordinary one with only four keys, and new, would have been the same price, and you must have waited two or three months for it. If, however (which is not probable), it does not suit you, I have settled that you may return it, particularly as the instrument-maker Bauer here is prepared at any minute to give the same money for it; but I hope you will not give up so good a bargain. Pray address your answer to Ballabene, as I am not quite sure whether your letter will still find me here. I sympathise with you much on the unfavourable remarks in high quarters about your cantata, and heartily grieve for all your vexation; I wish I could have heard it. When my appointment in Dresden is actually made, which seems very probable, you must come to me for a couple of months, and, if not, I must go to you. My cantata gets on rather better than yours, for the Emperor presented me with a handsome box and diamond cypher; but highly as I feel honoured by such a *souvenir*, I wish that the other great men would bestow ready money on me, as I have had an outlay of 700 florins, which rather embarrasses me.

I intend to go direct from this to Berlin, in order to finish my works there, and, if I have time before entering on my post in Dresden, to proceed to Hamburg and Copenhagen. I have no music whatever to send you, nor can I procure any concerto for the oboe. Apply, therefore, through Bärmann to Flad, in Munich. The Jungs have all been in Carlsbad; but owing to the bad weather, they received no benefit whatever from the waters. All send you their best regards; Liebich, too, who is not yet quite well, and my Lina. I cannot as yet say anything certain about the latter; for a long time she seems all that is good and excellent, and then all of a sudden the old demons of passion and jealousy come to life again with their temptations; I am really in a very unsettled state. God and time alone can help or decide the affair.

I am so glad that you liked the worthy Beers; they are, indeed, truly good people. You must yourself express your thanks at some future time for the braces and the *solfeggi*, as at present I see no one.

The society of the Firmians must have been a pleasing variety for you. I hear or see nothing of Minette; she appears to be angry with me. Giuliani [the celebrated guitar-player] gave a concert here, and Mdlle. Schmalz intends to give one. Farewell, dear brother;

the post is just going, so I must conclude in haste. Write soon again, and continue your love for your ever faithful brother,

WEBER.

39.

To Friedrich Rochlitz.

Berlin, Nov. 22, 1816.

My dear and esteemed Friend,

The bearers of this are the very worthy brothers Bender, clarionet-players from Petersburg, who wish to obtain your patronage and kind notice; they will certainly cause you much pleasure by their beautiful tone and mode of executing music together. I beg that you will do me the favour to accept the contents of the enclosed roll of paper, and give it a place in your family apartment, so that you and your estimable wife—your dear good daughter having left her paternal home—may often have your distant friend before your eyes. It is one of the first impressions.

Since I saw you in Konnewitz on July 11th, I have scarcely had a moment to myself, owing to the pressure of various matters that have engrossed all my time. I arrived at Carlsbad on the 13th, and found there such pressing letters from Prague, that I set off thither on the 17th, and directed 'Figaro' on the 19th.

I was then obliged to make a catalogue of all the music belonging to the theatre, and also, for the benefit of my successor, complete the books containing the notices and information about the conduct of the whole business, as I wished everything to be given up in a condition worthy of an honest artist, who is far from feeling maliciously pleased that he will be missed, and that all will come to a standstill without him. I also put Spohr's 'Faust' on the stage, and it gave satisfaction. Unluckily, I have been unable as yet to write any public notice of it, and unless I do so, it is not likely to be done at all. I could not even announce the happy result to himself, as I have no idea where he is to be found at this moment. A number of concert givers, Giuliani, Mdlle. Schmalz, &c. &c. helped to confuse my brains, and to absorb my small portion of spare time. At the end of September, I resigned my situation, and then first had the satisfaction of seeing how much I was beloved and esteemed, and more particularly how unwilling the members of my orchestra were to part from me. Not one of the works that I had undertaken by contract with Schlesinger to supply by 1st of December had advanced a single note; so I was obliged to make the firm resolution to be quiet for a long time, and to lay aside all thoughts of concerts. This I have strictly adhered to since October 13th, when I came here, and hope by December 1st to complete a good number of works, the materials for which have been long seething in my brain, only awaiting deliberate arrangement to be completed.

When I was in Carlsbad, I was spoken to about a situation in Dresden; the affair has been recently renewed, although it appears to me still rather distant. How go on theatrical matters at Leipzig? Is it the fact that Wohlbrück is to undertake the management? If so, I congratulate you, though I should like to discuss it further with you verbally. My plan for the present is to go from here in the middle of December to Magdeburg, Brunswick, Hamburg, and Copenhagen. If you thought that I could give a concert in Leipzig (without a new pianoforte concerto), which would repay the *détour*, as I must now unluckily look to profits also, I would go at once from here direct, and have my cantata performed. I am to give no concert here on this occasion, as I had one in summer, and do not wish to appear presuming; besides, it robs me of too much time.

I beg you will find a place for the enclosed short article as soon as possible in the 'Allgemeine Musik-Zeitung.' An impertinence of this sort is too absurd, and had it happened to any other person, I should probably have expressed myself still more strongly; but as it concerns myself, I always hold a moderate and simple style to be the best; besides, the sneaking conduct of the publisher and of Herr Ebers is sufficiently brought to light.*

* 'A Warning to the Musical Public,' referring to his clarionet quintett, op. 34, of which Hofmeister, in Leipzig, had published without Weber's sanction, a very deficient pianoforte arrangement by Ebers.

Have your new tales appeared yet? I hunger for new songs. Oblige me, my dear friend, by writing me a few lines, when I hope to receive the agreeable assurance that you and your excellent wife are well and happy. I beg my friendly regards to her, and pray remind her sometimes of one who will ever remain with lasting affection and esteem, your faithful friend,

WEBER.

40.

To Günsbacher.

Berlin, Dec. 17, 1816.

My beloved Brother,

In accordance with my promise, I mean to have a good chat with you to-day, and tell you all that has gone on, and is likely to go on. The last time I wrote to you was on September 12th. The delivery of my works and the preparations for my journey, the sale of my effects, &c., gave me enough to do. My career at Prague closed on the 29th with the 'Dorfbarbier,' and with no very brilliant result either. After having taken leave of my orchestra, some of these farewells being very touching, as they at length saw that I was in earnest, and remembered how often they had been led triumphantly by me into the fray, I left on October 7th, with my good Lina and her mother; We remained a few days in Dresden, where my affair was pretty nearly arranged, but not finally concluded even yet. We got to Berlin on the 13th, where Lina went to lodge with the instrument-maker Kisting, and I with Lichtenstein. Lina acted eight times with the most distinguished applause, and was, moreover, so good and kind that it caused me the most heartfelt delight. At last she is restored to peace and confidence. She sees how much I am beloved and esteemed, and the friendly footing on which I am with the women here, and, God be praised! the demon of jealousy is appeased. I plunged into work over head and ears, as I had bound myself to deliver a number of compositions to Schlesinger by December 1st; so I visited nowhere; I neither gave, nor do I intend to give, any concerts, from the loss of time they entail. Up to this moment I have written, since I came here, three songs; an allegro and adagio for the sonata in A flat, four descriptive songs—1st allegretto for clarionet and pianoforte; a new grand sonata in D minor; the third book of 'Lyre and Sword;' a divertimento for guitar and pianoforte. I am now writing a trio and two arias for Mdmes. Milder * and Fischer. On the 19th, I invited my dearest friends to an oyster feast, and was betrothed to my beloved Lina. If she remains steady all this year, and I succeed in getting a tolerably good appointment, she will then leave the theatre, and become my beloved wife. On the 20th she left for Dresden,

* Anna Milder-Hauptmann enchanted all Berlin at that period, especially in the character of Fidelio.

where she played five times. I stay here till January 10th or January 12th, when I go to Hamburg and Copenhagen.

So here you have all my sayings and doings; and now to reply to your letters. That of November 6th I received here on the 16th, and you may conceive my delight on hearing of the well-deserved decoration of your button hole. Thank God! integrity at last meets with its reward, and is doubly welcome from coming quite unexpectedly. May you wear it for a hundred years to come in health and happiness! I am glad that you were pleased with the oboe. I rejoice, too, that you have at last made an agreement with Haas, as I almost despaired of your getting anything, for usually nothing but honour is to be gained by such works. I had a letter from Minette before I left Prague, but have not yet been able to answer it. She is always the same good old soul, and you do her injustice in suspecting her of fickleness. I thank you for your congratulations on my nameday, and in return send you my heart-felt New Year's good wishes. You and I are just the same as ever to each other. I got your letter of December 4th on the 10th. It is singular that common report instals me in so many places, according to what you tell me that Stunz writes to you from Munich. Invoke the devil too often, and he is sure to appear at last. God grant that I may go to Dresden, which would, I think, be best of all, and you could then come and stay with me. There will always be a spare corner for you. The Italian opera having so entirely failed must be a source of great glorification to the Munich singers. So poor Mdme. Firmian has been ill again ? Pray remember me to her, but say to the Count that I must be quite out of favour with him, for during his stay in Prague I had not the good fortune to see him, which would have given me so much pleasure. When you are once more at home, dear brother, pray do be industrious, and establish a close connection with Schlesinger : in this way you might make a very pretty sum of money annually, and not only get rid of all your debts, but also make an honourable name for yourself. The Beers are in Rome, with which they are much pleased, and will scarcely return home before the spring. I will, however, send them your regards, as I intend to write shortly. Things are going on badly at Prague; Liebich might as well be dead; he has incurred a burden of debt amounting to 125,000 florins, which the Estates are to pay, and to undertake the whole affair. He now sees that everything has occurred just as I prophesied. These are his own words—Yes, yes ! I have a quick eye, and know mankind. I must conclude, dear brother, as the post is going. Write to me soon, or the letter wont find me here. May God preserve your health and your love for me. Ever your faithful brother,

WEBER.

41.

To Gänsbacher.

Dresden, March 10, 1817.

Beloved Brother,

I ought long ago to have written to you and announced my appointment (as Royal Saxon Capellmeister and director of the German opera), which I received in Berlin on December 27, 1816, but I have really had too much to do. I am at length fairly settled, and all my fine travelling projects dissolved into thin air. I have indeed annual leave of absence, but if I marry, God willing, in the autumn, all expeditions will be more difficult, and I shall no doubt become a regular *Philistine.* I was obliged to begin my career here with much annoyance, and many struggles against cabals; and in fact I was several times on the point of setting off again; but all this seems eventually to have done good, in so far that it is now evident to them they have to do with a man who will not permit himself to be trifled with, and who has sufficient independence not to submit to any kind of neglect or want of respect. Everything is at present going on smoothly, and those who do not like me at all events respect me.

Even the Italians have become pacific, from seeing that I am more likely to promote their interests than to undermine them. Art has no fatherland; and all that is beautiful ought to be prized by us, no matter what clime or region has produced it. Thus I have every reason to be satisfied, and my sole wish is that Heaven may soon bestow on me tolerable singers, for as yet I have actually none at all. Things go on miserably in Prague, where everything is hastening to decay. My 'Silvana' was given there, and created the most tremendous *furore*, while all deplore my loss and the golden time of the opera, when I was with them. Yes, yes! it serves them right, for at that period nothing I did was good enough for them. I mean soon to set to work at a new opera which the well known poet Friedrich Kind has written for me, the 'Jägersbraut' [the 'Freischütz'], a very romantic, mysterious, and beautiful work. My life, on the whole, here is very solitary, and indeed, I may say, rather dull also, for though I know a number of people, and am esteemed by all, still a true friend is wanting, and I have no one whatever with whom I can converse on musical subjects, which is melancholy enough. I hope, dear brother, that you will soon pay me a visit, when we can talk and work together famously; you will live with me, and our life will be like Heaven itself. Our holidays begin a fortnight hence, when I intend to make a run to Prague and take the people by surprise; an idea that delights me beyond measure. It seems that poor *D minor* has met with many misfortunes, but you are probably better informed than myself on these points; the half of her crops and her chateau have been burned. I wrote to her, but have got no answer as yet. I have news from Meyerbeer, who is in Milan; he is to remain all this year in Italy, where his address is, *Ferma in posta, Venezia.* He seems to have been working hard, and has written both a French and a German opera. Bärmann and Madame Harlas will probably soon visit me, as they propose making a journey to Berlin. I have heard nothing of Gottfried for a long time. No doubt, Schlesinger has meanwhile written to you. Send to him or to me the exact *opus*, title, and dedication of the three works. Do be industrious, dear brother, for your works are certain to sell, and you can thus make a good sum yearly.

My appointment is only for one year, which is the usual form, and though there never has been an instance of its not being followed by a life appointment, still I know my star too well not to dread, at least, some difficulties; but as God wills! I place my trust in Him, and fear nothing, although henceforth I shall have more than myself to provide for. The arrangement with my Lina's mother is at last completed; she is to go to her son in Mayence, and I am to allow her 100 dollars a year; it was better to make this sacrifice, and to have rest and peace at home. Write to me soon how you get on in Vienna; guard well your liberty, and do not allow *F major* to beguile you into making any promises. Independence is noblest and best for a man. It is said that Pixis is to leave Prague, and also most of the members of the orchestra and the theatre. Madame Liebich is to marry Herr Stöger. Clam tore up a bill for 40,000 florins; that was indeed being a true friend. The prices are raised, but the theatre empty. The departure of Mademoiselle Brand [Lina], and, please God, Madame Grünbaum also, (if I can secure her) will give the final *coup de grâce*. May God guard you, dear brother; write to me soon how you are, and what you are doing, and ever continue your love for your faithfully attached brother,

WEBER.

42.

To Gänsbacher.

Dresden, July 18, 1817.

Dear Brother of my heart,

It is long since I have written to you, and I blame myself for it, though I really have been so buried in incessant work and worry, that my health is seriously affected, and I have been very unwell for the last couple of months. I shall, no doubt, soon get better; so I will recount to you all I have been doing, and answer your dear welcome letters.

The last time I wrote to you was on March 10th. Wohlbrück came on the 13th starring, and lodged with me. Taking advantage of the Easter holidays, I resolved on a surprise, and set off with Bassi* to Prague, on the 22nd, at 9 o'clock in the evening, and we travelled so quickly that we arrived on the 23rd, just in time for the second act of the *Zauberflöte.* You may conceive the joy of my beloved Lina and all my friends. Your letter of the 13th I received on the 27th, and on the 28th I directed 'Silvana' myself. The moment my head made its appearance in the orchestra, the most uproarious applause and cries of Bravo! burst forth, and seemed never to come to an end. Every piece of music was applauded, and at the close of each act, 'Bravo! Weber!' shouted out, and indeed it did go off admirably, both orchestra and chorus being inspired with the old spirit, and all, as it were, electrified and intoxicated with delight; they then really felt for the first time what they had lost. I was obliged to leave again on April 1st. The separation was grievous, but still the long year was pleasantly curtailed by this surprise, and fresh strength given us for the remainder of the time. I arrived on the 2nd in Dresden; on the 3rd I arranged all my director's business, and on the 4th set off at an early hour to Leipzig, with Wohlbrück. On the 8th I conducted my 'Kampf und Sieg,' played a concerto, and drove back the same evening to Dresden, where I arrived on the 9th—in ample time for the performance of 'Adelina,' in which the Weixelbaums ap-

* Luigi Bassi, the singer for whom Mozart in 1787 wrote 'Don Juan.'

peared. During the night of the 12th, I wrote music for Müllner's tragedy of 'Yngurd.' 'Joseph' was given on the 13th; 14th, 'Yngurd;' 15th, 'Ostade;' 16th, 'Adelina,' when Thurmer played the oboe splendidly between the acts; the 22nd 'Helene' was given for the first time. The Grünbaums arrived on the 30th. 'Johann von Paris' was given for the first time on May 3rd; the 'Lotterieloos' on the 11th, and 'Blaubart,' for the first time, on the 18th. Madame Grünbaum sang in all these with the most enthusiastic applause, and went from here to Berlin. 31st, the 'Hausgesinde;' June 4th, the 'Waisenhaus;' 15th 'Das Geheimniss.' 16th, I received your letter of the 5th, and meanwhile Madame Grünbaum returned from Berlin. Owing to the absence of some of the company, the opera was rehearsed afresh, and Madame Grünbaum sang again in 'Johann von Paris.' On the 18th, an unprecedented event occurred. For the first time, in preference to the Italians, the German opera was summoned to Pillnitz, when Grünbaum sang in 'Lotterieloos.' That was a triumph! On the 27th, I conducted Naumann's 'Vater Unser' in the church, assisted by the whole orchestra, for the benefit of the poor, and it went famously. Papa Beer passed through here on the 28th on his way to Carlsbad, and Treitschke and Schreivogel from Vienna, who were touring about, recruiting; I talked much of you with them. On the 13th, I received another call to Berlin as Capellmeister; so now is arrived the important epoch of my life, when I am like the ass between the two bundles of hay, and do not know what to do. Unfortunately, my chief, Count Vizthum, is absent, but returns in a few days, so the affair will soon be decided. In any event, the offer is a good thing, for I intend to choose the best.

You see by this short sketch, in which I do not include hundreds of letters, articles, parties, corrections, theatrical stars, rehearsals, &c., how I have been overburdened with work, sufficient to make anyone sink under its weight. But to reply to your letter No. 1, of March 1st. My appointment here is, for the present, only for a year, but one for life invariably ensues; that is the custom in Dresden. Life is very tranquil here, and therefore favourable to domestic retirement; there are some admirable poets and some amiable men; but not one single musical soul such as we require, and much annoyance from the cabals of the Italians, and very uncertain prospects for the German opera in the future. The tenor Mieksch is still alive, and a very kind friend of mine, but Naumann is dead. I wish I could have been with you at the grand solemnity when you received your well merited medal; those are the glorious moments of life that counterbalance many others. I have not heard of *D minor* for ages: I wished to sympathise with her after that unfortunate conflagration, but have never since received one line from her. I have also shamefully neglected the letter to Schlesinger (in fact, I owe answers to all the world), but I have at length forwarded it. I confidently hope one day to perform some of your sacred music, as soon as I am fairly installed in office; perhaps, too, I might contrive to get you something for it, but time will be required for that; with us all goes on rather slow, but sure. In vain have I hoped, from what you said, that Count *F major* would come here. We have Count O'Donell instead, with Jung's sister, who is very like Haas. I have no time to go about much, and have only been there once. The Count and Countess, however, are a polite and agreeable couple. If you could only come to me, dear brother! Were the present church composer to take himself off, that would be the very post for you, but time will show. I was glad to find that you had been hard at work, and completed something new for the church. Let me know the effect when performed. It is indeed to be lamented that publishers are nourished by the sweat of our brow, but if works are made well known in the world, it is all right, and this will certainly be the case with Steiner and your 'Requiem.'

Meyerbeer is about to give, or has by this time given, an opera of his in Venice. He is to remain another year in Italy, and then goes to Paris. The Grünbaums introduced an aria and a hymn of his into their concert in Berlin, both of which were exceedingly liked. The hymn is very simple and flowing, and yet adorned with many novel features.

As for the Weixelbaums, they are wretched low creatures, and contemptible hypocrites. Here they have pursued the same system in borrowing money, both from me and others, and yet, in spite of their base conduct, it is possible they may be engaged.

I am working as hard at my 'Jägersbraut' as my many avocations will permit; four or five scenes are already sketched. What would I not give for my friend and brother's counsel and approval, to sustain and elevate my thoughts. As it is, devoid of all sympathy, I must write for myself alone. I am going to Prague the end of September, to marry my good Caroline, with whom I have daily more cause to be pleased. We are to take the mother to her son in Mannheim, and endeavour to make a few dollars *en route*, and then proceed to take possession of our domestic temple, whether here or in Berlin, God knows! Farewell, beloved brother of my heart. May the Almighty prosper you and your works: continue well and happy. Ever, till death,

Your faithful brother,

WEBER.

P.S.—It is long since I heard from Gottfried. He has begun an admirable theoretical work, which is constructed on our principles, and stands alone of its kind. The first part has already appeared. *Addio senza addio.* Constant practice in Italian is the best thing to do here.

43.

To Gänsbacher.

Hotterwitz, near Pillnitz, Dresden, Aug. 24, 1818.

Dearly loved Brother,

I dare scarcely venture to lift up my eyes before you; what must you think of my long silence? I trust you are not as irate as, I own, you have a right to be, for you well know your faithful Weber and his love for you. But such is the course of things in this plaguy world; I wished to write to you at full length, but could not find time, and at last the materials run fairly ahead of me, &c. You understand all this, so I cry *Peccavi*, and you will grant me your brotherly forgiveness; will you not? I now resume my diary, and at least note down the chief events.

The last time I wrote to you was from Dresden, on July 18, 1817. The numerous rehearsals, vexations, and toils, injured my health seriously, and for several months I suffered from severe throat complaint. My position, too, seemed very precarious; besides, the Italians were really too aggravating. I had hoped to be united to my beloved Lina by Michaelmas, but I was not destined to find this so easy a matter. The nuptial festivities of our Princess Marianne and the Grand Duke of Tuscany intervened, for which I had to write a grand cantata; then the preliminaries were much protracted, and I was in the most painful position. My poor Lina had no longer a lodging in Prague, and was forced to take refuge in a miserable hole, and I was obliged entirely to refurnish my own apartments; so these arrangements, and also having to compose a piece in honour of the royal wedding (being my first task here), were quite enough to drive me distracted. At last the celebration took place on October 29th, and on the 30th I was *en route*, arriving safely and long looked for in Prague on the 31st, where I received your kind letter of September 25th through Kleinwächter. November 4th was my wedding-day, which was kept in the quietest way at the Jungs', but in all cheerfulness and happiness. The only persons present were the Kleinwächters, Bomsel, and Lisette Frieser. I packed up the same evening, and on the 5th my young wife and I passed through the gate that leads to Mannheim, where we arrived on the 11th, and placed the mother under her son's care, with whom she now is, well and happy.

How forcibly was I reminded, both here and in Darmstadt (which I passed through on the 15th), of former times, and the gay charming days we passed together, but, alas! no longer to be found there. Yearning once more to see at least one member of our Triad, I hastened to Gottfried in Mayence. This was, however, the saddest moment of my journey, for I met him with all the old heart-felt love, and—he was no longer the same. I do not wish, however, to be unjust, having arrived at an unfavourable moment, when he had daily criminal cases, had just changed his quarters, and his wife recently confined, &c., and perhaps such was the origin of his no longer taking any interest except in his own affairs. He is also become rather dogmatical and dictatorial. In short, it caused me the utmost sorrow; I had so rejoiced in the thoughts of seeing him; indeed, this was the chief object of my journey. Well, all joys cannot be realised! I gave a concert in Darmstadt, and also one in Giessen, was most courteously received in Gotha by the Duke, and on December 20th reached Dresden, where I found plenty of secret intrigues and cabals. Notwithstanding all my work, I determined to write a mass for the nameday of the King, and I did so with care and good will. It was performed on March 8th for the third time, and evidently made a sensation. I wish I could have had the happiness of letting you hear it. At that period, I had a great deal of annoyance from my chief, and at times I was on the very point of demanding my dismissal, when I first learned how to prize the happiness of having by my side, as a companion for life, a sympathising faithful wife. I must not delay telling you, what indeed I ought to have said at the beginning of my letter, which is, how happy and cheerful I am in my domestic relations, and how much my beloved Lina embellishes my life, and assists me to bear its burdens. I am indeed a fortunate man, and wish you, my dear brother, similar happiness. No one could in the most remote degree discover that my Lina had ever been an actress; she is become such a busy, intelligent, and careful mistress of a household, and takes delight in her new sphere; we are both pictures of health and contentment. God be praised for this, and may He grant us a continuance of these blessings. Only come soon, and see for yourself. The parting from her mother was a most painful trial, but she bears it with quiet submission, and, to my great satisfaction, acknowledges its necessity.

Next to my official duties, I strove to work at my opera ['Freischütz'], but it was impossible; a succession of stars engrossed my whole time; so I asked for a dispensation from my service, to enable me to go to the country and work there. I had settled to do so on May 20th, when Bärmann and Madame Harlas took me by surprise, to my great joy; so I carried them straight off with me to Pillnitz, where we passed some very agreeable days together, and you may well believe that you were often thought of. On the 23rd they sang and played at Court with the greatest applause, and also received handsome presents. On the 30th they left for Berlin, and I was obliged in all haste to compose a cantata in honour of the Queen's nameday, for which festivity Bärmann unexpectedly returned on August 1st, stayed with us eight days more, and went back to Munich on the 10th. Between that and the present time I had to write a grand cantata, which is just finished, to celebrate the jubilee of our King, and it has left me in such a state of exhaustion that for the last two days I have been suffering from the most entire prostration of strength. This is the first day for a whole year that I have had one leisure moment, and even now I have granted it to myself on purpose to talk to you, dear brother. All hope of putting my opera on the stage this winter is at an end, as I remove to Dresden to-day, where my official duties take up the whole of my time. These compositions for special occasions, which are mere ephemera in the artistic world, belong to the dark side of an official position, and from their transitory nature are always dreary work, however devoted and loving and loyal one may feel towards the person for whom they are written. This is certainly the case with myself, for anyone well acquainted with our royal family must be devoid of all feeling and sensibility not to feel the highest reverence and the most faithful attachment towards them, which, indeed, makes me both content and cheerful. Everywhere there are drawbacks, which must be patiently borne, and time and perseverance can alone bring about more rest. The King gave me a handsome token of his approbation by presenting me with a beautiful and costly ring (value 200 ducats) in return for my mass, a distinction that no previous Capellmeister in office had ever obtained. My beloved Hänsel, you now know how matters are with me, and when I also add that I hope in December to welcome a young scion, you will then see the full extent of my happiness, heightened by the fact that my excellent wife enjoys the best health in her situation, and suffers from none of the usual maladies.

I heard two days ago from the Jungs after a long silence. They and their brother and children had all been wretchedly ill, but are now recovering. Death has made havoc too in the Kleinwächter family, which you, no doubt, already know.

To reply to your welcome letters, two of which, *horribile dictu*, I have yet to answer. My appointment here is for life. My little wife has a great regard for you, and sends her cordial regards; she can never forget the *l' amerò*, and invites him kindly to visit her house in Dresden. It would indeed be delightful, dear brother, were you to come. Perhaps you might present a mass to the King, and thus defray the expenses of your journey—reflect on this. Schlesinger, meanwhile, has, no doubt, corresponded with you himself. I also spoke to Peters from Leipzig, who was here, about you; he will be very glad to publish for you, and he pays honestly.

I hear or see nothing of *D minor*; she is quite dead to me, which causes me heartfelt regret. I may, however, be also to blame for this, as I write to no one; still, she owes me a letter. *F major* has disappeared altogether. I read with great interest of your brilliant performances, the compliments paid you, and your gay visit to Botzen. May it often fall to your lot to enjoy similar pleasures! What brighter fate can the artist desire than to see his efforts welcomed with enthusiasm. Think of me on September 21st, when my cantata is to be performed in church with a vocal chorus of about 100 voices.

Meyerbeer is still in Italy, and I understand he is writing something for Turin for the next Carnival. I nearly went to Italy myself (to Milan and Venice) for the same purpose, but I could not well be so long absent from here, nor could I leave my wife at this time; moreover, I neither can nor will write such *Klingklang dudeldum* as people like nowadays.

But what I cannot accomplish at this moment may perhaps be brought about at Milan a year hence, and then I shall come with my wife into your hilly country, and visit you, but first of all do come here like a good fellow. Prague is in a poor condition, and three days ago Clam wrote to me, 'The good star of Prague vanished with you.' It is said that Dr. Schaller is to marry Mdlle. Demmer. I wish him joy!! Schlesinger is sure to send your divertimento to Vienna. If the Viennese do not pay handsomely, let me know, for Peters will take it at once. I embrace you, dear brother, in imagination. May God bless and preserve you, and bestow courage and peace on you. My Lina unites in kindest wishes for my Hänsel, with your faithful brother, who will not again be so long silent, and will ever be devoted to you with the truest affection.

Yours wholly,

WEBER.

44.

To Günsbacher.

Dresden, Dec. 24, 1818.

Dear Brother,

Only a few words to-day, but joyful ones, and well assured of your sympathy. My beloved Lina gave birth to a fine healthy little girl yesterday, at 11 o'clock, after terrible sufferings, which she bore heroïcally; these must be witnessed, not described, rightly to appreciate the courage of a woman. Thank God! it is over, and she is as well as can be expected under the circumstances. What a singular feeling it is, dear brother. I am still very much agitated, but must answer your letters of the 8th and 15th. Lina sends you her cordial regards, and looks forward with much pleasure to the time when she may hope to do the honours of her house to you. Pray put this charming plan into execution; how we shall talk, and revel in art and friendship, and in the past and the present.

The idea of the mass for here is very good. Above all, make it as short as possible, and don't forget some pleasing finished soprano solos for our admirable *musico* Saparoli. You must, however, leave him a good deal of liberty, and write with great breadth for our church, as it has a tremendous echo, so that all rapid passages are apt to become confused; trumpets and kettledrums, too, must be very sparingly employed. It is true that the Court here like a very melodious style, but you will regard that as little as I do, for it would be unworthy of the sublime locality and words, and the heart itself can supply melody. Bring some other works also. I hope that at all events your journey will cost you nothing. I am heartily glad to hear that you are industrious, and do not allow the sword to make you forget the lyre. I know nothing whatever of *D minor.* I have not as yet received anything for my cantata, which made a great sensation here. I have just completed another mass for the wedding jubilee of our royal pair, January 17, 1819. The King and Queen are sponsors for my little daughter. My business goes on in its usual tranquil course; right ahead, but not recklessly, nor setting anyone aside, as I do not wish to take possession of the road to prosperity by force. This succeeds better too in the long run, and I have every reason to consider my position a good one. I hope you can say the same; but come! come! with heart-felt brotherly love are you expected by my little wife and your faithful old

WEBER.

45.

To Gänsbacher.

Dresden, March 28, 1821.

Brother of my heart,

What joy your welcome letter of February 22nd caused me. I would have answered it by return of post, had I not wished to give you some pleasure in return, so I now enclose printed evidence that it is my highest delight to tell the world something about you. I need not tell you the interest my Lina takes in you. We are very much concerned lest you should be obliged to go to Italy; so pray set our fears at rest as soon as possible. It is indeed long since we met, and I can as yet see no glimpse of hope in this respect, and you have even less command of your time than I have. Only be industrious, and write a good deal; I don't know why, but it always seems to me that your doing so may one day have an important influence on your fate. Man is thus constituted, and even the most ardent and glowing for his art requires an impetus.

I have all sorts of things to tell you about myself. Last year I travelled from August to November, going to Hamburg and on to Copenhagen, which turned out happily in every point of view, my reception everywhere being far beyond my most sanguine hopes, and I also made plenty of money. But I was obliged to leave my good Lina in Hamburg, as she expected her confinement, and a sea voyage was thought a risk for her. Man proposes, and God disposes; for notwithstanding these precautions, she had a premature confinement, but was so admirably nursed by kind people that by the time I returned from Copenhagen I found her quite brisk again; the good creature, too, not having written me one word on the subject to avoid alarming me. During our journey there had been great changes in Dresden. Count Vizthum, our intendant, had taken leave of us, and Herr v. Könneritz from Vienna had stepped into his place. He is the kind of man who goes with the stream, and is quite in the hands of the Italians, and thus I see vanish for ever all that I have with such difficulty accomplished during the last four years, for the German opera. There were times when I felt utterly miserable and desperate, but I now endeavour to take the matter as lightly as possible; I have the comfort of knowing that I have done my duty as an honest man, and the rest I leave to God.

I am going to Berlin the end of April, to conduct my new opera, 'Der Freischütz,' with which the theatre there is to open. From thence I go with my Lina to Alexisbad, which is necessary both for her and for me. I hope also about that time to see Meyerbeer again in Berlin. God grant that in Germany he may be what he formerly was, and not think in the same style in which he composes, when in Italy. I heard yesterday that B. A. Weber in Berlin is dead. It is very possible that I may be offered his situation, but I should be very unwilling to leave Dresden, though many things are exceedingly painful to my feelings—our royal family are indeed truly excellent, when well known—but as God wills.

I have just looked at your letter, and am shocked to find that you have had no news of me since the end of 1818. My dear brother, in the meantime I was at the point of death, and during the whole summer of 1819 dangerously ill; then my wife had another premature confinement, so instead of children I have a dog and a monkey—but God will no doubt replace our loss. My health since then has become very fragile, and I cannot yet get rid of a teazing cough; well! no doubt it will pass away in time. Bärmann passed through here before Christmas, when you were often spoken of. I got letters from the Jungs two days ago; he has just recovered from inflammation of the lungs, and his wife has had another girl. He also wrote to me about your ring, and hopes to hear from yourself. The old mother has got the arrears of her pension, which amount to a good round sum. I believe they require it all; may Heaven preserve him to his large family. I have heard nothing whatever of *D minor* or *F major*. Naumann's 'Vater Unser' is being engraved, and the subscribers can soon have it, for a louisd'or, I believe. Only the pianoforte arrangement of my 'Kampf und Sieg' is engraved; so I await your orders on the subject; perhaps you might also make use of the cantata that I wrote for the jubilee of our King, and which might be given with other words as a harvest thanksgiving. I am at present engaged in a grand comic opera, and an *opera seria* is to follow, with recitative throughout. Were you not glad to hear that Dietrichstein and Mosel had become directors in Vienna? At last that imperial city will no longer be quite closed against nature and talent, and what is really good will be preferred, instead of always Rossini. Moreover, I hope he will no longer be considered a standard, for he is cutting his own throat. May Heaven only send peace in a political point of view! A favourite plan of mine has long been to go from here to Munich, and thence by Salzburg and Innsbruck to Milan, and home by Vienna; but who can now venture to make any calculations? Besides, it could not be till next year, and by that time there may be many changes. May God dispose the hearts of our rulers to peace!

Dear old Hänsel, farewell!—may God keep you in the same health that you now, to my great satisfaction, enjoy. My Lina sends you her regards. I trust we shall ever continue the same, except indeed in writing—a point on which we might both easily improve. May each of us frequently take up the pen to send mutually happy tidings, for it is too tiresome to do nothing but complain. I embrace you, and ever believe me, with a loving brother's heart, your

Weber.

46.

To Gänsbacher.

Dresden, Dec. 25, 1821.

My much loved Brother,

What intense pleasure your letter caused me! Though I know how much allowance I must make for your praise, on the score of faithful friendship, yet so much remains, evidently emanating from profound knowledge, and a feeling heart, that I cannot thank you enough. The approbation of an honest man is cheering, and inspires courage for future labours. The praise of the public, highly honourable and desirable though it be, may often be supposed to spring from chance causes, rather than from the actual inner life of the work itself. God does bless me in a wonderful way, and I rely on His further aid, that my ensuing works may not disgrace the promise of my earlier ones.*

Your presence in Vienna first inspired me with the thought to go there soon myself, so that I might become well acquainted with those persons for whom I am to write, and, fortified by such impressions, to hasten home, and begin to compose. But you set off again on January

* On June 28, 1828, he wrote a little note to his friend from Berlin, in which he recommends to him the pianoforte composer Franz Lauska, and goes on to say: 'I return to Dresden to-morrow evening, after having won really great triumphs here; all the greater that the "Olympia" of Spontini, so long in preparation, and costing above 21,000 dollars, was very far from being received with the same warmth as my German "Freischütz."'

8, and I cannot get away from here till February, as the 'Freischütz' is being rehearsed at present by royal command. It would indeed have been soothing to me once more to repose on the breast of a friend. Every day one becomes more lonely in the world; I have met with ingratitude without end. Some do not approve of my being more esteemed than themselves, and so I live here quite deserted, in an artistic point of view, and in other respects happy only with my wife. I withdraw from all society, for frivolous conversations and tea-parties are no relaxation to me from my many labours. My health, too, has suffered severely, but we cannot always have sunshine here below. Is it really quite impossible for you to stay a little longer? Would that I could have the happiness of procuring for you a quiet little place in our Capelle as church composer! But so many lie in ambush for it, and the gentlemen whose names end in *ini*, and *elli*, know so well how to put every iron in the fire, and to take steps so long before, that my wish will probably only remain among the *pia desideria*. How happy should we be, living and toiling together! Your description of the Cecilia festival amused me very much, and the sympathy of the artists delighted me, for usually these worthies are hard to move.

Thank Lieut.-Colonel von Call in my name for his warm interest; I shall rejoice much to see him again. All good wishes to the respected Firmians; if I don't get to Vienna till the end of the summer, I shall miss them once more, which would really be provoking. The cantatas and your presentation copies are now ready to be forwarded. Do not be displeased, dear brother, at the delay, but my copyists were busily engaged in sending off my opera, which is still being transcribed, although I have already sent it to seventeen theatres.

I knew beforehand that the Lauskas would certainly please you. They are good, honest, warm-hearted people; indeed, I still have a number of truly loving and sincere friends in Berlin. This was in fact what rather disposed me to go there, but after all this place suits me better. I will thank you for the diploma when I send the score. The 'Jubilee Cantata' was given again a few days ago, and received with enthusiasm. Naumann's glorious 'Vater Unser' has not yet, alas! been performed, all sorts of obstacles standing in the way, but I now mean to take charge of it myself, and have already held a consultation on the subject with the widow. Doubtless your stay in Vienna and the many new impressions you received there have had a favourable influence on your mind, and you will again create and work at something new. What of the mass you were to write for our King? I hear little of Meyerbeer; he has become quite Italianised. Gottfried is grown dumb: where are the bright days of old?

My wife sends you her kind regards, and I must close. May God once more reunite us. Write soon, and believe me ever your faithful WEBER.

47.

To Gänsbacher.

Dresden, April 28, 1822.

Dear Brother of my Heart,

You must almost think that the tumult and excitement of applause have made me so worldly and time-serving, that I have forgotten my dearest and most faithful friend. Oh, no! I must ever be the same; but it is undeniable that the more I belong to the world the less can I live for myself, and must often renounce what I like best. But above all you must share my joy, purchased by long years of regrets and disappointed hopes. On March 25, at eleven o'clock in the forenoon, my Lina gave birth to a healthy boy.* She nurses him herself, and both are doing as well as possible. I too feel somewhat better, and expect much from my stay in the country, where I am going as soon as I can. Now as to your letter.

The joy of seeing you in Vienna would have been almost too great, so Heaven has thought fit to postpone it. What you write about 'Silvana' was quite my own opinion; so I formally refused that it should be performed. Do not forget the mass for our King; if it does no good, it can at least do no harm, and I have various little projects *in petto*. But, dear brother, so

* The present director Max Maria von Weber, in Dresden, the admirable biographer of his father.

long as you have no firm footing elsewhere, continue your present career.

The 'Jubilee Cantata' has been forwarded to you, at least so Lannoy writes. He is an excellent man, and I heartily like him. 'Kampf und Sieg' will soon follow, and along with it my thanks for the honorary diploma. I got your last letter in Vienna, two days before my departure. I have not seen poor Madame Firmian, for, when I arrived, her husband was ill, and after his death I could not bring myself to call on her. My own illness also intervened. It would certainly be one of the greatest joys in my life if I could in any way brighten your existence, but I could be of no use with the Archduke K. He only spoke to me once at Prince Friedrich's of Saxony, and though I know that he is favourably disposed towards me, still to apply to him with any good effect, I must be much and often with him. This will, however, induce me, during my second visit to Vienna, to present myself more frequently before him, which is besides quite in accordance with the high respect and love that I, and every honest German, cherish for him in our hearts.

How you put me to the blush, my good brother, by the modesty (to me most touching) with which you express yourself on this occasion! Your head and heart are worthy of the best place, and no one ought to take precedence of you. I saw nothing more of Madame Wolkenstein; she probably enquired for me after my departure. I found the Jungs, in Prague, well and cheerful: I was two days on the journey, and one day there, when we talked much of you.

After long years, I have at length got once more a letter from Gottfried, quite full of the old Mannheim love and warmth. This has given me intense pleasure, as I had quite given him up as lost. Bärmann has married again. Meyerbeer's last opera, 'L' Esule di Granada,' has pleased very much in Milan. I came back on March 26, and have been confined to my room for nearly three weeks. When all this is over, and when I go to the country, I mean to set to work busily at my grand opera 'Euryanthe,' which is to be finished by the autumn. May God grant it His blessing! May Heaven also soon fulfil your wishes! How happy would it make me! Do let me soon hear from you again, and ever continue to love your unchanging and faithful old

WEBER.

48.

To Frau Bärmann, Munich.

Dresden, Dec. 26, 1822.

I acknowledge with sincere thanks the kind terms of your letter, in which you address me as the true friend of your Heinrich [Bärmann]. As such I have certainly a right to your sympathy, and I would not have hesitated to claim it if your kind letter had not so agreeably anticipated me. But you also give me cause to reproach you a little; for is it right thus to overwhelm with flattery your husband's simple friend, so that he can only be silent in return? You must not allow yourself to be dazzled; do not look through the spectacles of my Bärmann, who has no doubt praised me far beyond my deserts, in accordance with the love he feels for me. I must now dread what I formerly wished—to become personally acquainted with you—for you will find a very ordinary mortal, only good enough not to be thought evil, rather more sulky than he ought to be, but full of fidelity to his friends and imperishable gratitude for their love. I cherish the pleasing conviction that I shall one day be deeply in your debt for making my good Heinrich happy, a debt that I beg you will heap on my shoulders without measure or end, and thus still further oblige your most sincerely devoted

C. M. v. Weber.

49.

To our Heinrich's Fame and Praise.

Zu unsers Heinrichs Ruhm und Preis,
Aber ich bitte mit bestem Fleiß.

unser Freund schon fab = ri = zie = ret, sie sol = len im = mer=
bar ge = deihn u. bald tret' auch der 4 = te ein.
Und während wir um Deine Rückkehr weinen,
Bereichre Dich mit Ruhm und Edelsteinen.
Zum Zie = le führt Dich die = se Bahn, nur
laß Dich, Freund, durch nichts ge = ni = = = ren, mach Dir die Menschen
un=terthan, laß re = den, schreiben, ca=ba = li=ren.

Kommst Du mit vol = lem Beu = tel an,
bis.
so wird Dir Deutsch = land ap=plau=di = ren.

Soweit seh' ich's, kann unser Wünschen frommen,
Noch mit der Kunst und mit dem Künstler kommen.

Recit.
Die Strahlen der Son=ne ver = trei = ben die Nacht, das
heißt, aus der Baarschaft wird al = les ge = macht.

Presto.
So geh' nach Ve = ne = dig und ho = le baar

50.

To Gänsbacher.

Dresden, Dec. 12, 1822.

Dearest Brother,

I have passed both a good and a bad summer: good, because God blessed my family with health, and the nursing mother prospered as much as the little wild Max, who a few days ago cut his first tooth; bad, because I could scarcely work at all, for, owing to the illness of the church composer Schubert, the whole weight of the official service was laid on me alone, and as we lived in the country near Pillnitz, one German mile from this, I was constantly on the high road, thus wasting both money and time. Morlacchi being ill at present, the Italian duties also devolve on me, and likewise all the festivities in honour of the nuptials of Prince Johann; indeed, I was obliged to conduct Morlacchi's new cantata. It was therefore quite out of my power to fulfil my promise to give my 'Euryanthe' this autumn in Vienna; so I thus lose an entire theatrical year. Still my position here daily improves, and I become more reconciled to the idea of living and dying here.

That fatal word *dying* is my chief reason for writing to you to-day. The continued illness of Schubert leads me to fear that his pilgrimage on earth is drawing to a close. I cannot, therefore, renounce the plan so essential to my happiness, of your living with me. If God would only grant me that joy, I should be at the height of felicity. Only yesterday I spoke again very urgently to my chief on the subject, and I have every reason to expect that some attention will be paid to my words. There is a project here to appoint two music directors, each with a salary of six or seven hundred Saxon dollars; they are to go hand in hand with the Capellmeister, to share all his duties, to rehearse and practise in his absence, &c. I would then earnestly beg of you, if the mass intended for the King is not yet finished, to send me the score of some of your earlier church compositions, overtures, &c., and write to me at once to say whether you would agree to accept such a situation or not. You could certainly live very well on the income, and your works would become better known from this place. My home would be yours, and your salary would be raised in time.

I conclude that nothing certain has at yet turned up for you in your own country, or you would of course have set my mind at ease about your fate. I therefore go on quietly paving the way for my favourite plan.

From my inmost heart do I deplore your unhappy family circumstances. May God give you strength, my beloved brother. I hear nothing of *F minor*; it is said that she wished Fanny to marry her steward, and people throw out all sorts of insinuations on the subject. Things do not go at all well with Angst. My Lina sends you her most cordial regards; her greatest wish too is to see you here with us. May Heaven listen to this innocent prayer! I should be ashamed to receive any expenses of copying from the Union. I enclose a letter about it. Answer me forthwith. I remain, with the most heartfelt love,

Your ever faithful

WEBER.

51.

To Gänsbacher.

Dresden, Dec. 26, 1822.

Dear Brother,

Our letters have crossed. You must have received mine of the 12th just after sending off yours of the 19th. I do not wait for your answer to the former, but hasten to give you information about the mass. As I have no thoughts of going to Vienna till next autumn, you are sure still to find me in Dresden : summer and winter are equally good for your mass. I wish, however, you could send it before you come yourself, that the King may previously know something of your being in the world: I spoke again last night to my chief on the subject. You cannot conduct it yourself, being contrary to custom here. Moreover, I can tell you nothing as to the leave of absence for which you stipulate. At the end of April I go to Pillnitz with the Court, who attend mass in town every Sunday. With regard to your own work, do not forget that our church is very large, and has a most unseemly echo ; short subjects become confused, a long *appoggiatura* swallows up the principal note. Cherubini's and Beethoven's music, for instance, being full of rapidly succeeding modulations, the voice parts much interwoven, and with rapid changes of harmony, would with us have the effect of a Dutch concert. Consequently large, broad subjects—all that is massive—is effective, though the occasional single sustained tones of a wind instrument have a fine effect. The vocalists are Italians, therefore never very firm, so make everything as easy as possible. The *alto* is miserable. The *soprano* admirable in the grand and noble style; breath like a horse. Do not forget to give him an

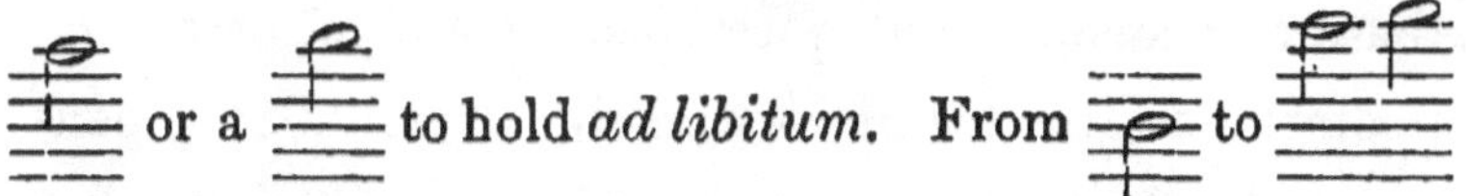

he sings with the greatest freedom. We are accustomed to solid fugues; so do as you like about this. You must inspire respect in the orchestra. Send also an *offertorium*; but as the texts apply to particular Sundays, I do not answer for its being performed. After the *gloria* we have a short instrumental movement and no *motett.*

I wish you joy of the ring; I had heard of it already from Lannoy. Send your mass as soon as you possibly can, and come when it suits you. I cannot tell you, brother of my heart, how I rejoice at the thoughts of having you with me for a time, and my Lina feels just as I do. May God prosper your work and my faithful efforts.

I am ever, with heartfelt brotherly love, your

WEBER.

52.

To Gänsbacher.

Dresden, Jan. 14, 1823.

I have received your letter of December 29, 1822, and likewise your compositions, in which I take great delight; they shall be made use of as time and opportunity permit. I hasten to answer your questions. All royal orchestral appointments are for life, with full salary. Being pensioned simply means receiving the pay from another treasury. The female pensions are small, and depend on the pleasure of the King, who leaves no one belonging to a faithful servant without a provision. Dismissal is unknown, except for the most scandalous mode of life, indeed there are instances of even such things being overlooked by too great indulgence. Of course, you are not prohibited resigning the office yourself. Leave of absence can be sometimes procured, especially if the music director is on good terms with the Capellmeister.

It is my duty once more to impress on you that neither my wishes, efforts, nor plans by any means ensure a certainty; I am only paving the way, and will do all that a man of integrity can do, to carry the affair through. At a court like this, innumerable people are on the watch for such a post, and they do not scruple to use any means. Go on, therefore, quietly with your Innsbruck affairs, and do not throw away any other chance. Even were all your wishes fulfilled there, you have always the power of accepting or refusing any offer from here. You must also be prepared for many things, and many annoyances, which would never occur to the mind of a straightforward Tyrolese, who has lived far from courts. But the man who steadily goes on his way, animated by pure zeal, will find himself respected here as elsewhere, and content. Besides, in me you have a friend who knows the depth of the stream, and who will be your faithful pilot.

Your sacred music, dear brother, is so clear and symmetrical that it will assuredly produce an effect here. Our intendant wished to lay all the pieces before the King, but I begged him to reserve the new mass that you wrote expressly for His Majesty. If our Sovereign wishes to see some more of your compositions, it will then be time enough to present the mass. If you have written any melodious Italian pieces, don't fail to send them likewise. So much for to-day.

Every kind wish from my Lina and your

WEBER.

53.

To Gänsbacher.

Dresden, April 21, 1823.

The cause of my delay in answering your letter of January 8, which I received on February 27, was solely my anxious wish, dear brother, to have announced to you some positive result. As it is, however, the affair continues to drag on, and the arrival of the Bavarian Court in the meantime not a little contributes to this. I have had your mass bound, but our chief has his own reasons for not yet presenting it to His Majesty. At what a creeping pace this business seems to proceed, to a heart glowing with friendship, and awaiting the result! Do not be disheartened, nothing shall be neglected, and patience is, above all things, indispensable in the matter. I had only yesterday an opportunity of impressing the affair strongly on the minister, Count von Einsiedel.

I studied your beautiful work with great interest and satisfaction. It does credit to the master and creator, being flowing, melodious, clear, novel in many passages, and rich and profound in harmony; but I dissuade you from having it performed in Innsbruck, as that would certainly be known here, where sole possession is valued. It will not be easy to find a publisher, for such a very bulky work seldom repays the great cost of engraving, but you will get one in time, no doubt.

I have the following idea with regard to your march. Send it to the King of Prussia, through Spontini, who feels flattered when his influence and patronage are sought. Request also that it may be performed, in which case Schlesinger will be sure to pay you for a pianoforte arrangement. Make use of my name to Spontini, and say that I highly extolled his impartiality in bringing forward foreign talent, and had advised you to apply to him. You must likewise write to the King of Prussia.

As we are on the subject of writing, it might be advisable, as you say yourself, to address my chief here about your mass, and your appointment. I have given Dr. Ek a copy of your march to take with him, but I do not think this will do much good. I had almost forgotten to write to you that we have no trombones in the church, I must therefore employ a double bassoon instead. Forgive my writing in this fragmentary style, but I am so often interrupted that I can only steal a few moments at a time. All are well at home, thank God! My Lina sends you her cordial remembrances, so adieu for to-day. Let me soon hear from you again. I embrace you with true brotherly affection, and am for ever and ever your

WEBER.

54.

To Gänsbacher.

Dresden, Dec. 1, 1823.

Much beloved Brother,

You must have been quite puzzled by my silence in return for so many letters which I received in a strange subversion of order. But when I tell you that I literally, from day to day, hoped for a decision about your affair, you will then comprehend that an irresistible power insensibly deterred me from writing to you. Now, thanks be to God and to my excellent chief, I have the intense joy of procuring for my King a faithful servant and admirable artist, an ornament to our artistic establishment: for you an honourable sphere for work, and for myself an attached comrade in joy and sorrow. I congratulate both you and ourselves from the depths of my heart, and rejoice unspeakably at the hope of soon embracing you. I pass over all the other points in your letter, as I reserve everything for verbal discussion; only I may say that you must not object to three months' probation, such being the invariable custom in our service, and no better conditions were offered either to myself or others. In order to be very provident, however, take your holidays at once, if not for three months, at least for two months, or six weeks. The rest we can manage from here through our ambassador in Vienna; arrange so that you can settle here at once, and not be obliged to lose time by again making the expensive journey here and back. As you will have all kinds of outlay, and probably must equip yourself entirely in plain clothes, for people here lay some stress on this, I entreat you to accept from me the enclosed advance of 200 gulden, C. M., which you can repay at your convenience, of course at a high rate of interest, in accordance with my Jewish disposition. I will dun you well. I must look out for a lodging for you, as unluckily I cannot offer you one; we hope, however, that you will kindly be satisfied with our family fare, which you are invited daily to partake of (such being the will and pleasure of the stern lady of the house), at least until you choose to make other arrangements.

Preindl's situation in Vienna [Capellmeister of St. Stephan's] would certainly have been more desirable for you, but from all I hear you have no chance of getting it. Your friend Kettel wrote to me here from Vienna, but forgot to enclose your letter, so I did not know what to do, and now the very thing I have so long wished is come to pass. May it cause you as much joy!

Answer this at once, or, still better, come yourself, for you are much wanted. I cannot bring myself to write more to-day, or on any other subject. I embrace you cordially in my thoughts, my dear good Hänsel, and am now, as ever, your most faithful friend,

WEBER.

You must drive to the 'Golden Angel' here.

55.

To Gänsbacher.

End of Feb. 1824.

I take the deepest interest in your painful position, but I cannot think it so very distressing. The place here is still kept open for you. It certainly cannot be compared with that in Vienna, where you would have an ample salary, here only a moderate one, but still enough to live on, especially if you would put off your marriage for a year, after which period you will certainly get an increase of pay. There are many highly respected official men here, whose income does not exceed from 800 to 1,000 dollars, and yet subsist on that sum. Everything depends on your domestic arrangements and economy; so, dear brother, do not give way to needless despondency. Had it not been for the prospect in Vienna, the situation here would have seemed to you most highly desirable, and you would equally have brought home your bride; so do not complain of Fate that has set before you two such bright prospects, and if the best cannot be had, then rest satisfied with the less lucrative one. Still, I do believe that your appointment in Vienna is secure, and may God grant you His blessing with it. But decide soon, as with the best inclinations, they cannot wait here much longer. I must also give you some comfort by . . . . . .

[*The rest torn off.*]

56.

To Gänsbacher.

Dresden, March 12, 1822.

Dear Brother of my Heart,

A few lines in haste. The church composer Schubert is dead. His situation, with a salary of 1,200 dollars, would in all probability devolve on you if you were here. All the *protégés* of royalty are applying again, unfortunately, though I have contrived to put them off. Our position is really painful to all parties. If you do not come, it is of course important to have a man of talent for my colleague. I therefore beg that, through my friend Schwarz, to whom you must show this letter, you will persuade Seyfried to apply to Herr von Könneritz for Schubert's place here. He is no doubt better paid in Vienna than by these 1,800 G. C. M.; but on the other hand, the salary here is for life, which ought surely to secure us against inferior men. For me the best of all would be your coming; but I pray to God for your sake, that the situation in Vienna may be secured; but make a final decision. Can you not in the above occurrence find good reasons to press forward the other? It is a very trying position. I am urged on by others, so I would fain urge you on in turn, and yet I am still more alarmed, lest you should allow yourself to be hurried into any rash or prejudicial step. Make my excuses to Schwarz, but I am overburdened with work and see no end to it. My friends must be indulgent.

Ever and ever, with faithful love, your

WEBER.

57.

To Gänsbacher.

Dresden, Dec. 29, 1824.

Beloved Brother and Colleague,

In haven at last! ! ! God be praised! who in the end does all things well. My most heartfelt good wishes attend you and your beloved wife. You have everything that can contribute to the happiness of life; an existence free from care, a sphere for work,* a faithful, prudent wife by your side, and loving friends;—now do not fail to prize all these blessings, and to enjoy them with gladness of heart. This is the greatest boon that I can wish for you and yours; for though God has bestowed so many rich bounties on me, beyond what most enjoy, I do not possess a cheerful spirit, to elevate these gifts to pure earthly felicity, and therefore I best know that, without such a boon from the Almighty, you may persuade yourself by force of reason to be happy, but —the heart feels there is something wanting.

* Gänsbacher succeeded after all in getting the situation of Capellmeister in St. Stephan's Church.

I should have liked to send your music by some private opportunity, as the carriage by post is so dear; if you really require it, write to me, and I will send it off at once. I am at this moment in treaty with London, but do not as yet know precisely when I may go there. The opera text which I am to write is not yet come, besides I am so oppressed by the work of my office that since 'Euryanthe,' I have not written a note. Your situation here has been divided, and Marschner and Rastrelli are come. Morlacchi is still ill. The 'Cecilia' is a very distinguished paper, and you will do well if you assist in promoting what is so excellent. I have good will for this, but little time.

My wife expects her confinement in the course of a few weeks. My Max, thank God, is well and merry. I am very delicate and suffering. Your new post cannot fail to exercise the best influence not only on your works, but also on their dissemination, especially as you live in Vienna, where there is such incessant activity and excitement, though at the same time singular enough in its way. Some of your instrumental pieces, among others your divertimento for pianoforte and violin, have been published in London and favourably reviewed.

Herr von Könneritz has been long minister in Madrid, so your letter to him is still in my possession. You had previously returned the letter of credit. I did not receive the letter that Countess Wolkenstein brought me from you till the end of July, in Marienbad, where I took the waters for six weeks, but without any great effect.

Farewell! may you be happy, beloved friend. My Lina sends you and your better half her kind regards, and I am, with the old love and fidelity, ever your

WEBER.

As a conclusion to this touching connection between Weber and Gänsbacher, a letter from their mutual master, the Abbé Vogler, may here be inserted, some interesting letters of his being now before me from the collection of Gänsbacher. The following one is addressed to the well-known Countess Firmian, in Prague.

Hesse Darmstadt, July 10, 1810.

Gracious Lady,

Your Excellency desires to have our Gänsbacher back again, whereas I wish that he could remain with me for a whole year, as I have good grounds for asserting that a genuine academy of music really now exists in this house.

It so happened that Carl v. Weber, whom I formerly taught in Vienna, and who has already put several popular operas on the stage, and is going to conduct one at the next autumn fair at Frankfort, met Meyerbeer here, a composer of great promise, whose grand psalms have been executed by the Singacademie at Berlin, and his ballet music at the royal theatre there, both with great success; he is the pupil of one of my pupils, the Royal Prussian Music Director Bernhard Anselm Weber; a *triad*, and certainly an harmonious *triad*, for they love each other cordially. Well! each produces every day his own composition. I frequently set before each and all a very difficult task; every morning and afternoon we hear and analyse one of my works, or those of some other persons, but always classical composers. I paternally impart to them the fruits of fifty-six years' study; nay, they frequently learn from the man of sixty-two what he did not himself know at sixty-one, because they helped him to discover it. Gänsbacher likewise has the privilege of free entrance into all the court rehearsals. How much, then, do I lament that he is soon to forsake this musical Areopagus!

Not the less, however, does the summons of your Excellency prevail; and, in accordance with your gracious command, he will set off next Monday for Bohemia. With this intelligence I conclude, begging you to offer my devoted respects to His Excellency, your husband, and I have the honour to subscribe myself, with sincere esteem, your obedient

Abbé Vogler,
Hessian Grand Ducal Geheimrath,
and Commander of the Hessian Order of Merit.*

* The signature alone is autograph, and is encompassed with the usual well-known comical flourishes.

58.

To Hans Georg Nägeli, Zürich.

Dresden, June 6, 1825.

Sir,

I acknowledge with all due gratitude your flattering proposal, and also the handsome manner in which you express yourself with regard to me. It, however, appears to me utterly impossible to promise you a pianoforte sonata in the course of this year. My dramatic works entirely absorb my time, and detach me from everything else. Besides, there are difficulties in the way, owing to my failing health and ungenial mood; the latter, no doubt, being the result of the former. I can, therefore, absolutely promise nothing, except my good will to co-operate with you in your new undertaking, as soon as my time, strength, and inclination permit.

It was, at all events, very pleasing to me to hear once more from my talented friend.

C. M. v. WEBER.

59.

To Herr Heinrich Bärmann,
First Clarionet to H. M. the King of Bavaria, Munich.

Bad Ems, Aug. 9, 1825.

My dear Brother,

I received your welcome letter of June 14, in Dresden, at the very moment when the physicians quite unexpectedly decided to send me to Ems: the preparations for such a journey, as well as the long separation from my family, prevented my being able to think of anything else, yet I hoped to be able to write to you in the early days of my stay here. But people at a watering-place are always so much occupied in doing nothing, that no leisure can be found, and I now see, with shame, that your second letter of July 10 has been in my hands since the 24th, and not yet answered. I have been here since July 15, and drink the waters and bathe regularly, without feeling any particular improvement in my throat complaint, although I am on the whole better and stronger. Well! we are told that the best effects of the baths are felt afterwards. God grant it may be so! To give me some pretext to find fault with you, I must reproach you for not replying in detail to my letters. It would have been gratifying to me at least to know that what I had done in Dresden to fulfil Poissl's wish was appreciated, and if not quite to the full extent he desired, still, though less in degree, it was flattering to him. I am quite convinced that, if Poissl does in Munich what I have done, he will arrive sooner at the goal, as with you they are not so singularly punctilious in the distribution of such distinctions. Instead of all this, I hear that I am to have the good fortune to be permitted to send my opera to the directors, and of course at a cheap rate. Heavens! what a happy man is a German composer!

'Euryanthe' is being transcribed. I have some idea of laying it at the feet of your gracious monarch, but I must reflect on this, and first hear your opinion on the subject. Thank Baron v. Poissl warmly in my name for the renewed performance of the 'Freischütz.' Probably his 'Prinzessin von Provence' will be placed on the stage next winter, if the machinery does not prove an obstacle. As I shall only stay here ten or twelve days longer, write to me to Dresden, whence I shall certainly despatch the score of 'Euryanthe' at once. I could also let you have the orchestral parts, but I recollect that your parts are written out in a different manner. If you advise me to send the opera to the King, it might perhaps be more agreeable to Baron Poissl that I should forward it through an ambassador? I don't know what your custom is; the best mode of proceeding with us I have already informed you of. But enough, and more than enough, of my own affairs.

God grant that you and yours may all be well. I gratefully thank your charming wife for her kind wishes, which I fully appreciate. Would to Heaven that I could once more pour out my heart to you. But I have been long accustomed never to consult my own happiness. Farewell! Let me soon hear from you. Remember me to all my friends, and continue to love your old and faithful friend and brother,

C. M. v. WEBER.

One year after this, on July 5, 1826, the great Master died in London, on the same night when his latest opera, 'Oberon,' was performed.*

* He fixed his departure for Dresden on the 6th. He was strongly urged to postpone his journey, but this solicitation only irritated him. 'I must go back to my own,' he sobbed. 'Let me see them once more, then God's will be done.' When, on the evening of the 4th, he sat panting in his easy-chair, with Sir George Smart, Fürstenau, and Moscheles grouped around him, he could only speak of his journey. At 10 o'clock they urged him to retire to bed. But he firmly declined to have any one watch by his bedside, and even to forego his custom of barring his chamber door. When he had given his white, transparent, trembling hand to all, murmuring gently, 'God reward you all for your kind love to me,' he was led by Sir George Smart and Fürstenau into his bedroom. Fürstenau, from whom alone he would accept such services, helped him to undress; the effort was a painful one to himself. With his own hand, however, Weber wound up his watch, with his usual punctilious care; then, with all that charm of amiability for which he was conspicuous through life, he murmured his thanks to his friend and said, 'Now let me sleep.' These were the last words that mortal ear heard the great artist utter. It is clear, however, that Weber must have left his bed later, for the next morning the door through which Fürstenau had passed was bolted. For a long time the friends sat together in Sir George Smart's, room filled with sorrowful presentiments, and earnestly consulting what means might best be taken to prevent the journey. About midnight they went asunder. On their leaving the house, all was dark in Weber's window—his light had been extinguished.

The next morning at the early hour when Weber generally required his aid, Sir George Smart's servant knocked at his chamber door. No answer came; he knocked again, and louder. It was strange, for Weber's sleep had always been light. The alarmed servant rushed to Sir George, who sprang out of bed and hurried to the room. Still, to his repeated knocking, no answer was returned. Fürstenau was sent for. He came, half-dressed and already anticipating the worst. It was now resolved to force the door. It was burst open. All was still within. The watch which the last movement of the great hand which had written 'Freischütz,' 'Euryanthe,' and 'Oberon,' had wound up, alone ticked with painful distinctiveness. The bed-curtains were torn back. There lay the beloved friend and master dead. His head rested on his left hand, as if in tranquil sleep—not the slightest trace of pain or suffering on his noble features. The soul, yearning for the dear objects of its love, had burst its earthly covering and fled. The immortal master was not dead. He had gone home.

It was decided that his funeral rites should take place with pomp in the Roman Catholic Chapel of St. Mary, Moorfields, and that Mozart's 'Requiem' should be performed. The orchestras and choruses of Covent Garden, Drury Lane, and the Philharmonic Society, solicited the honour of being ranked among those employed. Early in the morning of June 21, 1826, the long funeral procession left the house of Sir George Smart, in Great Rutland Street, in all the almost mediæval pomp of such ceremonies at that period. Crowds thronged the streets through which the hearse and a long line of mourning carriages wound their slow and weary way to the far distant chapel of Moorfields. Long before they reached the place of worship, the building, hung with black and blazing with wax-lights, was filled by a crowd of some two thousand persons. As the body was received at the entrance by the priests, the imposing tones of Mozart's splendid 'Requiem' burst out; and over the sleeping form of the great composer were poured forth the strains of the illustrious master he had reverenced and loved. The last notes of the 'Requiem' had melted away to the solemn strains of the 'Dead March in Saul;' the coffin was lowered into the vault; the lights were extinguished one by one; then silence and peace were around the dead, and there, far from home and love, and all that his warm, noble heart most prized in life, rested the body of Carl Maria von Weber. . . . .

Years passed away. But it seemed as if that yearning for home which had been the last feeling in Weber's heart had not died out with the death of his mortal portion. It continued to haunt the hearts of those he had so fondly loved. The time arrived at last. On October 20, 1844, Weber's coffin was landed at Hamburg. There all honour was paid to the remains of the great German master; and amidst the sounds of Beethoven's 'Funeral March,' and the thunder of cannon, with the flags of all the ships of every nation lowered around, the body was transferred to the smaller vessel which was to bear it up the Elbe to Dresden. On December 14, a delay having been occasioned by a sharp frost upon the river, it reached its destination. It was the dusk of evening when the coffin was conveyed through countless masses of human beings, who, in solemn silence, lined the streets from the black draped quay to the Catholic cemetery in Friedrichstadt, and amidst an interminable line of flaming torches, which dimly showed the black banner on which were inscribed the words 'Weber in Dresden.' Yes!

Weber's last wish had been fulfilled, and he was again to be at home. His now only son [the younger son, Alexander v. Weber having died suddenly] and all the musical corps of every institute in Dresden, followed, with an endless mass of friends. In the richly decorated chapel of the cemetery, all the ladies of the theatre, with Mdme. Schröder-Devrient at their head, awaited the body, and covered the coffin with laurels. The ceremony was at an end; the torches were extinguished; the crowds dispersed. But by the light of two candles still burning on the altar, might be seen the form of a middle-aged woman, who had flung herself upon the bier, while a pale young man knelt in prayer by her side. . . .

The following day Weber's body was conveyed to the family vault amidst crowds of spectators, even more numerous than on the day before. A funeral march, which Weber himself had composed in early youth at Breslau, accompanied him to his last resting-place. Richard Wagner and Theodor Kell spoke over his grave. Then amidst a solemn strain, composed expressly for the occasion by Wagner, roses and laurels were thrown into the depths, and now indeed, by the side of his youngest born, Carl Maria von Weber was at last at home. A statue by Rietschel was inaugurated on October 11, 1860. It stands on the open space before the theatre in Dresden.—*Extracts from the Biography of Carl Maria von Weber, by his son, Baron Max Maria von Weber.*

LETTERS

OF

FELIX MENDELSSOHN-BARTHOLDY.

Born 1810; Died November 4, 1847.

1.

*To Nägeli, Zürich.**

About 1826.

Sir,

I have received your esteemed letter of November 17, and I thank you sincerely for your liberal offers and agreeable proposals; above all, I must beg your forgiveness for not having long since replied to you and expressed my gratitude; still, my silence is not entirely without an excuse.

You wish, sir, to have from me a piece for the pianoforte, so I must at once confess that as yet I have never written anything for that instrument alòne; sonatas, with violin or tenor, quartetts, &c., have always had more attractions for me. I do not take into account a few minor pieces that I composed long ago, and which I have brought out on this occasion. I really could not, with a good conscience, publish them now; nor would they be in any degree worthy of the honour that you intended for me. Latterly, however, even before receiving

* From the autograph in the possession of Herr Nägeli, in Zürich. Date about 1826.

your respected letter, it frequently occurred to me that I had hitherto composed nothing for the piano alone, and it was my full intention to do so during my first leisure hours, and then came your kind offer, furnishing an additional impulse soon to apply myself to the work. Never having yet done anything of the kind, and being thus quite strange to me, I perfectly see that it will require some time to make myself at home in it. Your undertaking is on a rather extensive scale, and no doubt the time in which it is to be carried out has been fixed. I beg you will therefore, as soon as possible, let me know how long you can give me to complete the piece of music, and if I can accomplish it within the period, I shall then accept with the greatest pleasure your flattering proposal. Hoping for a speedy answer,

I am, sir, your obedient

FELIX MENDELSSOHN-BARTHOLDY.

2.

To Nägeli, Zürich.

Berlin, July 29, 1827.

Sir,

I must first of all thank you for the pleasure and honour you confer on me by renewing your offer of publishing one of my compositions; and then I have to solicit your kind indulgence for having been far too long silent. But, on the one hand, a number of the most important and somewhat disagreeable duties deterred me from writing; and, on the other, I was unwilling to write to you until I could give you a definitive answer, and so the thing has been delayed, and to-day is the first opportunity I find to send you my reply and my thanks, so long due.

I rejoice exceedingly to hear that my pianoforte sonata meets with your approbation. I would gladly have given you the piece when you some time ago made me the first offer; but you had expressly stipulated that there should be no tenths in it, whereas they occur repeatedly in this work. You also promised me more detailed information about your undertaking; so your silence led me to fear that either your friendly disposition towards myself, or some circumstance connected with your enterprise, had changed your sentiments in my favour. So thus it was that I gave this sonata to Herr Laue.

Now, however, being convinced, to my great joy, that this fear was unfounded, nothing can be more in accordance with my wishes than the renewal of your proposals; and although at this moment I have nothing in the shape of a sonata on paper, I can venture to promise that the sonata shall be sent in about eight weeks, inasmuch as I believe I have ample materials for one. Moreover, neither tenths nor fugues shall occur in it, as these were the conditions for which you previously stipulated, and I have only to beg you to let me know within eight weeks all particulars with reference to the revisal of proofs, the time of publication, &c. &c., so that I may make my arrangements accordingly. In the hope of a favourable answer,

I remain, sir, with esteem, yours,

FELIX MENDELSSOHN-BARTHOLDY.

3.

*To Heinrich Bärmann, Zürich.**

Rome, Feb. 14, 1831.

Dear Bärmann,

Long have I delayed fulfilling my promise to write to you, and indeed you have cause to be rather angry with me on this account; but when daily excited by novel impressions, and the objects around perpetually changing, the superabundance of material renders it quite as difficult to write a proper sensible letter as a dearth of subjects, while remaining in undisturbed quiet in one's old circumstances and neighbourhood; and as I now break silence, pray be good-natured also, and let me hear from you again, for indeed this letter chiefly originates in my wish to hear all about you, and to know how you are, and the tenor of your life and doings. But to describe what I have seen and experienced since we met, a letter is much too short, and in fact it is not easy to do so at all in writing; we might talk it over better

* Herr Carl Bärmann, court musician in Munich, possesses the originals of all the letters here given, except where another collection of autographs is expressly named.

at some future day, and who can tell how soon that may be? For it is a settled and favourite plan of mine to return to Munich for a few weeks this year, and, if all turns out as I hope, perhaps I may pay you a visit again this autumn, make my appearance unexpectedly at the Carlstrasse, eat dumplings, play the A flat major sonata, and then you will say, He drives me distracted! I should much like on this account to have a few words from you, to let me know whether you are to remain at Munich during the summer and autumn, or have any journey in prospect, for I prized the time we lived together there far too much not to wish once more to enjoy it. They were the jolliest days I ever passed, and I have you specially to thank for this, as you well know, and you may imagine how grateful I am to you. Life here is on a splendid scale, richer and more exciting than we can find it elsewhere; but a man like myself, who is after all essentially a musician, longs for music of merit, and none such is to be heard here. There are indeed other things in its stead, that bring beautiful music with them; the most balmy spring breezes, a warm blue sky, everywhere divine pictures, and nature and relics of past ages, more bright and abundant than the imagination can conceive; but just now, even while writing to you, I feel that a musical tone, and a musical friend, are both wanting, and I would give a good deal if we could talk together once more, even for half an hour.

Since I have been in Italy, my own music is all I

ever hear; orchestras and singers are really too miserable. People whom I knew in London as quite second-rate performers, sing the first parts in Venice and in Florence; Mdlle. Carl, of the Berlin theatre, was engaged in Rome as *prima donna* (she, however, was a great failure, so that the contract was annulled), and such persons as Pasta, Malibran, and David, are utterly out of the question, being either in London or in Paris.

It is therefore quite natural that the people themselves take no longer much pleasure here in music, and I might safely declare that nowhere in Rome have I felt so unmusical as at the opera. You must figure to yourself an orchestra like that of the most obscure Bavarian village; to describe it by words is not easy. Among others, there is a first clarionet in the Teatro di Apollo here. Oh! Bärmann, you really ought to hear him; I believe the race of Oerindur, 'the mighty pillars of our throne,'* would topple over, and roll on the ground with laughing. The fellow always starts off with an *appoggiatura*, when the third note sticks fast, and he winds up by a shake produced entirely by the elbow, and the man's tone is such that at the first moment I thought it was a very bad oboe; but then the oboe itself followed in a solo, when I saw it all clearly. The bassoons are exactly like so many combs, and no instrument is in tune except the big drum; every instant some one of them plays out of time, and all of a sudden the kettle-

* A quotation from a play of Raupach.

drums burst forth vigorously into the midst of a tender solo, when the first violinist calls *st! st!* and brings them together again. The double-bass is a formidable fellow, who wears a scarlet cap in the orchestra, and thick moustachios, lies on the watch for the notes, and strikes in, whenever by good luck he can descry a good-sized one. Thus all goes on 'with fire and precision,' as our critics say.

No symphony has ever been played in Rome. But their pride is that some years ago Haydn's 'Creation' was given here, and they declare that the orchestra managed to get through the affair very tolerably, for that such frightfully difficult music could be really well executed must be impossible even in Germany, where this learned style is understood. I then put on a face like that of St. Nepomuk, reminding myself that I am in the fatherland of music, where everything is to be found, except musicians; so I take refuge as much as possible with the young ladies, who talk very little about art, and are all the prettier for it. I must not forget to mention that the trumpeters, one and all, blow away at those infernal keyed trumpets, which always seem to me like a pretty woman with a beard; they are also without the chromatic tones, and sound shrill and unnatural. But variations are executed on them here. Now pray don't show this page to Stunz, or he will kill me as dead as a rat when I go back to Munich: besides, I am only speaking of Rome; elsewhere it may be different. When I, however, tell you that in spite of all this I lead a famous life here, and that the winter I have passed seems to have flown like moments, and that I enjoy the gayest and happiest time, you will possibly think that I have become a renegade to good music. We pass our time thus:—Every morning early I compose in my own room and work hard, that I may be able to show you something new when I return; so this is a great pleasure, and suffices me. Then I go out at twelve o'clock to look at Rome, some gallery, or ruins, or scenery, which is again a great pleasure. In the evening I always go into society—in fact, more than ever, and have seen a mass of people of different nations and lands, a gay assemblage, and not to be despised; to which I may add the mild air of spring, that makes one totally forget winter, and this is cheering in itself; and now I no longer heat my stove, but sit at the open window. The almond-trees are all in full bloom, the shrubs are coming into leaf, and already we seek the shade, which in the month of February is pleasant enough. A few days ago the mad Carnival commenced, when everyone runs about all day long in the open air. The most grotesque masks swarm on every side. The Italian ladies are in all their splendour, the crowd bombarding each other with sugar-plums like mad. This childish sport is everywhere vehemently carried on, and it is impossible to resist joining in it. The ladies have nosegays, roses, and violets thrown into their carriages, and in return shower down bonbons and sugar-almonds. You lie in ambush watching for an acquaintance, the men so covered with white dust that they look like millers, while intrigues and chaff are in full swing. Unluckily, we were cheated of the three last days, when the extravagance is at its height; for yesterday, on reaching the Corso, laden with sugar-plums, the place was black with crowds of men—no ladies, no masks to be seen; and at last I discovered in a corner an edict from the Pope, setting forth that the Carnival was at an end, owing to certain painful occurrences. It was pretended that a revolution had been discovered; and soldiers were posted in every street with loaded fire-arms, and in the evening some shots were heard, a few people arrested, and one severely wounded. Thus the merry game was changed into sad earnest; and though Lent does not begin till the day after to-morrow, the streets are quiet, and just as usual. But now, *basta*. Heaven knows you must be preciously tired of this letter. If it only induces you to give me an answer, its object will be accomplished, and you promised faithfully to reply to me at once—pray, pray, then, do so. One more request. I wrote a few lines from hence to Count Pocci,* in answer to a letter from him As,

* Intendant, until the last few years, of the Royal Bavarian Court Music, at present Royal Bavarian *Oberceremonienmeister*; well known as a zealous friend of music, and as having published various musical compositions.

however, scarcely any letter that I put in the post myself there seems to have reached its destination, I being deemed a dangerous spy, writing in cypher, on account of my written music, I should like to know whether he received my letter; therefore I beg, if it does not give you too much trouble, that you will enquire about this, and write to me about it. And how is Mdme. Vespermann? [the singer] I beg you will give her my kind regards. Let me hear of all my acquaintances and friends, and whether everything looks about the same as when I left Munich. You know how much every topic there interests me; but above all, tell me of you and yours; whether Carl and Heinrich [the sons] make satisfactory progress, and sometimes remember me. Give my heartfelt good wishes to all your family, particularly to your charming wife, and that I commend myself to your own friendly remembrance is a matter of course.

Farewell! may you all continue well and happy.

Your

F. MENDELSSOHN-BARTHOLDY.

P.S.—My address is, 'A M. F. M. B., Rome, Piazza di Spagna, No. 5.'

4.

*To H. Bärmann.**

Milan, July 9, 1831.

Dear Bärmann,

This is no letter, but a lecture that I mean, not to write, but to read you. Most faithless of men! not one line in answer to my charming letter of eight pages (exaggeration!). I had firmly resolved never to write to you again in the course of my life, as a punishment; but this evening it somehow all of a sudden struck me that I punish you far more by writing; hence I do so at once. But it is really the last letter I mean to write unless you answer me forthwith; and that you may not be able to do so, I take care not to send you my address. Your sins are crying out like an F clarionet or an increased seventh, the race of Oerindur is an unpunctual race, and does not reply to the race of Mendelssohn, when they write; nature resolves to put an end to this; it is bad, it is base, it is excruciating!

I have the honour to announce to you by these present lines—not my marriage by any means, nor yet the baptism of my youngest son, nor, further, that I continue to carry on the wine and ale-house of my deceased wife under the same firm, but what makes me happier than all these put together, namely, that, God willing, I shall

* The autographs of the next two letters are in the possession of Herr Röth, in Augsburg.

soon be in Munich again. In the course of six or seven weeks, I beg that your charming wife will buy up all the plums in Bavaria for dumplings, to be cooked for me, and then you shall see whether I have not learned something in Italy. But, seriously, I expect to arrive in the Carlstrasse the beginning of September, or about the middle of the month at latest, and rejoice already at the thoughts of it, for that you will be as kind and as friendly to me as on a former occasion, I feel well assured of—I know Heinrich Bärmann. I come to Munich prompted by the wish, before plunging into the mad wild life of Paris, once more to be with people whom I love, and with whom I can pass a few happy weeks, and because I long once more to have a downright good practice, and to hear music *con amore*, which I have not done since I have been in Italy, for at present no musician exists in this land, and I should like again to be renovated by something sound and solid. I mean to play to you as long, and as much of Weber as I can, or as you choose; but you must also bring out your clarionet, that we may take something in hand together, and then I must again hear the piece in E flat major and the F minor concerto [Weber], and even at this moment I am as happy as a child in thinking of it, for in my life I never did hear more beautiful tones than yours, old fellow! I do not forget that afternoon at Staudacher's when you played the concerto. I have never since been able to have such music—and this is why I come to you, so welcome me kindly.

I am going to remain here for a short time to finish a whimsical composition which I began in Rome, and one day I intend to play it and sing it to you (are you dismayed?). In the course of ten or twelve days, I set off for the lakes, to Como and to the Borromean Islands, then by the Simplon to Geneva, whence I cut across Switzerland in a straight line, and go on direct to Munich till I arrive there. Who the first man will be that I seek out, we both pretty well know, and if you don't know, you will find it out one day. But it is only vexatious to set one's heart too long beforehand on anything; there are far too many troubles afloat in the world, raging and threatening, and who can tell whether in the course of a few months all may not be changed and overthrown? God forbid! I trust the world will last yet a while, and if war and pestilence do not assail us at too close quarters, I shall be with you in September. Be sure you have Carl's piano thoroughly tuned. How is he? and what of the Basset horn? and how about Heinrich's painting? But it is stupid in me to ask these questions, for I intend to come myself for the answers, which is far better. Otherwise there are many persons whom I should have liked to ask for: the fat Moralt and Mdme. Vespermann, Mangotti and the Müllers, Von der Mark and Delphine von

Schauroth, Staudacher and Fräule in Keias, Ascher, half the orchestra, and the Himsel family. All this I shall be told when we meet. The sketch I took of you at the baths is now lying before me, your name written in one of the folds of your blouse; it is wonderfully like, my master hand is visible in it; you look particularly sweet. Do not take it amiss that I am writing you nothing worth hearing, for I reserve everything till we meet, and indeed I have abundance to relate. Give my best regards to your dear wife and sons, and to Mdme. Vespermann, if she is again in Munich, and has not allowed herself to be detained in Paris. Remember me also to the handsome Müllers (the dark one is by far the prettiest), and to Stunz and his wife, to Hector and the Staudachers. Place my homage at Poissl's feet, and greet Mangotti from me; in short, remember me to all at Munich, and one besides. My compliments also to your B clarionet, an excellent creature, and one that I highly respect. All the clarionet players I heard in Italy must have been born with a wooden leg, one always feels inclined to throw them something into the orchestra; it all sounds so feeble and miserable; but for Heaven's sake don't say this to a soul in Munich, or they might stone me. Germans can play a vast deal better, but it won't do to tell the Germans so, for they would take it amiss. May we soon meet, dear Bärmann. Think of me kindly.

By the bye, I quite forgot to tell you a most amusing

and interesting story. One day when, according to my custom for some time past [breaks off, see No. 6].

Perhaps you may no longer remember my name?

FELIX MENDELSSOHN-BARTHOLDY.

5.

To Intendant von Poissl.

Munich, Nov. 4, 1831.

Most respected Baron,

Permit me to express my sincere gratitude for your commission to write a new opera for this stage. I accept it with the greatest delight, and it is doubly welcome to work for a theatre producing so much that is admirable, and for a city where I have been received with so much kindness. I need scarcely add, that I willingly agree to all the stipulations you make, inasmuch as everything is set forth and included that I could possibly desire; so all I have to do is to promise on my side to occupy myself at once in finding a libretto, and then I will punctually execute in every point your commission. Before beginning the composition, I will not fail to apprise you of the subject and the poem, and I hope this may be soon.

Allow me once more to express my gratitude for all the courtesy I have experienced from you, and accept the high consideration of your devoted

FELIX MENDELSSOHN-BARTHOLDY.

6.

Paris.

. . . And now, to tell you the story at full length. The clarionet players here are in a miserable condition, so that in the orchestra of the Conservatoire, which is in most respects really admirable, there are two clarionets, neither of them fit to dust your coat, if tone, execution, mode of playing, and ordinary fairness still go for anything in this world. The first one recently, in the minuet of the Pastoral Symphony, commenced his solo a bar too soon, but went on puffing away as merrily as possible, never observing that it sounded quite infamous, and that some of the audience, and among others the undersigned, were making dreadful wry faces, and that the director had got stomach-ache ; the horn ought then to have come in, but took fright, and did not come in, on which the violins took fright also and played softer and softer, on which the thing every moment became more like a Dutch concert, for they were all out, and only a movement in $\frac{2}{4}$ time being close at hand, saved them from the disgrace of stopping short, and beginning all over again. So, as I was going home, it was but natural that I should think over the affair, and exclaim to myself 'This is beyond bearing,' and instantly resolve to write to you, and tell you all about it, and ask if you can look on quietly while the Parisian clarionet world is going on in such a shabby fashion. For this fellow is a professor in the Conservatoire, and I understand the best here. I believe his name is Dacosta. Seriously, however, do you really feel no inclination to found a clarionet seminary here? I think it would be a very good plan, and sure to succeed; besides, you had already a project to go to Paris, so I most strongly advise you to do so, for they have not the most remote idea of your instrument, and therefore would doubly appreciate it; it would also be a capital thing, in my opinion, if you were to bring one of your pupils with you, for instance, your son Carl, for I am convinced that he could easily find a good and respectable livelihood here. This is, of course, merely a suggestion, but I wish you would reflect on it. Besides, you told me to look round, and to write to you if I could find anything for Carl, and I do so now, as this seems to me a good opportunity. I hinted something of the kind last autumn to Leitrum, and said you wished to get an appointment for your son; he seemed much taken with his playing, and praised him highly, but I don't know whether anything resulted from it, as the orchestra appeared to be already complete. I saw a good deal of Lindpaintner during those few days, and felt a great liking for him. You are right in what you say of him, he is certainly very devoted to you, and if you had only accompanied me on that journey, it would indeed have been famous. At all events, I hope to return thither once more to enjoy with might and main music, flirting, and merry pranks, but then we must go there together. And now I will begin my letter.

Paris, April 16, 1832.

Dear old Bärmann and Friend,

The above is the continuation of the story I began in Rome [see No. 5], and Dohrn, who came in at the moment, wishing to put in something of his own, wrote the postscript. How long it is since I heard from you! But I must first of all apologise for not having written to you for such a time. Do not take it amiss, my dear fellow, for it was impossible. I was as sulky as a porpoise, and felt as miserable during the whole winter as a fish on dry land. There was always something amiss with me, and at length I became positively ill, and was obliged to stay in bed, and submit to have my stomach rubbed by an old woman, to have warm cloths applied, to perspire a great deal, eat nothing, and undergo a great many visits and much compassion, wishing everyone at the devil, swallowing peppermint pills, and bored to death; at last, by dint of constant perspirations, my bad humour and my stomach-ache were driven away, and likewise the dreaded cholera. Now that I have done with perspirations, I feel for the first time for many months light and cheerful, and so I write to you forthwith, you capital clarionet *bear* and *man*! At times (for instance now), I would give the whole of Paris to be able to hear even for a minute that sweet world of magic tones of every grade that stream from your wooden instrument so light and bright, so mellow and low, flowing and glowing, clear and dear, pure and sure, clinging and singing so sweetly. But without any compliments, the truth is that I am as glad as a *Spitz* at the thoughts of seeing you again. I have passed a very dull winter, what with illness and the stupidity of the circles here. Devil take them all! I never felt quite right, either as regards myself or others. Still I composed many new pieces, and am now publishing a whole pile of new music in Leipzig, designed to make a great man of me. Probably you will never hear any of it, and my fame will remain *incognito.* I have heard some of my things performed in public here, and played myself several times. The Parisians applauded and extolled me, and some of the musicians looked very savage at me when it was over, so I have certainly made effect! For some weeks past, however, everything has come to an end, for cholera has been raging fearfully here, and the people no longer think of music but of cholic. Whoever could get away, went away, and the rest do not now go out in the evening, and if I had not been forced to stay, and have my stomach rubbed by an old woman, I would have been off long ago myself. I hope to get away in a few days to London. There the cholera is quite gone; besides, all here agree that it can be cured, if the very moment you feel unwell you instantly stay at home, keep yourself warm, and are careful. Now remember, in case it attacks you (which I don't now fear), keep yourself warm, and treat the first symptoms of diarrhœa with respect, and then you will take no harm. After many pros and cons, Dohrn is reconciled to his family, lives a jolly life, is to become a merchant, and goes to England in the spring to learn his business. He sends you all his regards. Schätzler and Rost* were here, and also the Kerstorfs: is it really true that Fritz Kerstorf killed a man in a duel and has been obliged to fly?—they say so here. I have now a request to make, and if you love me, comply with it at once, and do it punctually, as it is of great moment to me; go immediately to Poissl, and beg him to send me to London forthwith an answer to the letter I wrote to him some months ago [see No. 5]. If he will not or cannot write himself, then ask him about it, and let me know by return of post. My address is 'Care of Messrs. Doxal & Co., London.' I wrote him about my libretto, and have not had a single line in reply. Now pray attend to this, and write at once. Perhaps you could enquire at my former lodgings, and find out what my pretty Therese is doing, and whether, after my departure from Schauroth's, she got the things she had left behind. If you can let me hear something about her, that would be famous. Now do this, and be so good as to write, for I shall anxiously expect your letter.

* A head with a very large thick dripping nose is sketched here.

My cordial regards to your wife and children, and to all who may still kindly remember me. Your

FELIX MENDELSSOHN-BARTHOLDY.

. . . .

derful how a little page is spotted by sundry Spanish flies, one of which is evidently afflicted with a sore throat. But Father Beer, after having rallied from the first shock, and once more shut his mouth, calls his family about him, and, opening his benevolent goose's bill, exclaims: 'Children! at last there are tidings of Felix!' At the first moment of surprise, the gallant son and heir blows off the mouthpiece of his Basset horn, the volume of Schiller's poems drops from the worthy mother's hands, and from the daughter's finger falls her thimble (*Digitalis purpurea*, Linn.). What can be more natural than that everybody should at least have four naps in three successive midnights, even if the text were the veriest trumpery and trash, and he who writes programmes for Reibel must either have nothing in the world else to do, or be a Royal Bavarian Chamber Musician, like myself, who am the same as I always am and always shall be.

H. DOHRN.

7.

To Bärmann.

My adored Heinrich,*

I can no longer guard my secret; indeed you must long ago have guessed it by my eyes, by the disquiet that assails me the moment you enter the room, by my whole demeanour. Away then, oh! virgin timidity, and may love alone guide my goose-quill! for, ah! I love you but too dearly! My father would be furious were he to know, for he destines the Crown Prince of Buxtehude to be my husband! but what matters a Crown Prince to a heart touched by love? Ever since hearing the dulcet tones proceeding from your mouth (I mean when you play the clarionet), since then, I say, I think of you alone. I must speak to you, and secretly too, in some retired spot; meet me then to-morrow at two o'clock at the Scheidel Coffee-house,† where your Isabella is to dine. There we shall be private, and may continue private, and that will be very charming.

The whim seized me to set to music my passion for you, and thus to elude the vigilance of my governess; so the chief master of ceremonies and head cook, Felix Mendelssohn-Bartholdy, has written the enclosed page for you.

* Outside is written, 'To Herr Heinrich Bärmann, first clarionet, private,' and a post-mark sketched with the word *Trapezunt*. The whole letter is written in the feigned hand of a lady.

† A frequented coffee-house in the Kaufinger Strasse in Munich.

Ah! how my heart palpitates! Forgive so many blots; they are tears that have dropped on the paper while writing.

To eternity I am and ever shall be your affectionately devoted

ISABELLA, PRINCESS OF TRAPEZUNT.

P.S.—I wear a cholera bandage at present; do so likewise for love of me.

8.

To Bärmann.

Berlin, Sept. 5, 1832.

Good evening, old Bärmann!

Now you ought to ask me where I have been for so long, and I ought to tell you that I have been so long away from you because I was obliged to go to London, and then to come on here, 'and so we live merrily on.' But properly I should first have thanked you for your pleasant, kind, circumstantial letter; it contained some rare nonsensical stuff, and had quite the flavour of some of our former expeditions. Pray don't take amiss my subsequent silence. I really had no time whatever for writing, and indeed I have none at this moment, but being this evening in my old Berlin room, where I have been pacing up and down feeling rather unwell, our jolly South German days suddenly recurred to my mind; o I must write to you, and ask how you are getting on, and beg you to send me a few lines. If you knew the pleasure it would give me, you would do so at once. Now pray, old fellow, let me hear from you, for I do long to know what you are about, and the whole of pretty Munich likewise. Would I were only there once more! then our happy days should be renewed. At present things look somewhat gloomy around me, and I have had rather a dismal disagreeable time of it! You already know that I had an attack of cholera in Paris that very much weakened me. Since then I continue to suffer from my stomach and nerves, and no day do I feel quite well or cheerful; moreover, I have lost a great many of my nearest relations and friends; I heard of the last death only a fortnight ago, and all this has made me feel much depressed: a few gay and cheering words from you, therefore, would be doubly welcome, so you will write, I feel sure, knowing how I long to hear from you. No doubt you continue to live as tranquilly and comfortably as when I was with you. You write that there was a great deal of music at the Kerstorfs, but this is, of course, all at an end now: I little thought, when I saw the old gentleman in Paris, that he would so soon be taken from us. It is a terrible loss to his family; I really believe he had the best disposition of them all; but I trust, with this exception, there is no other void in the circle of my acquaintances. Is your wife's indisposition quite gone? You do not say what her ailment was. I rejoice much to hear that your son Carl is now an actual though not a titular Chamber Musician; no doubt he will get on well in the world—'like father, like son.' The father, however, plays on the clarionet in a . . . . Here I omit a great many encomiums that might have made you, as well as your son, very conceited and inflated, whereas in your case nothing ought to be inflated but your cheeks in a *forte*.

I could not get your article into the French papers, not being acquainted with any of the editors, and I am at daggers drawn with their chief authority, Fetis; we do indeed hate each other heartily. Now, as he edits the only musical paper in Paris, and the others do not accept articles of the kind, I have translated it into English, and sent it to an editor in London, whom I know pretty well (Mr. Ayrton, of the 'Harmonium'), and hope it may have the result you wish. But I fear that in England the proposal will not meet with the sympathy you expect, for there, as you are aware, they cling very much to things as they are, and are shy of any novelty, and for this reason their clarionet player, M. Willmann, is all in all to them. Do you not think it would be wise to insert it in the papers here? Although I do not myself know the people, I could at all events manage to have it put in with some introductory words of commendation. They owe this indeed to themselves, for in Berlin every votary of the clarionet knows you; so I think far greater success might be looked for here. Write to me, then, whether I am to take any steps in the matter, and should you wish me to do so, send me a copy of your article, as I have left the former one in England. Tell me, too, a great deal about my pretty Munich girls: indisposed and out of sorts as I am to-day, and in spite of all the terribly cross looks I cast on my paper, I become somewhat more cheerful by even thinking of them. I should have liked much to see Therese in the black dress, her graceful figure must have looked charming in it; when you see her, give her many greetings from me, and if you don't see her, go on purpose to see her, and take them to her: you must pass her house every morning, whether or no. It would have been a pleasure to hear Delphine [von Schauroth] play; but no doubt the whole family are highly offended with me, for I have not been able to send a single letter. I began to write to her in Paris, finished the letter in London, and put it in the post, when, two days afterwards, it was returned to me because the postage, it appeared, was not properly paid. Since then I have made no further attempts. No doubt they will be very angry, but I have been all along in the worst possible humour for writing, as you will perceive by this letter, which is good for nothing, but if it brings an answer from you, it will be good enough. Farewell! I am as surly as an old tom cat; I should like the whole world to be hanged. But in spite of my miseries, give my love to all pretty girls, among whom

I include Margotti, Staudacher, Stunz, Poissl (Senior and Junior), Ascher, Schülein, Horn, &c.; also to all dear friends and worthy men, among whom I include Mdme. Vespermann, the Demoiselles Müller, Mdme. Haydn, Delphine, and Therese. Remember me to Legrand, and the whole Himsel family; don't on any account remember me to Chelard, but to your dear wife and sons instead, twice as often at least as they care to hear it. And now forgive this stupid letter, but answer it; so adieu! may you be well and happy, and wish for me that my cross mood may go far, far away! I do wish I were in Munich, but I cannot get off from here during the winter. Then, however, comes spring, and I to you, I hope. Farewell!

Yours,

FELIX MENDELSSOHN-BARTHOLDY.

9.*

To H. Bärmann.

Berlin, Jan. 19, 1833.

Dear Bärmann,

I herewith send you the duet you bespoke. 'None but a rogue will pretend to give more than he has.' The title is:—

* From the autograph in the Royal State Library in Munich. Date 1833.

GRAND DUO

COMMANDÉ PAR M. BÄRMANN,

COMPOSÉ SUR UN THÈME FAVORI DE M. BÄRMANN,

POUR MADAME BÄRMANN,

PAR

F. MENDELSSOHN-BARTHOLDY, ENTRE AUTRES,

for it might just as well be by any other indifferent composer. At all events, do with it what you choose; if you cannot make use of it, throw it into the fire, and if you can make use of it, alter it to suit your son, strike out and put in what you please, and make something good out of it, which means change it altogether. The following are my intentions: see the first movement, of which your theme forms the subject; my fancy painted to me Herr Stern, after you had won all his money at whist, and he had flown into a passion (you will soon see him, give him my compliments); in the adagio, I wished to give you a retrospect of our last dinner at Heinrich Beer's, where I was obliged to compose it. The clarionet depicts my ardent yearnings, while the tremor of the Basset horn represents the grumbling of my stomach. The last movement is purposely kept cold, because you are going to Russia, where the temperature is supposed to be ditto. May Heaven protect you by furs! I do not send the piece for your son to-day for several reasons, the first being that it is not yet begun, and therefore is not yet finished; but I will set to work at it early to-morrow. I beg you will write me a few words from Königsberg, to let me know your travelling route and your address, that, if necessary, I may forward the piece to you; for even if it were now ready, I should have to send it by the *diligence*, as it must be arranged with orchestral parts, which would cost heavy postage; besides, it would not reach you now. So write me everything minutely. At all events, I will do it as quickly as I can. Since I wrote to you, nothing new has occurred here; in the political horizon alone we have an interesting novelty. Madame Beer has sent me a large sweet cake, and when I eat a piece of it, I always think of you, as it is so good that I should like you to taste it. How does Königsberg look? *Kingly*, and *hilly*? Pray why did you so carefully conceal from me that you have such a pretty niece? If I had not gone to take leave of you, I should not know it now. I was yesterday evening with Hühnel, who asked so much about you, and had so much to say about your amiability, that I could have wished you in the land where pepper grows, were you not luckily bound for the land where russia-leather grows. God forgive this miserable attempt at wit, but I really don't know what more to write to fill up the page.

I enclose a letter for my Russian pianist [Kohlreif], who is a capital fellow. Ask David, in Dorpat, where he lives, for I don't know. And now a kind farewell to both, and may God send His blessing on your cold journey, and may it be attended with success and good fortune. We shall, I hope, meet in Munich next autumn, at the time of the October festival, and other jovial doings.

Yours,

FELIX MENDELSSOHN-BARTHOLDY.

10.

Berlin, Jan. 19, 1833.

Dear Kohlreif,

A favourable opportunity offers to recall myself to your recollection, and to convey to you my good wishes. I beg to make you acquainted with a very dear friend of mine, the celebrated clarionet-player Bärmann, of Munich, and I hope that you will receive him with all possible kindness. He is one of the best musicians I know; one of the few who carry everyone along with them, and who feel the true life and fire of music, and to whom music has become speech. And as I feel quite certain that his playing will enchant you, as much as it enchants me, and that it will be also a pleasure to you to become acquainted with such an amiable and kind-hearted man, I give him this letter to you, though I don't know how to address it. I hope it may reach you, and that you will make a great deal of music together, for he too must hear you play much and often.

It would be very kind to write to me direct, but

only till April, when I leave Berlin to wander about. I have heard the most contradictory details of you and of your life and doings. You have, however, only yourself to blame for this, if you still like hoaxing people as you formerly did; but in those days you usually undeceived them yourself: so let me know soon whether you are now a preacher, a pianist, a Capellmeister, or dead, for I have been told all these things concerning you.

No doubt there may be a variety of contradictory reports about me also, but Bärmann can tell you far better verbally than I can in writing, how I have been living, how I am actually living, and what I propose doing. Now once more let me commend him specially to you. Farewell! Is there any chance of your coming to Germany? I hope so, for then we may meet again, as it is scarcely probable that I shall ever go to Russia. My family send their best regards. Once more adieu.

Yours,

FELIX MENDELSSOHN-BARTHOLDY.

11.

*To Baroness Pereira, Vienna.**

Düsseldorf, March 17, 1834.

My dear Cousin,

Were you aware that you had a correspondent in Düsseldorf? one too who would gladly write to you

* From the autograph album of Fräulein Marie Countess Brunswick, in Marton-Vasar, in Hungary.

often if he were not a mighty man of business, directing, composing, playing, &c., through thick and thin, till quite late at night. After all, you may think me very indiscreet in recalling myself to you by writing. In the letter of introduction to Hofrath Chervais you declared that I was a little rogue; I answered you poorly enough, and after that set off on my travels again, became altogether dumb, and now I am a finished *Cartouche* or a *Käsebier.* But that would be a bad compliment to your knowledge of mankind; on the contrary, you well know how often I think of you, and how gladly I would write to you, if indeed I could write at all properly. I have now quite forgotten how to do this; but it suddenly occurs to me to ask you to-day where you intend to pass your summer, spring, and autumn, for I should so much like once more to pay you a short visit, were it at all practicable. Vienna, to be sure, is too far east for me, and being a *Kaiserstadt*, and very musical, I should be obliged to do something else there than talk to you all day long, though that is my chief object; or if you are going to make a tour, and I knew of it beforehand, and could possibly arrange it, I would join you, and try not to miss you, as I did in Ischl, and we might then pass a few pleasant days together. Will you then give me an answer? Pray do, for I think few of your correspondents would be so much pleased as the one in

Düsseldorf. It is very long now since I have heard anything direct from my Vienna friends. My mother from time to time writes to me that you are well, and have written to her, but says little more; besides, you can describe all that is going on and your own life so famously, that while reading one of your letters, one seems to be living for the time with you. If you once more give me this pleasure, pray answer my question, and add a few words. I could also tell you a vast variety of things since I last wrote, but I could not bring them before you so graphically, and then you would be bored; still this I may say, that my life here is most agreeable, and that I am contented and in good train for work. Should I ever succeed in writing something entirely to my own mind (it need not give pleasure to anyone else), then I shall be able once more to write a becoming sensible letter, and gladly tell you about myself; but as yet I am much dissatisfied, and should like to try to write better, for my works often please others better than myself. The more I work, the more this will pass away, and the reason I have so little spare time is that I make so much use of it. Does it at all interest you to hear anything of our school of painting or our theatrical union? Although there is a good deal to remind one of the *Deutsche Kleinstädte* [petty German towns], yet many things are not to be despised. If you will only say so, I will then write away at a fine rate. But you perceive that I am rather alarmed, and first of all wish to know if you mean to receive me into your good graces?

The last time I heard directly of you was through Katherine's very welcome letter. Farewell! may you be happy.

Yours,

FELIX MENDELSSOHN-BARTHOLDY.

12.

To Bärmann.

Düsseldorf, July 7, 1834.

My dear Friend Bärmann,

Do you still know the man who writes this letter and writes music, and would gladly be in Munich, and loves you with his whole heart, and is of the same name as myself? It is indeed nearly a year since I have written to you, but I have thought of you daily. Since then you have been in ice and snow with Emperors and Empresses, have pocketed roubles, and preached the gospel of the clarionet to the heathen. I don't grudge it to them at all, but I wish I too could have been there to hear you. Twice, however, I thought of you so vividly that I seriously contemplated a journey to Munich, and if some favourable circumstances combine, I still intend to go there this autumn, or if not, certainly next summer. Heavens! what music we shall play together (although no doubt you will not care, and will make me play alone), and how I delight in the thought of besieging you all day long! The first time this project occurred to me was last year in Coblentz, when I was calling on a king's counsel, who said he had been in Munich. I asked if he had heard you. He said no, but he had seen you, and that during the whole opera you were leaning in an attitude against one of the pillars in the gallery, looking very merry, and smiling whenever there was a hitch. Then I thought, why had I not been standing beside you and laughing with you, &c.

But the second time was still worse. The devil prompted a clarionet player here to play Weber's F minor concerto in public, I having previously told everyone that now they would hear the most wondrously beautiful piece, and all were eagerly looking forward to it, when he scrambled and puffed through the whole thing till I was in an agony, and the people said, 'Ha! a very queer composition;' and I thought, 'If only the *Bärvater* could be here for half an hour, and place that reed of his in his lips!' I often thought too about the solo I was to write for the Basset horn—it was to have been in C major—but I do not even know whether 'little' Carl can or will make use of it now, or if it was only to serve for your journey. I therefore beg he will send me a few lines on this subject, for as he told me in his last letter that I should certainly be detained at the gates if I came to Munich without a new duet and the solo, and as I am anxious at least to get as far as the Carlstrasse, I mean to be guided accordingly. His letters were most quaint and diverting, and often for days brought back my cheerful spirit [Frohsinn], in which mood you no doubt are when you receive this letter, and are drinking beer in Frohsinn [name also of a tavern in Munich], so you may as well despatch me another epistle, and let me know at once how you all are, how things are going on at Munich, what music you are having there, what is given at the theatre, and further—about all my acquaintances; further—about dumplings—whether Carl still tunes his piano, whether he has heard anything more of Stern or of Prince Wallerstein, or of Mark—but really and truly about all Munich. Dohrn passed through here recently; he is going to America, and was a long time in Sweden and Norway, but he is just the same as he was at the Neckarschwaige. We talked over old times, and drank your health repeatedly in Rhine wine: if your ears tingled half as much as our glasses, you must know this already. Stern's whist parties, too, and the programme of my fête, and Zacharias von Poissl, who is now starring (for Heaven's sake, tell me what has happened; why did he resolve to become a singer?), and the swimming-baths, and your little dog—everything, in short, connected with those days was discussed. Pray what did you think of my being a fixture here for two years? You were furious, no doubt, being quite determined that I should travel about a few years longer;

but you must know that each year I stay here I have three clear months for travel, and even more if I choose, and capital time to work quietly for my own benefit, which I now turn to right good account. Besides, I have only to direct the concerts (six yearly), and the opera *en gros* is under my 'circumspect management' (which gives me practice in that also); but above all (and this is the chief point), I have the forenoons free till one o'clock, and my three months' leave besides: what can any man wish for more? I believe this is the first letter I have written for forty years not in answer to another. Give me very great credit for this, but above all, by every Grecian sage! by every music page! (an oath quite as lofty in the eyes of a clarionet player) and by the golden age! answer; and answer what follows.

Give me the whole account of your journey from Petersburg; how you found Munich and your belongings, and whether your son's playing is perfected, and he is contented with his situation. What did you say to Delphine's [von Schauroth] marriage? and what did I say to it? I said *Donnerwetter*! Is she still in Munich? Has her mother ever married again, or her sister? What is Madame Vespermann about? Give her my kind regards, and say that I hope she is well. Much love to the Müllers; remember me to Stunz (does he still wear a tuft on his chin?) and Josephine Lang [a singer], and pretty Therese, at my former lodgings, and Count Pocci, Horn and the Staudachers, and old Pappenheim; *à propos*, is the tenor Hoppe with you? and has he been singing? Write me your opinion of him; I should like to know how he has turned out, for some years ago he showed much promise. Greet old Poissl from me. Where is Ascher now? still in Greece? And Eichthal? also there? Be sure to answer all this punctually, or tell Carl to do so, and sign your name, adding a short postscript; above all, give my best love to all belonging to you.

Yours,

F. M.-BARTHOLDY.

13.

To Bärmann.

Berlin, Sept. 27, 1834.

Dear Bärmann,

I leave this the day after to-morrow, and go straight back to Düsseldorf, but I must write to you again, however hurriedly, to thank you warmly for your kind letter. So you tried to console my fair friends? Oh, traitor! you could certainly do so better than anyone; and at length the consoler made them no doubt quite forget that they were inconsolable; and thus I served as a convenient screen to shelter you, &c. &c. Pray look at the biography that I send you *sous bande*, and which is very nice. In it I read: 'He knows the loftiness of humanity, he knows what earthly happiness is better than any man.' Now pray what is the meaning of this 'loftiness,' and 'earthly happiness,' and all that kind of thing? Surely not merely princes and gold boxes? We know better. I wish, though, that I had been in Munich to listen to you. Who can tell when I may again see the Carlstrasse? but that I daily wish myself there you well know. It is famous that I am so soon to see you in Düsseldorf; in December, you say? If it really does not suit you to lodge with me, you shall find comfortable rooms when you arrive, either in an hotel or elsewhere, as you please; but believe me when I say that your staying with me would not put me to the slightest inconvenience; so if this notion weighs with you, dismiss it at once, and pitch your tent with me. But just as you like best. I will make every necessary arrangement for a concert in Düsseldorf, and as I am now going through Cologne, I will concert measures with some of my musical friends there, and the authorities, with whom I am acquainted, that you may find all in readiness when you come; I should be glad therefore to know as soon as possible if you will positively be there in December, and in what part of that month? I beg likewise that you will write to me a fortnight before you set out, fixing the day for your concert in Cologne, that it may be properly advertised. Is Carl to be with you, or do you travel alone? If I can find time, I might even be able to go with you to the Hague for a few days, having received many invitations from thence, and once more to play with you in public would indeed be jolly. But all this slumbers as yet in the lap of time, and can only take place if Fate wills it, and your reed wills it, and the theatrical intendancy of the Stadttheater at Düsseldorf wills it, which gives me more work to do than is fair; but more of this when we meet. I like your biography very much; it seems truthful and accurate, and what pleases me most of all is, that there is neither exaggeration nor bombast in it; on the contrary, its tone is that of genuine sympathy and appreciation of your music and yourself. Some of the passages made my mouth water for the sounds of a good clarionet. Here, where I have been several times at the opera, they puff away at the clarionet as if it were mere wood; a sort of pea-shooter, for each time the clarionet comes in, the noise is like a shower of blows, and quite startles you when they cut in sharply, so coarse and clumsy and screeching, and yet tame.

When Marschner was last here, Tausch took him aside at a general rehearsal, and told him that the whole instrumentation of his opera was bad, and that he ought to be more careful in his future works. If I ever write an opera for this stage, I will write it entirely without instruments, and without singers; and as I cannot endure a ballet, the scenery alone shall sing, and play, and dance. Now answer me accurately the following question:—Where is Wilhelm v. Eichthal to be found, who was in Greece? I wish to write to him, and do not know his address. Many kind regards to your wife, and thanks for the dumplings, which are still in prospect for me;

also my compliments to 'little' Carl * (here I, as a bachelor, bow down before him as a married man). Is Delphine still without her husband? Would I only had a chance once more to see the charming creature! and when does she return to England? What is Madame Vespermann doing, and where is she, and has she not yet quite forgotten me? and little Lang, do you sometimes see her? Above all, what is going on in Munich? You write about Prince Wallerstein, but nothing of her, which is of more moment. Make up for lost time, and answer me soon—that is at once, and now farewell!

Yours,

FELIX MENDELSSOHN-BARTHOLDY.

14.

To Bärmann.

Leipzig, Oct. 30, 1835.

Dear old Fellow,

You have done well in not forgetting your old companion and announcing your visit to him. For this you deserve to be praised, and warmly thanked, and eagerly longed for. How gladly would I have come to you this year, and all was in readiness for it, when my mother, who was staying with me in Düsseldorf, was taken seriously ill, and it was several months before she recovered, so I was obliged, as a matter of precaution, to escort her back to Berlin myself, and give up my

* Here again a little sketch with a pen.

journey altogether; so this year again I have been deprived of seeing my beloved Munich, but feel all the more delighted that I am to see my dear Munich friend here: such an idea is worthy of you, that is, quite superb! If I only knew when you are to come, for you say nothing decided on this point. Unfortunately, I cannot at present renew my invitation of last year, to stay with me, for my quarters here are very limited, compared to my house in Düsseldorf, where I had several spare rooms; but still I hope we shall be together the whole day, and talk and make music to our hearts' content. If you speak me fair, I will write just such another piece for your journey, with pianoforte accompaniment, as the former two duets in Berlin; but in return you must previously promise to play the F minor concerto [Weber's] again and again for me. I spoke to the directors of the subscription concerts here [the Gewandhaus] about the concert you propose to give; they said that the new year would be the most favourable moment, but I think that you would prefer coming soon, and felt embarrassed at not being able to name any fixed time.

Why should you not also play in one of the subscription concerts? We might, perhaps, fire off a duet together; but more of all this when you arrive here—I trust very soon, and to stay as long as possible. I like this place very much indeed, and musical life is most stirring here; we might spend a few famous days together, so do come, my good fellow, and come for a good long time. Excuse these hurried lines, which I am forced to scrawl between sleeping and waking, as I have passed the last eight days in an incessant drive of concerts and rehearsals, besides having much to compose. Farewell, and may we soon meet. My regards to your wife and to Carl; remember me to all Munich and to my pretty Therese.

Yours,

FELIX M.-BARTHOLDY.

15.

To Bärmann.

Berlin, Nov. 25, 1835.

Dear Bärmann,

I received your letter yesterday here, where I have been summoned by the most grievous misfortune that can befall any man. I have lost my father; he has been taken from us without any previous illness, quite calm and free from pain, just as he had always wished. My mother and my brother and sisters are well in health, but none of us can as yet realise this blow, far less think of the future, or recover composure. On the evening of the 18th, my father was still with them all, cheerful and happy, and on the 19th, at half-past ten o'clock, his life was at an end. I mean to strive to fulfil his wishes while he was still among us and occupy myself and do my duty, however difficult I may find any other thought; but this is the only way, so far as I can see, to live in conformity with his will, and therefore I shall attempt to do so.

I enclose you a letter for the music director in Düsseldorf, who can give you the best information and assistance about a concert; I doubt, however, whether a long stay there would requite you, for almost all these concerts bring only very moderate receipts. When I was in Cologne, I spoke to President Verkenius about a concert; but he dissuaded you from giving one of your own, and thought your best plan would be to play once or twice at the winter concerts there, where indeed they only give a small fee, but you would at least be saved all trouble. Leibl is a personal acquaintance of mine, so he will at once do all he can for you; and if you choose to write to Verkenius (reminding him of my former correspondence with him), I feel sure he will arrange so that you need only go there to play the same day you arrive, without prolonging your stay.

The subscription concerts in Leipzig go on till Easter. Whether I shall remain there after that period, I cannot say. Concertmeister Matthäi is dead, and his place is soon to be filled up. I regret not meeting you there at present, but in these first days of sorrow, I could neither think of music nor take pleasure in it. Herr Schindler, formerly an acquaintance of Beethoven, is music director in Aix-la-Chapelle, but I know very little of him, and I doubt whether a concert there would repay the trouble. Certainly not in Elberfeld. I wish to answer every point in your letter, but I can write no more to-day. Farewell! May all good fortune attend your journey.

Yours,

FELIX MENDELSSOHN-BARTHOLDY.

16.

To H. Bärmann.

Leipzig, March 25, 1838.

My dear Friend,

I do not feel quite sure whether you know or care to know anything of me, but I am about to ask you a favour, the fulfilment of which will very essentially oblige me, and therefore I hope you will grant it. The son of Heinze, our first clarionet-player, who has for two years held the situation of second clarionet in the orchestra, and evidently shows much talent for that instrument, is to be sent by his father's wish for half a year, or three-quarters, to some first-rate master, to receive the necessary finish, in which he is as yet deficient, in spite of his facility of execution and musical steadiness. The father, not grudging the greatest sacrifices to cultivate properly the talents of his son, proposes sending him to Munich, and I have undertaken to apply to you to ascertain whether one of the distinguished clarionet-players there would bestow regular instruction on him for a fair remuneration; and receive him as a musical apprentice. Who the person is that we should prefer, you well know, but my fear is that either you never give lessons, or only for a sum higher than the father could afford. If, therefore, you cannot or will not do this, say whether you would recommend Faubel, or some other in Munich, and let me know the usual rate of lessons. You may imagine that this affair is of the utmost importance to these people, and as the father is a most upright man and a sound musician, I venture to hope that you will oblige me by giving him the best advice in your power; of course, if you could yourself superintend his studies, it would make me feel most grateful, but, at all events, let me hear your candid opinion on the subject, that the young man may act accordingly. He could set out in the course of three or four weeks, so I beg you will answer me by return of post, and by so doing you will exceedingly oblige me, as I have already said.

I had many and various things to write to you about, but I scarcely know whether I ought to do so, or whether you would care to read about them. Let me know how this is in your answer, when I will forthwith write you a circumstantial letter about my wife and my little boy, about my life and my music, and then you must write to me in your turn about yourself, and all your belongings and doings. I hope, dear Bärmann, that you will do this, and with kind regards to your amiable wife and your two sons, and hoping soon to hear from you,

I am ever your old friend,

FELIX MENDELSSOHN-BARTHOLDY.

17.*

To Herr Bauernfeld,
a celebrated author in Vienna.

Berlin, July 10, 1838.

Sir,

Frau von Göthe has added a most essential obligation to the many for which I am already indebted to her, in having been the cause of your writing a letter so highly agreeable to me. I am sincerely grateful to you for it, as well as for having sent me your poem; and as it has always been one of my chief wishes to obtain a really poetical *libretto*, I need not add how much I feel indebted to you for bringing me so much nearer the fulfilment of this wish by your friendly advances. The main point is, as you remark yourself, the happy choice of a subject. I confess that on this matter I would rather ask your opinion, than offer any suggestions of my own. I don't know whether the ideas I had myself formed of opera texts may coincide with your

* From the valuable collection of Herr Fritz Baron v. Reden, in Linz.

views, whereas I am convinced that this must be the case on my side with regard to yours. I would only presume to name one restriction—I do not wish to begin with a fairy opera, or rather, I do not venture to think that I have sufficient talent in this sphere, while I would work with greater confidence in the purely serious or purely gay style. If a serious historical or stirring plot, or a gay and natural subject, should occur to you, I beg you will communicate it to me. Should this not be the case, and you do not choose to confine yourself within such limits, I beg you will in that respect, as in all else, give me your candid opinion. You will always cause me pleasure by doing so. I can see from the accompanying text that your mode of treatment suits me thoroughly and in every respect, and many passages in the poem seem to sing and play of themselves. Were it not a magic plot, I would request you to let me have this very poem, as it requires only a few alterations to become thoroughly dramatic and effective. But, as I have already told you, I should scarcely succeed with such a subject; I therefore hope that you can and will propose another, and beg for a speedy compliance with my wishes. Even should other works at this moment demand your attention (which is precisely my own case just now), still, our distance from each other, and likewise the many points of discussion which cannot fail to arise, even under the most favourable circumstances, as well as the length of time that must elapse before the work could be begun, make me wish soon to hear from you, and hoping for the fulfilment of my request, I am, sir, with high consideration,

Yours,

FELIX MENDELSSOHN-BARTHOLDY.

18.

To Herr Bärmann.

Leipzig, September 14, 1839.

My dear Bärmann,

I heartily rejoiced, after so long space of time, once more to receive some lines from your hand, and to find from them that you are, as ever, my dear, unchanged, kind friend. I only found your letter on my return from a journey to Brunswick, or I would not have so long delayed my answer. Give Lachner * my best thanks for his friendly invitation; I would accept it with great pleasure if I had a little more time for my expedition, but as it is exactly four weeks after the beginning of our concerts, any prolongation of my absence would be very difficult. Besides, my journey to Vienna is by no means settled, and in any event, all the time I could contrive to spare for a visit to Munich would be a few days on my return—somewhere between December 20 and 30. Do you think that so short a

* Franz Lachner, Royal Bavarian General Music Director in Munich.

period would suffice? After such a lapse of time would not so shabby a visit be worse than none? Tell me your honest opinion on this point. Further (of course, *entre nous*), are they prepared to defray the expense of my lengthened journey and absence, and of my stay there, and in what way? How much I should rejoice to see at length once more all my dear Munich friends, but above all yourself, dear Bärmann, and to have a chat with you again, to make music together, and to walk about, &c., I don't need to tell you, for you know it already. Now answer me as soon as possible by a few lines, and rest assured that so long as I live, I am, and ever shall be,

Your old friend,

FELIX MENDELSSOHN-BARTHOLDY.

19.

To H. Bärmann.

Leipzig, September 30, 1839.

My dear Friend,

Much as I should have regretted at any other time to have received the letter I have just got, still it is easier than usual for me to reply to it, because I was on the point of writing to you to say that all hope of our meeting this autumn was at an end. My circumstances have assumed such a shape since my return, that even my visit to Vienna during the time of our concerts could only be purchased by great sacrifices and annoyances on my part. I am in considerable perplexity how to adjust all this, as I certainly cannot deem it unreasonable that my personal presence should be exacted here during the winter, when I have seven months' leave of absence in the summer. At all events, it is now quite out of the question to dream of prolonging my absence by any *détour*. The worst part of the affair is, that we could and would have passed such very happy hours together, instead of which our meeting is now postponed for an indefinite period. Herr Panofka and Rosenhain from Paris are here just now; they tell me a great deal and much that is charming of you, and praise Carl and his playing, and his talent for composition, with such enthusiasm, that my mouth began to water again to make music with you, and to play all sorts of nonsensical pranks. They cannot sufficiently extol a clarionet concerto of Carl, and likewise speak with so much affection of yourself, that it quite gladdened my heart. May we soon meet somewhere in this world, and till then continue your regard for me, as I do for you, for I was, and am, and ever shall be,

Your old friend,

FELIX MENDELSSOHN-BARTHOLDY.

20.*

To Herr Wilhelm Speyer, Frankfort.

Leipzig, November 18, 1840.

Dear Herr Speyer,

I can recommend young Eckert to you in every respect, and in the most unqualified manner. Of all the young musicians with whom I have for a long time been brought into contact, I do not know one who, both as regards talent and a spotless and upright character, deserves a more favourable testimony. Those compositions of his that I have had an opportunity of seeing, all show a highly cultivated artist, and one well versed in treatment and forms. There could, therefore, properly speaking, be no question of instructions from me; he is besides a clever pianist, a good violinist, and a sound musician, such as you, and all who wish well to art, like and love. With my whole heart do I wish him a successful career in the cultivation of his talents. He may attain the highest degree of excellence, or merely continue in the sphere of sound and solid work, but with his industry and perseverance, one of these two may with confidence be predicted of him. Should the scholarship be conferred on him, you would not benefit an ungrate-

* From the autograph in possession of the composer Wilhelm Speyer, in Frankfort-on-the-Main, who, as president of the Mozart-Stiftung, had been making enquiries about Eckert. Eckert is now Court Capellmeister in Stuttgart, and had been recommended by his foster father, Regierungsrath Förster, in Berlin, to compete for the first stipend in the Mozart-Stiftung.

ful man; and I am firmly persuaded that his conduct, as well as his capabilities, will at some future day redound to the honour and credit of your admirable institution.

You must, however, excuse me if I am not able to act strictly in accordance with clause No. 27. Eckert's connection with me is by no means, as I already said, that of a pupil to a teacher, and I quickly discovered on his arrival here that he was a thoroughly independent musician. Besides, with my many pressing occupations, it would have been utterly impossible for me to set him to work at something under my eyes, in order that I might hereafter certify this. Could you not sanction his sending his tasks direct? If required, I will gladly bear testimony that they are *bona fide* his own, and composed without assistance from anyone. The compositions of his that I know are the best security for this, and his own character sufficient, without any further guarantee.

Many thanks for your friendly communications. When shall we again make pleasant music together in Frankfort? I passed through it twice this autumn, but could not stay even for a day. I need not tell you my regret—you know how dear the Parrthorn * and all connected with it is to my heart.

Farewell, and ever think kindly of your devoted

FELIX MENDELSSOHN-BARTHOLDY.

* Parrthorn, in the Frankfort idiom, instead of Pfarrthurm. A fragment, copied by Herr Speyer from a Leipzig letter, February 12, 1838,

21.*

To Hofrath André, Offenbach.

Berlin, December 9, 1841.

Dear Herr Hofrath,

On my return from a journey of several weeks' duration, I found your welcome letter, and after having looked over the list of the Mozart MSS., I hasten to say that it would assuredly cause me great pleasure to see the whole collection purchased for the library here. I would also willingly take the necessary steps to ascertain whether the King is disposed to agree to this, but for that purpose it is necessary first to learn the sum total demanded for them. You write that I can easily make the calculation from the prices of the several pieces, but this I do not quite understand. You cannot mean by adding up the price of each individual piece, but in no other way could I arrive at a sum total; so pray write what you mean by return of post, when I will at once proceed to try what can be done here, and I need not say that the more you reduce the sum total in proportion to the price of the single numbers, the more hope shall I have of the purchase being completed.

appears to us worth giving here: 'I would gladly send you something for male voices, to serve the desired purpose, but that is a style which I have never attempted, so I should not like to display my first attempt in it to all eyes and ears, as must be the case there.'

* The originals of the two next letters are in the possession of Herr J. A. André, in Frankfort.

As the matter is urgent, and you have fixed the limit of the 31st, I write you these few lines at once, before I can give you a decided answer about your other proposals.

Count Redern, by the bye, knows nothing whatever of the music in question, nor of the music of Frederick II. either, and he could not recall anything of the kind, though I read him your letter. I shall now enquire about them from the intendant of the palace, Hofmarschall Massow; if he also knows nothing of them, then I fear the thing is nearly hopeless.

I have not yet been able to call on Mdme. Ilgen, but intend to do so in a few days.

Meanwhile, I hope to hear from you, and beg my very kindest regards to your wife and to your sons; my wife also begs to be recalled to the remembrance of Mdme. André, and sends her best wishes.

How delighted I was to hear from you, and once more to see your well-known handwriting, dear Herr Hofrath. Few days pass without my thinking of you with the most sincere and heartfelt affection. May you also retain the same kindly remembrance of

Your ever sincerely devoted

FELIX MENDELSSOHN-BARTHOLDY.

22.

To Hofrath André, Offenbach.

Berlin, February 3, 1842.

Dear Herr Hofrath,

Your letter, just received, reminds me of a debt with which I daily reproach myself, yet without managing to acquit myself of it. I earnestly beg you to forgive me. I live here in such a whirl of business and society, that more leisure than I can command is required to enable me to get through my affairs punctually. The most absurd part of it is that I long ago executed your commissions, although unable to write and say so.

I had no opportunity to speak to the King himself about the Mozart MSS., as he also has no small burden to bear from the complications of business and society; I therefore placed the matter before the minister Eichhorn, and placed it too in the light that every friend to music must desire, likewise specifying the reduced price you had named; but he did not agree to the proposal, and although he did not positively say no, still I could not get anything like a definitive assent from him. He said that if he were urged further at that moment (this was some weeks ago) he must refuse; at the same time he left it at your option to apply direct to the King or to him, when he would take the matter again into consideration. Such was the purport of his answer.

I also called on Mdme. Ilgen about a fortnight since, and delivered your message, which pleased her very much, and she promised to write to you herself in the course of a few days, though I perceive she has not done so. It is true she complained a good deal of her eyes, which made all occupation difficult, this alone being the cause of your not having long ago heard from her; in other respects she seemed well and cheerful. She became visibly animated while talking of you, while her complexion and her whole appearance seemed to me bright and healthy. She complained of nothing but the weakness of her eyes.

I have not, unfortunately, succeeded as yet in procuring any writing for you, either of my grandfather or of those others whom you mentioned. That of my grandfather is so rare, that I do not myself possess a single page of his writing, although I have long been trying to procure it,—if I meet with any hereafter I will send it to you at once; nor have I been able to discover, either through Count Redern or others, any trace whatever of Mozart's two pieces to 'La Betulia:' I much fear they must have been long ago lost or destroyed in the before-named confusion.

I exceedingly regret that I cannot give you a more satisfactory answer on most of these points, but I hope to do so on some future occasion, which I shall gladly take advantage of. I hear with heartfelt sorrow such a bad report of your health. I do hope you may not be absent from Frankfort at the very time I go there this summer. But this is not likely, as it will probably be in May. At all events, I trust I shall find you in better health, and with the same kindly feelings as of old towards myself. My wife sends her regards to you and yours, and I am always, with high consideration,

Your devoted

FELIX MENDELSSOHN-BARTHOLDY.

23.

Berlin, October 15, 1842.

Sir,

I herewith return with my best thanks the translation of 'Medea.' In compliance with your wishes, and with a view to its future performance, and especially the musical treatment of the choruses, I have carefully read and studied it. I regret to say, however, that I have again arrived at the same conclusion that I had the honour to impart to you verbally; the difficulties in the way of a representation of this piece seem to me to be so great, especially as regards the choruses, that I cannot rely on my own capability satisfactorily to accomplish this task, so I must decline undertaking the composition.

Allow me at the same time to assure you that in this, as in all else, it would always cause me the utmost pleasure if by the aid of my music, so far as my powers extend, I could contribute to the fulfilment of your plans; and I sincerely desire that an opportunity may soon present itself to prove this to you, not only by words, but deeds.

I am, sir, with sincere esteem,

Your obedient servant,

FELIX MENDELSSOHN-BARTHOLDY.

24.

To Carl Bärmann.

Leipzig, March 6, 1843.

My dear good Bärmann,

For some time past, even before I got your letter, the subject of your concert had been on my mind, so I hasten to answer you to the best of my knowledge and ability.

You played so charmingly, and pleased so universally, that it really would be a pity not to give a concert or a *soirée*. Much will depend on your selecting a suitable time, otherwise (owing to the small size of this place, and the limited circle who attend concerts), you could not reckon on a well-filled hall.

In this present month, this day week (the 13th) is the only free day; but I would dissuade you from that, because on Thursday next, the 9th, the centenary of the subscription concerts is to be celebrated, when the hall will certainly be crowded to overflowing, and on the

Saturday after (the 11th) there is to be a grand concert for the benefit of the sufferers in the Erzgebirge, when also a great crush may be expected. Monday, therefore, which would otherwise be a good day, thus becomes a very unfavourable one. On the ensuing week, from the 13th to the 19th, no concerts can be given, on account of the fast-day which occurs in it, and when this is the case, no public amusements are sanctioned for several days. The week following begins with a concert, for which the hall is already bespoken (Monday, the 20th), and as the concerts at this season succeed each other so rapidly, I want to know whether you could not arrange your journey so as to give your concert here in April? Our last subscription concert takes place on March 30, and no public ones are as yet announced. Besides, in April strangers begin to assemble for our fair, greatly increasing the number of the visitors to theatres and concerts, so that I believe you might rely on a far better result in the first week of April, or immediately after Easter, than now. Think the matter over, and if you agree with me, the best plan would be when you are present on Friday next, to bespeak your day, and settle it all with Küstner. In this, as in everything else, I am entirely at your service, so far as my power goes; anything I can ever do for you will always be a true pleasure to me; but this you already know, so I need not assure you of it.

May we soon have a happy meeting, my dear kind old friend.

Ever your devoted

FELIX MENDELSSOHN-BARTHOLDY.

25.

*To A. Schüssler, Mannheim.**

Berlin, September 21, 1844.

Sir,

Your very friendly communication arrived here during my absence, otherwise I should have answered it long ago. Pray, first of all, accept my best thanks for the flattering confidence you place in me, by requesting my opinion of a work so long pondered over, and so carefully completed, as that of your collection of texts for composers. I have had the greatest pleasure in becoming acquainted with them, and as you have so kindly and properly made the first advances to me, as a true friend to art, I will, as you desire, tell you with entire sincerity the impression the work made on me. It may possibly be connected with my individuality, that in artistic works which have once captivated me, I cannot bear the slightest alteration, and I have had much controversy with musicians on this very subject; but it

* In the possession of Herr F. Heckel, Jun., music-seller at Mannheim.

is a feeling I cannot conquer, and therefore it would be more agreeable to me—personally—if you had not given in some passages a new version of Schiller's poems. I perfectly see your design in so doing, and that such alterations are intended solely as hints to guide the composer; but I do not believe that you will in this way attain your laudable object. Those who require indications of this nature, can scarcely be capable of rightly appreciating Schiller's splendid poetry, or of representing it by music; others would venture to make the attempt, but at the same time rather wish that this or that verse had been left untouched, and thus probably again alter the alteration, and I believe all would feel some difficulty in overcoming the prejudice at once aroused when the bass begins to sing, 'Wer wagt es, *Ritter* oder Knapp,' when a voice within cries '*Rittersmann* oder Knapp.' I feel the same with respect to the 'Bürgschaft,' the 'Dichterweihe,' and others. It would be very different if you were to give the poems in their integrity, placing your hints to composers, in the shape of notes, at the bottom of the page, either before or after; somewhat in the mode you have adopted in the 'Götter Griechenlands,' where you have marked the omitted passages, in which case many would thus receive several very welcome suggestions. It is the change in such popular words, so well known and beloved by everyone, to which I cannot reconcile myself.

This collection, however, contains much that is valuable, and will certainly be gladly welcomed everywhere. Several of your versions of the Psalms seem to me peculiarly successful. Could you not, in your happy idea of appointing a Psalm for each period of the day, find some more suitable and touching for noon and night? The 148th does not seem to me expressive of a noonday mood, and is not the 134th more appropriate for night?

But pray pardon my many remarks and objections. You see what free use I make of your kind permission to speak quite candidly. May this also show you the interest with which I have read and re-read your work, and my sincere gratitude for the kind confidence in me evidenced by your letter. I am, sir, with high consideration,

Yours truly,

Felix Mendelssohn-Bartholdy.

26.

*To Ludwig Tieck.**

Bad Soden, July 18, 1845.

Dear and honoured Herr Geheimrath,

A thousand thanks for your kind letter of the 8th, which I only received yesterday on my return from a

* Taken from Carl Holtey's collection of letters to Tieck (Leipzig, 1864).

short journey, and now hasten to answer. Herr von Küstner already has the score of my music for 'Œdipus' in his hands, and will no doubt take charge of its transcription and all further preliminaries, so that my personal presence will only be necessary at the actual rehearsals of the music. As you tell me that His Majesty the King has appointed the end of this month or the beginning of the next for its performance, I have arranged to arrive in Berlin about the middle of August, that is, three weeks previously, and therefore no obstacle will be offered on my part to the fulfilment of the King's commands. But I should be very thankful to you, respected Herr Geheimrath, if you would cause the appointed time to be strictly adhered to, both as regards the preparations for the tragedy itself, and the actors who are to appear in it, and also, if possible, to urge Herr von Küstner not to delay the performance beyond the term fixed. Herr von Massow wrote to me that in any event the King returns to Sanssouci the end of August, but goes early in September to the manœuvres, and does not return till the end of that month. If the representation then be delayed, it must necessarily be so till the very end of September, which would place me in very great embarrassment, as it would be difficult, if not impossible, for me to be in Berlin at that period, whereas, as I said before, I have already settled to go there at the time now fixed.

I therefore most earnestly and urgently entreat you, dear Herr Geheimrath, to begin the preparatory studies of the actors at once, and also to prevail on Herr von Küstner to take the most energetic preliminary measures, so that on our side, at least, the time His Majesty has named may be adhered to. You will personally oblige me much by doing this.

How I rejoice at the thoughts of meeting you face to face once more, and expressing the gratitude I feel for the great and intense enjoyment I owe to you, and all my delight in your works!—but to be silent were best, for words would not suffice to express this, and I least of all men could succeed in doing so. I hope to find you in restored health, and unchanged in cheerful spirit and vigour of mind.

Always your devoted

FELIX MENDELSSOHN-BARTHOLDY.

27.

To Ludwig Tieck.

Leipzig, September 4, 1845.

Highly esteemed Herr Geheimrath,

My best thanks for your esteemed letter just received. My presence is no longer necessary at the pianoforte rehearsals, for during my last visit I explained minutely to Herr M. D. Elsler, as well as to the chorus singers, all details about the *tempi* and mode of execution, and therefore I only wish to make my appearance again when the rehearsals on the stage take place, and when the music has been fully studied. Should you meanwhile learn anything more decided as to the time of the performance (which, according to your statement, and that of the committee, is still quite uncertain), I beg you will write me a few lines at once, as I wish to arrive ten or twelve days at all events before the representation, and to have at least as many rehearsals. I trust there is no chance of any day between the 20th and 30th being fixed upon, for these are the only days during the whole year when it would be difficult, or in fact impossible, for me to be present.

I am always, with the highest consideration,

Your devoted

FELIX MENDELSSOHN-BARTHOLDY.

28.

To Herr Joseph Krejci,
*Organist in the Stiftskirche, Order of the Knights Templars, Prague.**

Leipzig, Oct. 7, 1846.

Sir,

I with pleasure respond to the wish of the Cecilia-Verein, and place at their disposal the two scores of

* Joseph Krejci is now director of the Organ School and Conservatorium in Prague. The above letter is in the possession of Herr Dr. Schebeck.

the 'Festgesang' and the 'Antigone.' The former, however, being composed expressly for a brass band (and intended to be executed in the open air), I cannot tell how far brass instruments may sound to advantage in a concert-room. But if you still wish to have the score, you can borrow it from Breitkopf & Härtel (whose property the MS. is), so that you will not even have to pay the cost of copying. I must request in return that neither now, nor at any future period, will you allow the parts to leave your own hands. I could only send you the score of the 'Antigone' choruses at the price already fixed, of ten friedrichsd'or, for which sum the copy and the right of performance (but, of course, not the right of sale on your part or of publication) would belong to the Verein (the same as with the Männer-Gesang-verein in Vienna). I could not possibly make an exception in this instance, for, owing to other previous applications, I should expose myself to many annoyances. I thank you much for your notices as to the reception of the 'Midsummer Night's Dream,' and for all the kind expressions in your letter.

I am, with the highest consideration,

Your devoted

Felix Mendelssohn-Bartholdy.

29.*

To Wilhelm Wauer, Herrnhut.

Leipzig, February 15, 1847.

Sir,

Pray accept my best thanks for your very obliging letter You cannot conceive the pleasure you confer on me by saying that my music has gained personal friends for me in your vicinity, that you like to sing and play my compositions, and thought of me so kindly on February 3. A thousand hearty thanks for this.

The chorus parts and the pianoforte arrangement of my 'Elijah' are to be published in May at the latest, by Simrock, the orchestral parts are also soon to follow. The score, however, will not appear for some months yet, though not likely to be delayed beyond July. Its performance in Dresden on Palm Sunday was obliged to be given up, because the parts could not be procured by that time; but in the autumn I trust that either there or here this performance will certainly take place, and then I should much rejoice to make your personal acquaintance, and again to repeat my best thanks for the kindness of your letter.

I am, sir, with high consideration, your obedient servant,

FELIX MENDELSSOHN-BARTHOLDY.

* In the possession of the gentleman to whom it is addressed.

30.

*To Doctor Martin, Frankfort.**

Interlaken, August 26, 1847.

Dear Herr Doctor,

Your friendly letter gave me so much pleasure that I cannot defer expressing my thanks till I see you in Frankfort, though, God willing, this will soon be the case. I am anxious to tell you without delay how grateful I feel to you for attaching any importance to my co-operation in your Singers' Festival, and that I will make every effort to comply with your flattering proposal, and occupy myself in a composition for male voices for the festival. You have obviated the greatest difficulty by saying that the dimensions (that is to say, the length) of such a composition shall be left entirely to my own will and pleasure; whereas I had understood from the letter of the committee that a piece of some magnitude, sufficient to occupy at least one whole part of the concert, was what they desired to have. There are, however, many other obstacles, especially in my present mood, which then stood, and still stand, in the way of a positive assent, so it is not in my power to give a more decided answer. We can discuss the matter verbally when we meet in Frankfort (where I intend to be in two or three weeks at latest), and till then, pray do not mention either your letter or my reply

* In the possession of Dr. Martin, Frankfort.

to the committee. You may rest assured that I will most gladly respond to such a request as yours, if I find it at all possible to do so; and I hope, therefore, to conclude our interview by giving my consent. But even were I to find this impossible, pray do not doubt my inclination for the task, nor my heartfelt gratitude for your friendly letter, and the continued good will of your devoted

FELIX MENDELSSOHN-BARTHOLDY.

Soon afterwards, on November 4, 1847, this noble master died.

INDEX.

INDEX.

LONDON
PRINTED BY SPOTTISWOODE AND CO
NEW-STREET SQUARE

www.ingramcontent.com/pod-product-compliance
Lightning Source LLC
Chambersburg PA
CBHW032015110726
47901CB00004B/1094

* 9 7 8 3 7 4 4 7 1 8 0 8 0 *